On Becoming a Family

On Becoming a Family

THE GROWTH OF ATTACHMENT

REVISED EDITION

T. Berry Brazelton, M.D.

A Merloyd Lawrence Book
A DELL TRADE PAPERBACK/SEYMOUR LAWRENCE

A Merloyd Lawrence Book
A Dell Trade Paperback/Seymour Lawrence
Published by
Dell Publishing
a division of
Bantam Doubleday Dell Publishing Group, Inc.
1540 Broadway
New York, New York 10036

Library of Congress Cataloging in Publication Data

Brazelton, T. Berry, 1918–
    On becoming a family : the growth of attachment / T. Berry
Brazelton. — Rev. ed.
        p.   cm.
    "A Merloyd Lawrence book."
    Includes bibliographical references (p. 201) and index.
    ISBN 0-385-30768-3 (hc.) — ISBN 0-385-30770-5 (pbk.) — ISBN
0-440-50644-1 (Dell pbk.)
    1. Parent and infant.   2. Attachment behavior.   3. Childbirth—
Psychological aspects.   4. Infants (Newborn)—Care.   5. Infant
psychology.   I. Title.
BF720.P37B74   1992
155.4'22—dc20   91-47567
                                                                  CIP

Manufactured in the United States of America
Published simultaneously in Canada

September 1992

10 9 8 7 6 5 4 3

MVA

All photographs in this book, except where otherwise indicated, are the work of Michael Lutch.

Photographs on pages xv, 8, 19, 31, 45, 53, 65, 81, and 88 courtesy of Beth Israel Hospital, Boston, Massachusetts. Permission to publish elsewhere may be granted by Beth Israel Public Relations.

Photograph on page xviii courtesy of Lori and Jack Foley.

Photographs on pages 55 and 56 from H. Als (1975), "The human newborn and his mother: An ethological study of their interaction." Doctoral dissertation, University of Pennsylvania. Photographs on pages 103 and 105 from H. Als (1980), *Infant Individuality: Assessing Patterns of Very Early Development.* Proceedings of the First World Congress on Infant Psychiatry, ed. J. D. Call and E. Galenson, Basic Books. Photographs on page 172 from H. Als and T. B. Brazelton (1980), "Assessment of Behavioral Organization in a Preterm and a Full-Term Infant," *Journal of the American Academy of Child Psychiatry.* Photographs on page 74 from H. Als, M. B. Lester, and T. B. Brazelton (1979), "Dynamics of the Behavioral Organization of the Premature Infant: A Theoretical Perspective," in T. M. Field, A. M. Sostek, S. Goldberg, and H. H. Shuman (eds.), *Infants Born at Risk* (New York: Spectrum Publications), pp. 173–93. Photographs on page 119 from H. Als, E. Tronick, L. Adamson, and T. B. Brazelton (1976), "The Behavior of the Full-Term yet Underweight Newborn Infant," *Developmental Medicine and Child Neurology,* 18: 590–602.

Photographs on pages 142 and 143 have been reproduced with the kind permission of Dr. Michael Yogman and were taken from research that has appeared as follows: M. W. Yogman, S. Dixon, E. Tronick, L. Adamson, H. Als, and T. B. Brazelton. "Father-Infant Interaction." Paper presented to American Pediatric Society, Society for Pediatric Research, St. Louis, April 1976.

To
Gertrud Reyersbach
and
Ralph Ross,
remarkable pediatricians and generous friends

This book was written while the author was supported by the Robert Wood Johnson Foundation, Carnegie Corporation, William T. Grant Foundation, National Institute of Mental Health (#MH 14887), and the National Institute of Child Health and Development (#HD 18099).

Contents

Foreword

This book is written for parents. The ideas in it are backed up by forty years of research and pediatric practice. In those years I have learned daily from my patients, and many times I have learned from my coworkers and my research as well. However, the major sources for this book are the daily reports of the patients and their families for whom I have cared. I am grateful for their trust, which is demonstrated both by the richness of their reports and by the frankness with which they get me back on track when they disagree with me. Our ability to share the ups and downs of our relationship has provided numerous insights for this book.

In addition to this kind of practical experience, I have had the good fortune to learn about the process of attachment between parents and infants in several settings. The first of these were the Putnam Children's Center in Roxbury, Massachusetts, where I worked with such creative and exciting psychoanalysts as Marta Abramowicz, Myriam David, Dorothy MacNaughton, Marian Putnam, Beata Rank, Eveoleen Rexford, Gregory Rochlin, Samuel Kaplan, and the Massachusetts General Hospital, working with Gaston Blom, John Coolidge, Renata Gaddini, Jane Hallenbeck, and Lucie Jessner. Because of these connections, I learned of the remarkable work of John Benjamin and of René Spitz in Denver on the importance of early experience in the nurturance of infants. Spitz's work provided the necessary understanding of what constitutes a nurturing environment, as well as the research base which delineated the threat to the developing child if this kind of environment was missing. Sybille Escalona, Lois Murphy, and Sylvia Brody carried this work further in the Menninger Studies in the early 1950s.

John Bowlby's classic volumes, *Attachment* and *Loss,* have become cornerstones for the study of attachment and separation on which this volume is based. Mary Ainsworth's extension of his ideas, and more recently Alan Sroufe's confirmation of the importance of her research, have helped to identify the outcomes we would wish for all the children in this volume. Margaret Mahler's work on attachment and hatching has provided an underlying base for our exploration of the early stages of mother-infant development.

My own involvement with this research began to come to fruition at the Center for Cognitive Studies at Harvard in 1967, guided by Jerome Bruner. Barbara Koslowski, Mary Main, Martin Richards, and Colwyn Trevarthen made solid contributions. When I set up our research team in the Child Development Unit at Children's Hospital Medical Center, Ed Tronick split from Harvard to join me, and today is Director of the unit. Heidelise Als, Suzanne Dixon, Barry Lester, and Michael Yogman added their elegant contributions. The work of Dan Stern in New York, Louis Sander in Denver, and Marshall Klaus and John Kennell in Cleveland has illuminated the questions which lie at the base of these chapters.

More recently I have examined the earliest parent-child attachment together with Bertrand G. Cramer of the Service de Guidance Infantile at the University of Geneva in Switzerland. Our collaboration led to a book entitled *The Earliest Relationship* and to new insight for the present book.

Last, but not least, my own family, led and inspired by my wife, Christina, has taught me to respect and work for the bonds of a family and to value the depths of attachment in which these bonds are embedded.

Introduction:
The Agenda of Attachment

Attachment to a new baby does not take place overnight. It is tempting for parents to believe that having a baby and bonding to it are instinctive and that everyone is "ready" for the parental role when it comes. Young parents-to-be welcome the widespread notion that if one does everything right at labor and delivery, immediate bonding to the baby will be assured and this bonding will be intensely rewarding. Delicious pictures of mother, father, and beautiful, smiling baby

further romanticize the parental role. To a very large extent, of course, bonding *is* instinctive, but it is not instant and automatic. In order to be aware of its complexities and possible pitfalls, one must see it as a continuing process.

As one gets closer to the decision to have a baby and begins to pay attention to friends who are already new parents, several observations can be made. Those friends have virtually withdrawn from an outside life. They are tired; they can talk of nothing but the baby, endlessly bragging about how great he or she is. They cover up his* disagreeable crying with apologies for his being hungry or tired or teething. Boringly, they are interested only in whether they are doing the right thing by his colic or sleeping or eating. Their whole world seems centered on the baby, and they seem to want to spend all their time either with him or thinking about him, giving up their own personalities in the process. Their attempts to adjust to the new baby seem excessive. Can they really believe that everything they do matters so much? Must one really give up one's life to a new baby? For a young man or woman considering taking such a step, these become real concerns.

The pressure to "do everything right" and the concept of a brief critical period at birth for bonding to the baby have placed extra burdens on young mothers and fathers. On top of this the overemphasis on immediate reinforcement, or offering the right responses at the right time, diminishes the composure and confidence of new parents.

Few of us become parents with any real awareness of the nurturing side of a parent-infant relationship. Most of us remember the struggles as well as, or better than, the joys in our relationships with our parents. But in that instance we were the recipients of their dedication. As infants we made the demands and were adapted to, and as infants we adapted as best we could to the complexities of our own parents. Despite the romantic mythology that surrounds mothering and fathering, learning to be a parent is likely to be a complex process for most people. The role is demanding, and our approach to it has already been shaped, for better or worse, by our own past experience—that of being mothered and fathered (Brazelton and Cramer, 1990).

Most young parents today will have grown up in small families with no babies around at a time when they were old enough to have learned about them. Few practiced or learned about parenting as chil-

*Though I shall often use the generic masculine pronoun in speaking about babies in general, female babies will appear as often as male babies in this book.

dren. Few young parents come from extended families that have exposed them to caretaking responsibilities. Nor are the extended-family cultures in other parts of the world, which hand on the customs and practices of child rearing from one generation to another, available to parents in our society. Instead, they read and read, in an effort to absorb the vast amount of cultural wisdom and theory that surrounds child rearing today. But there is likely to be no one who can help them sort out all this information and put it into perspective. The sense that one must be aware of the critical periods of an infant's development as they occur can make young parents too uptight to enjoy their baby. Of course, they will spend all of their time comparing notes with other parents. Of course, they will question every move and every decision. But no one can really enjoy this kind of infancy—least of all the infant.

I would like to free parents from some of this pressure to do everything right. I would like to suggest that the essence of parenting does not lie in what one does for one's baby, but rather in the exchange, in the intensely rewarding feedback one can establish between the baby and oneself. The different ways to achieve this exchange are numerous and highly individualized. The timing of each step toward a close and rewarding attachment varies greatly from parent to parent. The best asset for parenting may be the freedom of knowing oneself, of following one's *own* inclinations. And the best signals for knowing when one is on track with the baby are found in the baby himself. I would like to help parents understand the stages that are "normal" in preparing and adjusting to the new baby. I hope to elaborate on as many of the baby's reactions as we presently understand, so that new parents can observe these for themselves and can look to him for the behavioral language that will tell them when they are in synchrony with him.

John Bowlby (1969), the great pioneer in the study of attachment, concentrated upon the behavior of the baby more than upon that of the parents. He also spent relatively little time on the first few months. "We can hardly say that there is attachment behavior until there is evidence that the infant not only recognizes his mother but tends also to behave in a way that maintains his proximity to her."

In our research at Boston Children's Hospital over many years, we have been analyzing several stages in the earliest development of attachment and reciprocity that are critical both to the infant and to his parents. We see that the infant is a surprisingly well-organized individual at birth, ready to signal to his environment when things

are going right and when they are not (Brazelton and Yogman, 1986). As his caregivers respond to him, they offer him the necessary control over his reactions that he lacks, giving him a base from which he in turn can attend and respond to important events in his environment. These in turn fuel him to go on to learn about himself. Robert White (1960) called this latter kind of learning a "sense of competence." The experience of learning from a combination of the inner excitement of achieving each developmental step and the reinforcement of responsive parents drives the infant toward a rich sense of mastery over both himself and his environment. Meanwhile, maturation of his nervous and motor systems is forging the basis for further progress.

The parents, too, are learning about themselves as they learn about the baby. As the baby reacts "successfully" to their care, they are rewarded by the feedback of this success. They are learning about themselves as nurturers. When they do not meet with a successful reaction in the baby, they learn about frustration, about the "other side" of being a parent. Attachment and parenting are not simple matters of caring but are also processes of learning how to deal with anger, frustration, the wish to escape from the role, and even the wish to desert the child. Learning to live with these feelings and to look beyond them for the simple but profound rewards of nurturing—the smiles, the developmental milestones—teaches parents a necessary balance. This balance becomes the "agenda" of attachment. If it were not for the negative feelings of disappointment, failure, and frustration, the feelings of success would not be as rewarding. Falling in love with a baby may well happen at first sight, but staying in love is a learning process—learning to know oneself as well as the baby. That is what this book is all about.

Pregnancy: The Birth of Attachment

Having a first baby is one of life's most challenging events, perhaps the most challenging. It is an opportunity for personal growth and maturity, as well as an exciting opportunity to nurture and become responsible for another being. It is a chance to perpetuate oneself and to "have another chance at life." A baby presents a person with the opportunity to "become a family." The rewards of participating in the growth and development of an infant are indescribable. But so is the feeling of responsibility. The feelings of being overwhelmed, of being anxious, of not knowing what is best, of caring too much, of being inexperienced and inadequate are universal ones for all new parents. In fact, the amount of anxiety that a new parent experiences may parallel how much he or she cares about doing well by that baby.

In our present culture there are few ways to be prepared for this overwhelming event. Most parents have not come from families where they witnessed birth or participated in the care of a new baby. Grandparents are not always nearby, and one's desire to do it by oneself may increase the generation gap at such a time. Society provides insufficient backups for most new parents. Childbirth education groups are trying to fill part of the vacuum. Pediatricians and family physicians are among the few professional sources for advice and help to which inexperienced parents can turn. But physicians are busy people and are both somewhat unavailable and too stressed by "real emergencies" for new parents to feel comfortable about calling on them for help with these feelings of inexperience.

I have been trying to ascertain the special times of stress when a pediatrician or family physician should be available to new parents—when he or she can represent a larger support system that, though it may still be inadequate, cares and is there when the parent needs it. I have been trying to identify the times when a little bit of understanding, an opportunity for questions and for unloading of anxiety can make a big difference. For I would like to see pediatricians play a more helpful role in the early development of babies and their parents. I would like them to take an interest in the babies' total development, not just in their physical progress. I would like them to understand and participate in the hard work of attachment and caring. Hence I have spent a good deal of my professional career looking for the most effective "touchpoints"—times when parents and/or baby are open to outside help, times when a pediatrician can get into the family as a participant and, in the short time available, help them learn about and enjoy each other. I have called such times touchpoints because just a touch from an understanding observer can help the family draw closer together and can give them the insight or direction that fuels their attachment to one another.

THE PRENATAL VISIT

The first touchpoint, and perhaps the most effective of all, is a visit with parents in the last trimester of pregnancy. In fifteen minutes we can get to know a little bit about each other. This short time with parents-to-be is, for me, equivalent to the work of ten to fifteen hours spent establishing a doctor-parent relationship after birth. The prenatal visit is a reach touchpoint—invaluable to my work with prospective parents and, I hope, invaluable to them in that they can begin to see me as a supportive figure after the obstetrician's job is done.

> *A Mrs. Dorn called to make an appointment for a prenatal visit with me. She was seven months along, and since everything seemed to be going well, she said she really didn't need to come, but she had heard from her obstetrician that I liked to meet parents before they had their new baby.*

Such a visit gives us a chance to know each other before we must, between us, concentrate on the baby. Not only can parents-to-be look me over and make a better choice about whether they feel good about me as their doctor, but I can answer some of their questions and participate in the turmoil of preparation for the baby that I know is inevitable for them. By seeing them before the event of delivery (or, in the case of adoptive parents, when they learn that the adoption is imminent), I can tap in on some of their problems and let them know that I understand the depth of their concerns and the reasons behind them. I can indicate that their turmoil is normal and even productive. For the very turmoil they are experiencing serves the important purpose of energizing the new relationship with the baby. By identifying it and stripping it of some of its negative connotation, I can help them channel it into the work of attaching positively and effectively to the new baby.

In this visit we can start a relationship with each other that will serve as well after the baby comes. Most obstetricians and nurse-midwives find it difficult to share with other practitioners the important relationship they have with their pregnant patients, so it can be a big step in our present specialized medical system for parents and pediatrician to be able to get to meet each other before delivery. Parents have resistance, too, for they are already pretty overwhelmed by all that is happening and they know how important it is to concentrate on the relationship they have with the person who will be delivering the baby. In order to overcome these natural resistances, I try to emphasize how valuable this visit will be to them later.

> *I assured Mrs. Dorn over the phone that I did like to get to know parents beforehand so that I could know them as people, not just as parents. Her voice became more intense as she said, "Well, when do you want to look me over?" I tried to let her know that I wasn't seeing her to look her over but rather to get to know her and enable her to know me. After all, she might not like me, and this way she could decide ahead of time whether she wanted to work with me. "Do all pediatricians let you look them over this way?" I assured her that many were prepared to see new parents during pregnancy, and it was a good time for her and her husband to make a choice among them.*

It is true that many physicians don't like to be "looked over" and haven't really accepted the value of a prenatal visit, but many have, and they are worth "looking at." They will probably be the kind of physician who will be interested in the parents' and child's development and will be a participant with them in the child-rearing process.

She said, "Well, when do you want me to come? I work, you know, and I can't come during office hours." She said this as if coming to see me were a burden, as if I were demanding it of her and it seemed an unwelcome demand.

I understand this reaction as a natural reluctance on the part of expectant mothers to enter into one more important relationship at a time when all of their energy is being saved for the new baby and for the coming changes in their lives. They have already made a relationship with their obstetrician, and that's a critical one for them. One more may be too much. But seeing me as their baby's advocate may help them focus on the baby.

When I assured her that I kept office hours after her working hours and that I did want to know her, she seemed relieved. I promised her that the visit need be only a few minutes, "to touch base." I thought she seemed relieved also that I wouldn't be delving into too many questions, invading too much of her privacy. I asked her whether she could come at a time when the father of the baby could come too. She assured me that she was married, but she wasn't sure he'd want to come: "After all, he works, and he can't just go to see doctors when it isn't necessary." Again I pointed out that I had office hours after his working hours and that I thought she should ask him. She called back to say, "He does want to come!" as if it were a surprise. We made an appointment for them at the end of the day.

Again, I understand a mother's reluctance to bring her husband as a kind of economy—a kind of protection against getting in too deeply before the baby comes, a protection also perhaps against sharing with him any relationship we might make. But the importance of getting to know the father at such a time far outweighs any danger of diluting our relationship. By including him, I help ensure his participation later on. He will feel important in contributing to my understanding of the developing family. But more crucial, he will feel necessary to the baby's optimal development, and I hope to help him see his role in that.

When they arrived, Mrs. Dorn was a rather quiet, demure-looking young woman with short black hair. She was not tall, and her pregnant abdomen dominated her. Swaying from side to side as she walked, she kept her hands on her belly, as if to maintain contact with the baby inside her. She had a rather patient, restrained look on her face and seemed to try to maintain a distance as I introduced myself. Her husband followed her quietly. He was a tall, slender, sandy-haired young man who looked eager and somewhat callow at first sight. He wore glasses, through which his bright, inquisitive eyes shone, and he watched appreciatively as I reduced my voice and toned down my approach to meet his wife's quietness.

As I asked them into my office, he squeezed her hand a bit, then let her lead him in. She moved in to sit in the deep, soft chair facing my desk. Her legs barely touched the floor, and her abdomen pressed up into her chest so that she had to breathe more quickly. She looked very uncomfortable, and I asked her if she wanted a straighter chair, but she nodded my question away. She answered by sitting up straighter and looking at me as if to say, "Go ahead."

Her husband had walked over to the chair behind my examining table, and I had to lean out to see him at all. He sat upright and completely quiet, as if this were his wife's show and he knew it. So I met a rather stiff, unyielding pair in my office.

Many couples demonstrate such reserve at a first meeting. It is the beginning for them of an important relationship, and their protective facades hide their awareness of the significance of this step. Instead of accepting this reserve at face value, I look upon it as a play for time—time to size me up and to see where each of us fits in the new scheme.

DECIDING TO HAVE A BABY

When a couple comes to my office and tells me that they are having a baby, I know they will be going through a certain number of expectable reactions. The future is exciting, and it opens up in a thousand new directions. It also closes down in others. The latter surprises most parents-to-be and may even interfere with the excitement that carries them along toward that new baby. I try to touch upon these inevitable conflicts that arise in pregnancy in the hope that by sharing them, by seeing them as normal, parents can look forward to the baby without some of the more draining aspects of this conflict.

Deciding to have a baby is a more complex step today than it was in the past. The ability to control fertility through contraception has brought added responsibility. Most couples these days feel that they should limit the number of babies they will have. If they're only going to have one or two children, the burden (of pressure) to nurture those one or two optimally is intense. In a family of six to eight children the older siblings helped with the child rearing. The pressure to nurture and be nurtured was diluted. Making mistakes with one or two is more of a threat. Hence contraception and choice add to the responsibility for making this baby perfect in all respects. Also, the challenge of timing pregnancies to fit the careers of two working parents adds to the complexity of the decision.

> *My first question to Mrs. Dorn was: "And when is your baby due?" She told me that it was only six weeks away, and she really didn't feel ready. She said, "One of the reasons I didn't want to come to see you yet was that it meant facing up to being 'ready.' But then I realized I probably never would feel ready."*

Who can really feel ready for such a step? Part of feeling ready to have a baby is feeling the equal of one's own parents. Young parents also have a concept of an ideal parent against which to measure themselves. They look back on their own childhoods and reconsider them in the light of this ideal. If their own parents had been better prepared or informed, would they have made as many mistakes as they did? These doubts force young parents to feel that if they put off the decision to some future time, they *might* be better prepared or ready, even though they know somewhere within themselves that this is not so. When a relationship with parents has been fraught with trouble or when the struggle for independence is still not resolved, it may be even harder to decide to risk reproducing such a relationship with one's own baby. A difference in early experiences is often behind some would-be parents' greater readiness in contrast with that of others.

Yet the pressure to reproduce oneself, to see one's own offspring, to complete the adult cycle, is enormous.

Despite the enormous effort that has gone into shaping a public scene that is more accepting of women, fitting a baby into a career is still very difficult. Women still feel a conflict between wanting to be good mothers and wanting to be available for their careers. The very real worry of being unable to support a family if they have to give up their jobs also has to be faced. There is an implicit put-down built into the professional world for women who must stop what they are doing to have and nurture a baby. We do not offer social support for women to stop their careers temporarily without losing out on their opportunities. Most businesses label women as halfhearted if they want to work half-time after a new baby.

Many European countries have maternity and paternity leaves, which require employers to grant at least a six-month leave for the mother and a three-month leave for the father. This implicitly acknowledges their responsibility to nurture their babies and equates it with their responsibility toward their jobs. Although important new legislation has been proposed, we have nothing like that yet in the United States. When a woman realizes that she will have to be back at her work soon after delivery, she must face the prospect of having to share the new baby with a sitter or a day-care center. The confusion around women's roles and the increasing pressure on both men and women to give themselves to a competitive world seem to undermine the energy and time necessary for nurturing a family properly.

Then there are other societal pressures that conspire to unsettle young parents and to urge them away from childbearing. The divorce rate threatens most families' hopes of being able to make it over the long run. Many of their friends are already divorced or are in the process of getting divorces. The cost of divorce to a child is enormous, and the difficulty of raising a child as a single parent also gives one pause. The facts of population explosion and depleted world resources as well as the threat of environmental pollution each loom over the future of a baby being born today.

In the face of all this, if a couple has decided to have a baby today, they must really want it. A certain amount of conflict is liable to be present for most young couples today. I see such conflicts as not only normal but as reinforcing to the caring that is being generated around the baby.

Mrs. Dorn seemed a bit chagrined that she had made such a revealing statement to me, so I hastened to reassure her: "I don't believe anyone is ever ready. It's a big step for you both. It probably seems pretty unreal and even scary right now." At this she planted her hands on her belly again, as if to feel the reality of the baby all over again. Mr. Dorn nodded enthusiastically as I included him in this statement.

Fathers can have an even tougher time facing the reality of becoming ready, it seems to me. Whereas the mother has the constant

reminder of the baby growing and moving insider her, the father has to imagine all this and prepare himself without the reality of a baby to feel and respond to.

NEW ADJUSTMENTS

Mrs. Dorn brightened a bit and looked at me with a clearer, more direct look, as if grateful for the understanding. "I just feel so tired and depressed all the time. I feel I should be on top of the world, and I am, but I feel drained a large part of the time too. I don't quite understand that."

Being pregnant is a physical strain. The readjustment of bodily mechanisms takes a lot of energy. Added to that is the psychological readjustment. Dreaming about the new role and preparing oneself for it begin to absorb a major part of a mother's waking time.

Most women experience a combination of feelings of helplessness, anxiety, and pleasurable anticipation. The energy that is withdrawn from their daily lives is used in trying to sort out these feelings. They may seem alternately depressed and giddy to people around them and also a bit dreamy and remote.

A woman may need to visit, observe, and even question her own mother about her childhood. She may revive old conflicts with her mother yet find herself hungrily observing and needing her mother again. This need to absorb all she can from her own mother may come as a surprise to them both. The hunger for being mothered may make her somewhat oversensitive to her mother-in-law. She may want just as much nurturing and advice from her husband's mother, but she may also feel she has to defend herself from that need. And she may lash out unexpectedly at other mother figures around her.

She will find herself intently watching her friends and peers who already have babies. Certainly the time of pregnancy is a time for learning as much about oneself and the new upcoming role as possible. Among the most valuable are the classes of the Childbirth Education Association and the La Leche League. Individual hospital and maternity centers generally offer childbirth preparation classes. Not only are these classes valuable for the information they offer about the birth process itself, but they also help clarify the parents' roles in future child rearing. And more important than either of these, they offer young parents a chance to identify with, and to know, others in the same role. Couples who are about to embark on such an exciting venture need others who are adjusting to this step and who can listen to their concerns, letting them feel that they are not going overboard as they adjust to the new job.

Mrs. Dorn: "I can't do my work well, and I am afraid of losing my job. At the same time I am really ready to quit just to have time to think about the new baby. I don't know what to do." All of this came out with a rush, as if she were ready to talk it over. I could sense that she wanted to talk at length about working and mothering and how to fit them together.

What must a working mother do? When should she leave her job in order to prepare for her new role? Many women do not have this option or would prefer to keep busy at such a time.

The anxiety about whether she and the baby will make it through the pregnancy is great, and for some it is hard to live with. If she needs a job and is geared to an active life, it will be much easier to continue working as long as it is physically possible to do so. But she must give herself the space and the time to do some preparation too. "Nest building" is a nice part of this period. And the psychological preparation for the new role is a necessary part of it. I see the anxiety and the turmoil that are an inevitable part of pregnancy as a process of readying the young parents' emotional energy for the most important step—that of attaching to the new baby. Unless a woman allows herself the freedom and the time to experience this turmoil and to address some of the questions about her new adjustment beforehand, she may find herself overwhelmed by her new job of mothering. In that case her best energy may not be available to the new baby.

Most women want to be pampered, to be taken care of during childbirth and the following days. They may not like to admit to a longing for dependency, and it may be harder for a woman who has been successfully independent before. But this is a time when they can learn again the comfort of being cared for and cared about. It may even pay off in other ways. At such a time a husband may have increased needs, too, and if they are recognized, he may respond with tenderness and nurturance that will strengthen the marriage. One's own mother certainly will want to play such a role, and even though it may revive the old struggles of growing up and of separation, it can be a good time to try out the dependent role again. For one thing, allowing oneself to regress and become dependent will conserve energy for the new, bigger adjustment ahead. The very process of experiencing dependency all over again can give a mother-to-be a more sympathetic understanding of the importance of it to the new baby. Most of us have struggled so hard to become independent from our parents and have learned to value the rewards of autonomy so much that we have forgotten or suppressed the lovely cotton-wool warmth of being taken care of, the bliss of being dependent. This is an appropriate time for falling backward into dependency, in order to be better able to value it and offer it to the new baby. For most of our lives we are under a lot of internal pressure to succeed, to get ahead, to do a perfect job, and we will pass this kind of striving on to the baby, whether we mean to or not. If we can cushion him with the other side, our nurturing side, we will give him a necessary balance.

New parents must adjust their lives on several levels. Independence from one's own parents may have been won at a price, and to allow oneself to realize that one needs them again comes hard. One's job and success in one's profession are too important to endanger willingly. And last but not least, the adjustment a young man and woman have made to marriage, to a sharing relationship, is threatened. Having to share each other with a third person, the new baby, is a challenge. Each of the parents may seem delighted with the prospect—on the *surface*. But underneath, each is likely to have fairly predictable concerns. It may help to share them with each other.

"Do you believe in mothers going back to work after they have their babies? If so, when do you think I can—without hurting the baby, I mean?"

I feel that this is a question that really shouldn't be answered with a general answer, and I told her this: "Wouldn't it be better to see how it goes for you and the baby and answer this later? If you need to tell them at work when you will come back, tell them that you will need at least three months at home. That will give you a good start, and you can make your own decision as you go. You may even want to be out longer."

The first three months are made up of so many adjustments that unless new parents can get beyond them into the fourth glorious month, they may never feel a sense of completion. Sometime during these first months the baby will smile and coo *to them*. To share the baby with someone else before that moment is to endanger a feeling of intense communication and belonging. Many women and most men must go back to work before this cycle of turmoil and closure is complete, but it isn't ideal for their own sense of fulfillment as parents.

As for the baby's development, we really haven't the research or follow-up necessary to know for sure when it becomes less important for the baby to have a protected relationship with his parents. The kinds of crises that must be met in the initial months and the stages of attachment that are reached all will be discussed later. And of course, a lot has to do with the kinds of individual arrangements that can be made.

Since I don't know how to give a general answer, I attempt to answer it at an individual level whenever I am pressed in advance. I am sure that the first few months are critical. At least six months and even a year might be the ideal time span. I feel that this stage is as important to the parents' development as it is to the child's, so any decision should be based on an observation of this development, which is hard to guess in advance. The dangers of separating a mother from her baby before she is ready to share him can dilute her feeling of competence and importance to that baby. Ideally she should be freed of rigid practical considerations in order to make such a decision at her own pace.

BREAST FEEDING

Mrs. Dorn seemed quite relieved at my answer. She said, "If I ask for three months, I can certainly try breast feeding. I want to very much, but I figured that if I were going back to work right away, then I might as well not even start to nurse the baby. I hear it's not easy to get one's milk started. If I feel under a deadline, I know I won't get milk."

I could see that she needed encouragement to breast-feed, and I gave it to her. "With your first baby, it takes four or five days to establish your milk, but this time is rewarding to both you and the baby. He is learning to suck effectively while he is stimulating your milk to come in."

I urged her to begin to prepare her nipples, to toughen them up. "If you wash them carefully first and wash your hands to eliminate germs, then you can gradually toughen the areolae by massaging them daily between your fingers, without endangering them by rubbing in an infection. When the baby starts to suck, he won't be as likely to hurt them if you've toughened them up. And then, if you start him off slowly, increasing the timing of sucking gradually, you'll get your milk going without getting a cracked nipple. The main thing is to be determined to make a go of it. Nowadays there is a lot of support for breast feeding in hospitals, so you are likely to find nurses and physicians who will help you if you want to breast-feed."

There is a natural competition for a new baby that always invades nurseries. New mothers feel vulnerable to this competition. Until recently this (often unconscious) competition took the form of undermining the resolve of a new mother in her breast-feeding efforts. Now the climate of most rooming-in hospitals has changed. In large part because of the rather militant efforts of such organizations as the Childbirth Education Association and La Leche League, nurseries in maternity hospitals have become geared to support breast-feeding efforts. The importance of breast feeding to the mother, to her physical recovery and to herself as a person (bringing a feeling of completeness through the use of her breasts), is coupled with its physical and psychological importance to the baby. There is no question in my mind that both participants profit enormously from the mutuality implicit in the act of breast feeding (Raphael, 1973).

The value of breast feeding is so widely recognized these days that I worry now about the implicit criticism of mothers who don't want to or can't breast-feed. The pressure is on to nurse your baby, and the implication is that unless you do, you are going to lose out on critical aspects of attachment and the baby will suffer. That isn't true, of course, for the overall climate of the feeding matters most to the baby; the kind of feeding is less important. I am a firm advocate of the value of breast milk to the infant for many reasons, but if a mother feels under pressure to breast-feed, I am sure that the baby will suffer because of her ambivalence. Breast feeding can be, and should be, pleasurable for both parties.

Mrs. Dorn asked me to help her make the decision about whether to breast-feed or not. I asked her about her past experiences and why she felt undecided. Although she said, "I really haven't thought about it," I felt that she was likely to be covering up her concerns. She assured me that she wanted to be able to nurse her baby, for she "knew it was for the best." I wondered why she was so sure. She said that she'd read that breast milk was safer from the standpoint of infection, less allergenic, and that one felt closer to the baby as one breast-fed than one did with a bottle. I agreed with her on all of these points and wondered why she still felt undecided. Her face became pinker, and she looked concerned as she said, "My mother never nursed us, and I wonder if that means that we can't do it in our family. My sister tried, but she gave up when her milk didn't come in right away. Now you've just told me that one must wait four or five days for it to come in. Will I give up too? I'd rather not take the plunge and then fail, for I would feel like I was starting off with a failure with this baby, and it means so much to succeed." I agreed that it would be a tough time to fail, even in something like this, but that all new mothers felt this same self-doubt. I was grateful that she'd been able to confide in me, and I assured her that knowing about her reasons for indecision would help me to help her more effectively.

Many women feel pressed during pregnancy to make a firm and unrelenting decision about breast feeding. Their conflicts about whether they will be adequate as parents, their memories of their own mother's way of feeding her babies, their concern about the shape of their breasts—all may interfere with a rational decision. I usually urge mothers to wait until they have the baby in their arms to decide. Often the baby's reactions and the mother's own instinctive urge to nurture him will help her make the decision afterward.

A FATHER'S FEELINGS

I felt it was time to include Mr. Dorn. I asked him how he felt about his wife's breast feeding. With a burst he spoke out, his voice high-pitched with excitement as he started to speak. He leaned forward and urgently said, "I'd love for her to feed the baby herself. In fact, when we talk about it and she wavers about whether she will try or not, I find myself getting angry with her. Why not try? I will surely help her if I can. I guess I care so much that I may even push her harder than I should. It's as important to me that we do all of this perfectly as it is to her! I guess I sound competitive, don't I?" He blushed as he voiced this latter feeling.

The feeling that surprises most young parents-to-be is that of competition—competition for the new baby, competition for the nurturing role, even competition with the baby for each other. These feelings are to be expected. The more you care about each other and the new baby, the more these feelings will present themselves. They surface in all sorts of ways. When his wife withdraws into her dreamworld, the father-to-be may feel left out and jealous of the baby. At the same time she may resent his freedom to come and go without the real burden of pregnancy, and she may find herself projecting her resentment onto him, excluding him even more. She may even wonder whether he will ever be a good enough father for "her" baby. She may find herself comparing him with her own father, unfavorably. All over again she may have to remind herself why she married him, and she may return to disturbing oedipal feelings about and wishes for her father. This kind of competition can frighten both parents-to-be unless they understand the source of it and can realize that it is a necessary part of the beginnings of attachment to the new baby. These very competitive feelings stir up energy for attachment to the baby. And if they are understood, they can become a renewing force for strengthening rather than weakening the parents' attachment to each other.

I reassured him about how natural were his feelings of competition for the baby and for doing everything perfectly for that baby. I also told him that I thought the best predictor that I could see for this baby's future was how much they cared—about each other and for the baby. With this his voice softened, and he said, "I've felt pretty shut out at times. She spends a lot of time dreaming and holding on to that baby with her hands. I can't get close to either one of them."

The feelings of being excluded are real ones for a young father in our culture. Not only is his wife likely to withdraw some of her energy and attention from him, but she becomes the center of everyone else's attention. No one asks him how he's doing in this period of adjustment. Everyone is concerned with her health and her feelings. They all want to take care of her. When he is around, she wants to be taken care of by him. Even when he's doing his best to please her, she may be actively resentful about being pregnant and about giving up her old roles. Since he feels responsible, often to an irrational degree, for having made her pregnant, he is quite vulnerable to her feelings of resentment. Whatever goes wrong in the pregnancy appears to him to be his fault. If she's sick in the morning, it's his fault. If she feels heavy and achy at night, it's his fault. If she's tired and doesn't feel like taking care of him, he mustn't feel resentful, for it's his fault in the first place. So all of his loneliness, all of his own resentment about being displaced tends to get turned on himself. He did it all to himself, and although he may wish he could be angry or show some outward sign of resenting the intrusion of the pregnancy, he must remind himself of his own responsibility in it. These are heavy feelings, particularly if there's no one around to unburden them to.

"You sound as if you have been feeling pretty lonely these days." He assured me that these feelings came and went. But as I encouraged him, he exploded: "Even my own parents came to see us just to find out how she's doing. No one ever asks me how I'm doing!"

No one seems to care what a father-to-be is going through. His wife or mate has her hands full with her own adjustment. Her parents and his are concerned with her and the new baby. All of their friends surround her to ask how she's feeling. The doctors and the childbirth groups are more interested in her and how she's doing. No one seems to care about the father-to-be.

Pregnancy: The Birth of Attachment   15

What is he going through? He is having to make an adjustment similar to hers for his prospective role. He is having to worry about the possibility of new, major expenses. Will he be adequate as a provider? He finds himself dreaming a lot at work, and his work is suffering. Will he lose his job? If he has an absorbing career, will he be able to free up enough time to be available when the new baby comes? He has already found it demanding to be more available to his wife in her pregnancy. Will it get worse when the new baby comes?

Sometimes he even finds himself wishing he were out of it all. His fantasies of flight, of getting away completely, of wondering about and desiring other women may be particularly heightened and disturbing right now. And they do peak at such a time. Partly because of his feeling of being left out, partly because he might wish to be left out, he finds his competitive feelings about her even more disturbing. She is having it all—the baby, the attention, the chance to regress and be taken care of. He is having to become more of a man. He has no one to turn to. When I see prospective parents in my office for a prenatal visit in order to get acquainted with them and they with me, I always draw the father into our discussion by asking him a question or two about his side of the adjustment to the new baby. His surprise at being included matches his hunger for attention. Later he always tells me that *no one* has asked him a question about himself during his wife's pregnancy.

> *Mrs. Dorn looked at him with surprise and concern. "Stan, I didn't know you were having all of these feelings. Why didn't you tell me? I can understand, and anyway, it makes me feel better to know you are going through all these questions too." He looked gently at her. "I can't load you down with my problems. It wouldn't be fair. I know how many worries you have on your mind. And I want to be a help to you—not a drain."*

A man feels he should handle his own turmoil. Will he ever be able to father a baby? In more ideal extended-family communities, there are institutionalized ways of learning what a father must be. We could easily provide education and practice for young fathers-to-be in our culture. But there is still an unstated feeling in our culture that men should be strong and "masculine." It is weak to give way to one's feelings. At such a time it becomes extra important that he be a "he-man." How can he let himself face up to feelings of weakness and indecision? The struggle against such feelings can be draining. There is also a new awareness that to nurture is all right for men. This latter feeling is still on shaky ground, and men who act on it have little support. We must create more opportunities for fathers to face up to and work out their own feelings of conflict about whether they can dare become fathers or not.

Even a father's protective feelings about his wife mask doubts and questions. Do I really want her to have my baby? Will she be a good enough mother? Unreasonably he, too, is wishing for perfection. Because of the importance of this baby to him, he begins to wish for his own mother to be nurturing that child. The natural competition for the baby is already surfacing in this wish. The questions about her competence as a mother really cover up questions about himself. If he were allowed to voice these questions, that would become apparent, and their universality could be reassuring to him. Most men probably need to hear that they are not alone in these fears of incompetence as they prepare for their first offspring. Men rarely feel competent until they've had a chance to try this role.

He looked at me and said, "I guess you feel like I'm making a fool of myself now, don't you? I really want to help with this baby, though. And no one has given me a chance to talk like this. It scares me to realize how much I care about her and our baby already. It makes me feel sort of weak. Men should be strong in our family. I remember my father always running away or getting angry when we cried as children or seemed emotional at all. It isn't okay in our family to feel like I do right now."

I remember the high school classes for juniors and seniors in which we showed them an infant and explained his behavior. The adolescent males were even more "hooked" on the infant than the young girls were, wanting to know all about him, how to take care of him, what it was like to be an infant. If you asked them, they all admitted that they'd had no real experience. But all of them admitted that they wished they had the guts to "baby-sit for a baby." To me this represents the hunger for nurturing that lies dormant in most men in our culture. Now that we need men to play a more active role in rearing their children and in participating with their wives in the baby's care, we must begin to give them opportunities to play with a baby and to care for one during or before their wives' pregnancies. A little experience would reinforce their sense of competence. Otherwise, men will continue to question themselves—and their wives—at a time when they are particularly vulnerable to such questions. With a little experience men can begin to look forward to the exciting side of being a father. They can help in nest building and prepare themselves for the experience of playing with their *own* babies.

A man's very need to understand what his wife is experiencing will make him feel competitive with her. When my wife was pregnant, I used to use my stethoscope every night to listen to the fetus's heartbeat—not just to see whether the baby was all right. I wanted to know that baby, to have some experience with it that paralleled my wife's. So clear was the longing to know all I could about the baby and what he was experiencing that I began to realize how attached to him I already was. In the process of longing for an experience with the fetus I began to sharpen my awareness of every baby in my office, on the subway, on the street. And not so curiously, I began to feel jealous of the intimacy with my baby that my wife was already experiencing. Every evening I pressed her to tell me what it was like, and I found myself listening jealously to her accounts.

One can see the longing for attachment to the baby in this struggle. The pressure to identify with one's wife is energized by the desire to know what the baby is all about, as well as by the self-questioning that is part of the preparation for becoming a parent.

> *After this outburst and my encouragement of him in it, Mr. Dorn became a real participant in our interview, inadvertently pushing his chair forward. He sat on its edge, his face was serious, and his childlike look had disappeared. He appeared to mature in front of my eyes. He was a part of the family now for sure.*

Each time I have such an experience in my office, I marvel all over again at the progress which can be made when a father has a chance to talk about himself and what he wants for himself with his baby. I knew Mr. Dorn would feel closer to me as his physician and would participate more in all of my future work with the family after his "outburst" and the chance to examine himself a bit.

THE BEGINNING OF A RELATIONSHIP: THE FETUS RESPONDS

> *Mrs. Dorn seemed to take his outburst as a kind of reinforcement for herself, and she, too, began to speak more confiden-*

tially. She said, "You know, Doctor, I already feel that I know this baby. He seems to respond to things the same way I do. When I get excited about something, he waits till I'm calm again; then he reacts too. In fact, he seems to let me know that he agrees with me. Do you think I'm crazy to believe this? I want to believe in our relationship so much that I can't separate the truth from my wishful thinking." Her face had become intense and pleading, as if she wanted me to agree that she was already getting to know her baby. I assured her that recent research bore out just what she was saying and that indeed, attachment to a fetus begins long before birth, and that was what she was experiencing.

Throughout pregnancy the fetus is experiencing and being shaped by the experiences of the mother. As it moves in response to these experiences, its activity gives her feedback that tells her how it reacts, perhaps even gives her a sense of what it is like, and begins to shape her to it. For generations mothers have said (when asked) that their unborn babies respond to music or to their anxiety or to loud noises in the vicinity. Now we can confirm these observations by monitoring fetuses' movements and their heart rates.

In the last few months of pregnancy the fetus will respond to many different stimuli administered from outside the uterus. If a

loud noise goes off near the pregnant woman, the fetus will startle, even when she doesn't (Rosen and Rosen, 1975). The mother experiences this sudden but complete startle and can tell you about it. The fetus will also respond to being poked by starting and moving away from the poking finger. A sudden bright light placed next to the mother's abdomen in the fetus's line of vision will evoke a startle. In other words, the fetus already sees, hears, and responds to touch (Brazelton, 1981). At certain times even his mother's sudden movement will set off a startle in him, and he will tend to move in synchrony with her as she walks or runs. She becomes aware of these synchronized movements only if you urge her to think about them, for she has long since become used to them and unaware of them. But she depends on them, for when he does *not* move or when he moves unexpectedly, she will unconsciously register the difference. She is becoming tuned in to him and his responses.

We are now able to detect at least three states of consciousness in the fetus in the last half of pregnancy. The earlier work was done by Geoffrey Dawes (1968) in England with fetal lambs. He was able to differentiate between states of deep and light sleep. The states of consciousness observed in fetal lambs can be translated to human fetuses. We are now beginning to identify states in human fetuses as well.*

There is a deep-sleep state, in which the fetus is quiet and relatively unresponsive to experiences around him. In this state there are occasional jerks of the extremities, but rarely of the entire trunk. In lighter, or REM (rapid eye movement), sleep there are more movements. Although the fetus is essentially quiet, there are periodic jerks of the body, of the extremities, or of the diaphragm. The mother will call these hiccups, and they may come in regular trains of activity. These hiccups may consist of a jerking of the diaphragm and may even represent abortive attempts to practice breathing in utero. They are accompanied by jerky startles of the body as well. There is little flowing motion in this state, and the baby is still relatively unresponsive to outside stimuli. Finally there are two awake states, in which the fetus is likely to be moving about. Movements can be slow and liquid or more active and vigorous. In this state the mother may feel as though the fetus were climbing the walls of the uterus, and indeed, when visualized by ultrasound techniques, the fetus is moving

*In a normal newborn there are at least six identifiable states of consciousness: light sleep, deep sleep, semialertness, wide-awake alertness, fussiness, and intense crying (Brazelton and Cramer, 1990).

around in the uterus like a hamster on a wire wheel. Humphrey (1969) and Hooker (1952), in England, described the movements and reactions of the fetus in great detail. Their descriptions were the result of careful observations of fetuses who were still alive at the time of abortion. Now we can monitor movements from outside the uterus, both electronically and by using ultrasound techniques, to confirm their remarkable observations. With this equipment, we can visualize, measure, and observe the fetus. The technique, which has become more and more refined, is used at present for detecting fetal growth and fetal abnormalities in order to improve care in the uterus. We (especially Dr. Barbara Howard of our group), along with the radiologist at the Boston Hospital for Women, Dr. Jason Birnholz, observed fetal reactions at various ages. Movements can be visualized, and there is a wide range of spontaneous and responsive movements, all of which seem to be related to the baby's state of consciousness.

Now that we have the capacity to determine these different states of reactivity in the fetus, we can begin to record and understand the way the fetus and mother join in their daily experiences. We can confirm what mothers tell us about the fetus's activity: how it comes at certain times of the day and is related to what they themselves are doing. When they settle down at night, the fetus becomes very active. When they are active, the fetus is quiet. When they sleep, it sleeps. And within these broad rhythms are smaller ones in which the fetus comes regularly up to activity for a short period and then quiets down again in regular and predictable cycles. At night, when she is in bed and quiet, a mother is more likely to notice these regular cycles of quiet and activity within the fetus's broader adjustments to her daily rhythms. It has rhythms of behavior of its own, and hers and its are being locked together in a synchrony in which each is getting to know the other. All through pregnancy a mother is experiencing this locking in of the fetus to her and is feeling its reactions to her experiences.

Not only does the fetus respond to light, sound, and touch, but it can respond differentially. We have done some experiments that seem to indicate that the fetus is already making choices between stimuli and responding to them in appropriate ways. This came from our work with newborns and their ability to make choices (see Chapter 5). In our study, we presented seven-month-old fetuses in a quiet-alert state with a buzzer eighteen inches from the mother's abdomen. The fetuses jumped for the first buzz, less for each succeeding one. Finally, by the fourth or fifth, they stopped moving at all. One fetus, closing its eyes, put its thumb up to its mouth and turned away from the buzzer. When we used a soft rattle next to the mother's abdomen, fetuses would open their eyes, alert, and turn toward the rattle. In these responses they showed the ability to habituate to the intrusive stimulus, and to choose to respond to the more appealing one. If a bright light is flashed next to the mother's abdomen in the fetus's line of vision (once we have determined which way it is facing), it will startle, and the mother can feel its jerky movements. If a soft light is then placed in the same spot, it will not startle but will turn smoothly toward it. If one continues to administer the bright light, the fetus will adapt and will become very quiet inside the uterus. If the more "appealing" soft light is repeated, it will get more active in turning toward the stimuli, as if attracted to it.

A fetus will even lock its movements in synchrony if a noise is repeated in a rhythmic fashion. Doesn't this explain the reports that mothers give when they tell us how the fetus "dances" during a concert? They tell me that the fetus will dance one way for a rock concert and an entirely different way for classical music. These observations demonstrate the fact that the fetus is learning from its environment and that it is feeding back that fact to its mother. She can tell that it is sharing her experiences with her. She is learning about her unborn child all the time.

It won't surprise anyone that a newborn baby will actively prefer a female voice to a male voice at birth. If he is held up in the air with his head resting on one hand of the examiner and his buttocks on the other, looking at the ceiling, he will turn repeatedly toward a voice and look for a face after he turns. If a male and female compete by talking quietly at the same time, but on different sides of his head, he will turn to the female voice every time. Of course, this is likely to be a result of months of earlier experience inside the uterus.

A mother who is a concert pianist gave me another example. She said that she was learning a concerto in the last months of her pregnancy and had to practice one phrase over and over and over again. After the baby came, she was too busy to play again for the first three months. When he was three months old, she placed the baby in a playpen next to her piano and began to play. He kicked and gurgled on his back, looking around contentedly as she played. When she came to the phrase she'd worked on so hard months before, he stopped kicking, became absolutely still, and looked wide-eyed toward her piano, as if to say, "I know that bit!"

Constantly learning from these intrauterine experiences, the fetus is all the more ready to be shaped by the environment later on. Learned behavior and important experiences begin in the uterus, and a fetus, in turn, is already shaping its mother by its responses. No wonder a father is jealous, longing to be a part of this synchrony!

Mothers always ask me whether there is a correlation between the activity of the fetus and future activity. If it is very active, will it continue to be active? If it is quiet and slow to respond, will it be a quiet baby? Now that we have established a working concept of temperament in babies (Thomas, 1963; Chess and Thomas, 1986), we can, in part, predict from the way they respond to their environments what kinds of children they may be later on (quiet, active, or moderate). I wrote my first book, *Infants and Mothers,* to outline the different tracks that these three types of babies might take and the tracks along which they'd lead their parents. Parents often want to know whether they should prepare themselves for one of these types of babies and want a prediction based upon the kind of fetal activity they experience. There have been a few studies that demonstrate a correlation between the kind of activity and responsiveness of the fetus and the kind of baby that is produced. Tjossem (1976) at the National Institutes of Health in Washington, D.C., found a rather high correlation between very active babies in the first year and mothers' reports of very active fetuses. Perhaps the extremes of activity—high and low—can be used to make a prediction. But in general there are several reasons why there can't be a direct prediction. One is the matter of interpretation. Unless a mother has had several babies, her ability to interpret what is "active" and what is "quiet" may be limited. But even more pertinent, some fetuses are responding with reduced activity or even overactivity to intrauterine conditions that are slightly stressed (not enough to hurt them in any way, but enough to change their responses). Outside the uterus they achieve a different balance, and their personality types become clearer.

FEARS OF DAMAGING THE FETUS

After I'd described some of the recent research on fetal activity to her, Mrs. Dorn brought out her real concern. "If I've been tense and anxious during pregnancy, will I have made him tense? Whenever I'm upset and worried, he seems to get more active. I feel guilty for ruining him already."

A question that mothers always ask, or wonder about and don't dare ask, is whether their own tension and activity will influence the baby. If they are anxious and tense, will the baby be tense? If they are too active, will the baby be hyperactive? First of all, all pregnant women are anxious and tense. The sense of responsibility inherent in pregnancy and the natural concern over whether things are going well make it almost inevitable. How the fetus adapts to the mother's tension and activity may complicate any simple correlation. Sontag (1966) monitored fetal heart rate in the last trimester by placing a belt on the mother's abdomen that could register the fetal heartbeat through the abdominal wall. He registered a baseline of heart rate before exposing the fetus to three kinds of stimuli: setting off a loud sound, having the mother smoke a cigarette, and presenting the mother with an emotionally shocking statement. In each of the three cases the fetal heart rate changed in response to the stimulus. It sped up, slowed down, and came to rest in a homeostatic curve of adjustment, returning somewhere near the initial resting level.

Then he presented the same three stimuli to fetuses of mothers who were already chronically stressed—mothers of many small children, mothers who were chronic smokers, and women who had been through and adapted to unusual and chronic emotional stresses. In these cases the fetuses responded with similar but significantly foreshortened responses of heart rates. The rates sped up, slowed down, and returned to rest—all in a much shorter period. In other words, the babies of the latter group had "learned" to adapt more rapidly to these same stimuli. This adaptation is both self-protective and conserving of energy and may well be shaping the fetuses of anxious or active mothers in the uterus. We do not know whether such a fetus may indeed be more jittery and active after delivery or whether it may have learned to remain quiet and to shut out a tense or disturbing environment. The result may be a quiet, relatively protected baby who can handle anxiety and an overactive environment very well.

This discussion led to deeper concerns about having damaged her infant. "I can't control myself. I worry a lot about whatever I do. It seems as if I think about the baby as if he were a picture-book baby but spend all my time worrying about whether I've done something to hurt him. Will he have Down syndrome? Will he have brain damage from something I've done? Is there any way to stop these incessant concerns? I'm afraid I'll hurt him by my worrying." As she talked, she seemed more despondent, and

I truly wished I could dispel her worries. But I knew I couldn't, for all caring parents have concerns. It seems to be the other side of caring so much.

All prospective parents worry about the kind of baby they will have. Will it be a boy or a girl? Will it look like anyone in the family? Will it look like me or like my spouse? And, then, the question that comes up in the middle of the night after the mother wakes up with a startle or the question that races through a father's mind when he finally sits down to rest—a question that is quickly shoved back into his unconscious: Will the baby be normal?

Mothers and fathers rehearse this unspoken thought over and over again. Old wives' tales are built around it. For example, intelligent people believe that if a black cat crosses your path, your baby will be marked. If you see blood, your baby will have a bloody mark on him. If you eat hot foods, your baby will be burned. In cultures less inhibited than ours, such fears are rampant and are expressed openly. Other cultures give a pregnant woman permission to voice such fears or even institutionalize them with elaborate reasoning that can help to assuage a young woman's guilt if she does produce a marred baby. All women expect something to be wrong with their babies. They feel lucky if there is no flaw. If anything goes wrong, it is inevitable that they should feel responsible. Irrationally, any mother will blame herself for any illness, for prematurity, for birthmarks, for any defect that may turn up in the baby. So common are these worries that they drain most young women (and men) during pregnancy. The worries are a measure of how much they are already feeling responsible, and beginning to care, for that baby. They cannot escape such feelings of responsibility or the fears that go with them. It does help to know how universal they are and to talk about them. Husbands and wives have them—each for his or her own reasons—and it helps to share them.

However, there is an unstated, rather superstitious fear that keeps two people from talking about the possibility of having a damaged infant. They are afraid that if their concerns are brought out into the open, they are more likely to come true. On the contrary, the anxiety these fears generate when hidden may be more harmful. I have known young women who felt a change in their fetuses' behavior that suggested the fetuses might be under stress. Their fear of facing it prevented them from talking about it or even reporting it to their physicians. It would have been much better to ventilate these fears in order to gain some objectivity about them.

No one can really tell whether a baby will be normal. The medical profession is getting close to such answers. By means of amniocentesis (tapping fluid from the uterus), floating cells can be examined for known defects such as Down syndrome, spinal cord defects, and several other serious conditions. Such a procedure and/or another called chorionic villous sampling should be considered by women (over thirty-five, though this is an arbitrary figure and age is only one small factor) and by parents who have in their families a history of certain hereditary disorders, such as Tay-Sachs disease, amino acid disorders, or neural tube defects. Ultrasound visualization of the fetus can also tell whether there are certain kinds of defects and whether the fetus is developing properly. All prospective parents should discuss these worries and techniques with their obstetrician and, if necessary, with a genetic counselor.

THE PURPOSES OF ANXIETY

Underlying these normal, healthy fears is a basic conflict in all prospective parents. The opposing wishes to have the baby and to be rid of it are always present. Most prospective parents will feel that they must deny *ever* wanting to be rid of their baby. The wish then gets translated into more acceptable fears, such as fears for the health and safety of the baby. *Of course,* a woman worries about and resents losing her figure, her body's shape, her old image of herself. *Of course,* she will worry about giving up her old adjustments and her balanced relationships in the service of this new invader. *Of course,* a man will worry about the increased responsibility and the necessary changes in his relationships that a new baby will bring. This conflict, between the wish to escape the situation and be rid of the baby and concern for the baby's welfare, produces anxiety, but it need not be destructive. Without the energy mobilized by the negative side of this ambivalent struggle, the positive forces for caring would never be as strong (Brazelton and Cramer, 1990).

Negative wishes tend to dominate one's unconscious thinking. It is inevitble that a parent-to-be will worry about whether the baby will have allergies if a father or a mother or one of their families has them. It is inevitable that both will dredge back into their families' pasts and begin to worry about the baby's inheriting any disease that may have turned up in either family—even in remote kinfolk. It is inevitable that they will worry about Down syndrome or congenital defects in the baby. Each will rehearse these possibilities over and over again at odd times throughout the pregnancy. They will crop up unexpectedly, making the hearts of parents-to-be speed up as they let the inevitable fears come to the surface. The fears will not harm the child. They simply reflect the enormous adjustment that must take place. Out of this turmoil will come a stronger sense of responsibility and caring (Crowe and von Baeyer, 1989).

In addition to the benefits of airing these feelings, rehearsal of what they may do if the baby is damaged may serve a purpose for parents if the baby is, indeed, born with a defect. For each parent will have been through that rehearsal, which will help with the adjustment to that baby. If they can then seek help in sorting out their feelings of responsibility, of having damaged the baby, they will be better able to cope with caring for him and his problems.

As I tried to reassure her, Mrs. Dorn seemed to feel that she was exposing herself too much. She sat back in her chair and subsided for a bit. I talked to her about this and reassured her that all women did need to expose these feelings but rarely had a chance. I assured her that it was safe for her to tell me, for I saw this turmoil as a necessary part of pregnancy, and in fact, it even played a major role. "I feel that the turmoil you are experiencing is common and will give you the energy to do a better job with your baby when he or she does get here. I'm glad you've included me in this. If you get a very quiet or a very active baby or any kind that you may not quite expect, you'll need all this energy to help you work out your relationship with him. And now I know I can help you both as you care for him."

Mr. Dorn took up the questioning. His wife worried about whether she should eat more or should diet. "Which school of thinking should she believe these days?"

A HEALTHY FETUS

Women today are confused with the current controversies about how much and what to eat during pregnancy. Do we know the answers, or do the arguments reflect unfinished research? Probably we do know enough to guide most women in our country. Overeating does not appear to be dangerous for the baby, although obese women have more difficult labors and deliveries. Their abdominal musculature is not likely to be as effective in labor, and their obesity can interfere with a pelvic delivery, making a Caesarean section more likely. The tendency of overweight women to develop diabetes and hypertension in pregnancy may become a problem for the baby, but these diseases are associated only with severely obese women. Overeating in pregnancy is easy, for one tends to be extra-hungry and low on blood sugar. The natural depression is likely to make one want to eat frequently. The obesity that results is hard to get rid of after the baby comes, but probably doesn't affect the baby. Overeating should be curbed, but not for the baby's sake. It can undermine a mother's health, and if a mother allows herself to get too fat, she is liable to blame the baby for it later on, and her feelings may affect him.

Strict dieting, as opposed to eating a well-rounded but moderate amount of food, should be discouraged. Severe weight restriction has been associated with low birth weight, which in turn can be associated with developmental problems after birth. The Institute of Medicine currently recommends a total weight gain during pregnancy of twenty-five to thirty-five pounds for women of normal weight.

Undernutrition of any important dimension is difficult for healthy women to achieve in our country. It looks as if moderate dieting won't really affect the baby. I feel that a mother should be careful to serve her own needs—both nutritionally and psychologically. Then, indirectly, she will be serving her baby's needs. If she needs to diet to curb her weight or to protect herself against the danger of hypertension or toxemia, it is safer for the baby as well.

More severe malnutrition, which occurs among the underprivileged and in chronically ill or addicted women, certainly can affect infants' development. Malnutrition in pregnancy can interfere with the number of replication of cells in the brain, the linear growth of the bones and of the rest of the body, as well as the size of all the baby's cells. Winick of Columbia University (1976) thinks that there may be as much as a 40 percent reduction in the number of brain cells in the baby of a severely and continuously undernourished woman. Not only would the baby's growth be affected then, but his brain development would be limited. Other organs, such as the thyroid and the adrenals—organs that are involved in activation, motivation, paying attention, and so on—would be affected by a lack of proper nutrients. Thus a baby whose mother may have been deprived of critical nutrients may be small and short, with difficulties in learning or in adapting to the demands of our complex society. We must not allow poverty or undernutrition of pregnant women to continue in our ghettos, for they affect the future of the unborn at a critical time with irreversible results.

The malnutrition that accompanies alcoholism and drug addiction is another serious and increasingly widespread concern. Both interact with the mother's starvation diet to affect the baby's development in the uterus seriously. As a result, the baby may be less than optimally responsive, and this becomes a vicious cycle, affecting the mother's responses to him. Drug addiction poses the additional threat of HIV infection for mother and baby.

For most young couples expecting a baby, however, especially intelligent and concerned ones like Mr. and Mrs. Dorn, fears about malnutrition or obesity can easily be put to rest. The same sensible diet that would keep them in good health—emphasizing vegetables, grains, and fruits and downplaying sugar, animal fats, and refined carbohydrates—would also be the best one for their baby.

> *"What about coffee and cocktails and smoking?"* Mr. Dorn had *heard that these could interfere with the fetus's optimal development.* "One reads both sides of these arguments, and we just *don't know what to believe."*

Many medications as well as hard drugs ingested at critical periods of cellular division in the developing brain of the fetus can cut down on numbers of cells and on the complexity of the developing brain. Alcohol in large doses in early pregnancy can do the same. Smoking has been associated with low birth weight, and large amounts of coffee with miscarriage. Quite apart from the effects of these on the mother, which are known to be harmful, the possibility of harm to the fetus should encourage great caution.

In order to have optimal health in the baby and in order to feel that she has done all she can to give the fetus an optimal environment, a mother must consider the effects of all these substances on her baby in the uterus. What makes most sense is to eat wisely, avoiding all drugs, including alcohol, caffeine, and tobacco, especially in early pregnancy.

> *"As long as we're on the subject, what does intercourse do to the baby? We have become afraid of any real show of affection. We certainly don't want to have a premature baby."*

As far as we know, intercourse during pregnancy does not have a harmful effect on the fetus, unless there is already a great danger of miscarriage or early labor. While orgasm stimulates contractions of the uterus, it will not induce labor or abortion unless these are imminent anyway. Even in the last trimester nonpainful intercourse will not start labor. If it did, very few pregnancies would come to term. Since the tendency for a couple to pull away from each other at such a time is already great enough to be a threat, it would be better not to place the strain of abstinence on their relationship.

Because the dangers of worrying about what you might do to your baby far outweigh the real possibilities, it might be worth reevaluating each of your "worry areas" with your husband, physician, or midwife at each visit. Worrying is normal, but it does interfere with the joy of pregnancy.

> By this time in the interview, we all felt close to each other, and when I assured them that I'd be in to see them as soon as their baby came in order to help them get going, they were delighted. Their reluctance to terminate our interview showed me how important it had been to them to unload all of this, but also that they now anticipated a kind of gap in the opportunity to share their questions about the baby. An obstetrician is primarily interested in the mother's well-being. Our discussion had been focused on the baby and the couple as parents of this baby. I urged them to take childbirth education courses together. I expressed the thought that the opportunity to share in the classes, to learn about labor and delivery and how to handle it, was a marvelous opportunity, and I knew that they'd find them very rewarding.

Support groups for pregnant couples such as those fostered by the Childbirth Education and Lamaze associations can play an important role. Not only do they offer a couple educational tips about pregnancy—what one can do and what one should be careful about, where the fetus is in its development, what to expect at the time of labor, and so on—but the mutual support of others who are going through the same kinds of anxieties is of immense value. Being able to talk about mutual concerns, to share questions and realize that most of them are universal, can be of real value in freeing both parents-to-be to get as much pleasure as possible out of the pregnancy and to be as prepared as possible for the next step.

MAKING NEW CONNECTIONS

The interview that I have quoted lasted longer than many, for the parents had used it as a chance to unload many of the questions

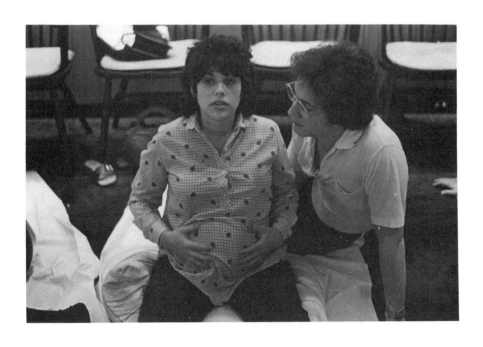

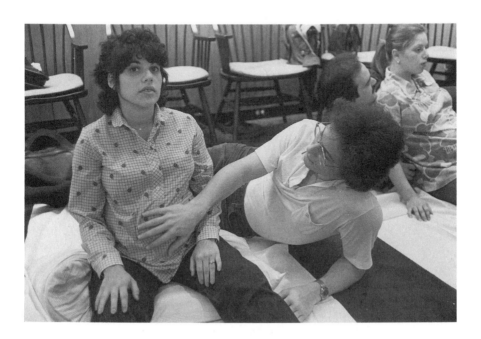

and concerns that had been building up, unanswered, for the prior seven months. For the pediatrician, too, this kind of interview is invaluable in helping to institute a working relationship.

The emotional energy that is mobilized during pregnancy does more than fuel a mother and father to make this major step in their lives. The metaphor of electric shock helps to describe what I feel is going on emotionally during pregnancy. Anxiety, like shock, shakes up old, no-longer-useful connections, allowing for reorganization. New connections will form; new combinations in relationships are possible; new kinds of relationships are all available because of the openness of these circuits at such a time. If parents get a quiet baby, they can adjust to his quietness. If they get an active one who makes demands all the time, this very turmoil in the latter part of pregnancy mobilizes the energy needed to handle the demands. Parents can break out of the limits of their former selves; they do not need to be a reproduction of their own parents; they can be opened up by this anxiety. The energy that it stirs up is needed by the new individual that they have produced. The turmoil of pregnancy serves a major purpose in preparing them for attachment to the baby and for their own new relationship as parents.

SHARING THE ATTACHMENT WITH A SIBLING

Mrs. Clark brought her two-year-old in for a routine checkup. Alice was a delightful little girl who charged into my office as if she were going to take over. She walked in with her curls bobbing and looked up at me when I spoke to her. She looked at me again, looked away quickly, and mumbled, "Hi," into the corner. She began to busy herself, pulling out one toy after another, turning them over, loudly running the wheels of the automobiles, kissing the dolls, and talking gibberish to them in a loud voice. She seemed to pay little attention to either her mother or me as we began to talk. Competence marked her every move. Her mother addressed a comment to her from time to time, but she ignored this except to speed up her noisy investigation of the pile of toys.

After responding to the first few routine questions, "How is she?" "Has she been sick since I saw her?" "Is she eating all right?" Mrs. Clark suddenly became quite serious. No longer presenting a gay, engaging exterior, she sat forward in her chair, her face drained of color, her hands picked at her clothing, and

*her voice dropped to a strained, urgent level. "I'm pregnant
again." She said this as if it were some sort of jail sentence. I
remembered how joyful she'd been with Alice's pregnancy and
what a really nice time she and Alice had had. It was hard for
me to reconcile this with her mood now.*

*As she changed her tone, Alice stopped playing and began to
watch her mother. Her eyes and face were as serious as Mrs.
Clark's. She leaned forward in imitation of her mother, forgot
her toys, and slowly inched her way toward her mother.*

*I wondered why Mrs. Clark was so serious. Was she feeling
all right? "Oh, yes, I'm fine, and we want another baby. My husband's delighted, and he hopes it's a boy! I'm glad too—I guess.
But how can I leave Alice?" She blurted this last statement out
as she unconsciously reached out for Alice, who was now cling-
ing to her knee. They had changed from a competent, carefree-
looking pair to two lost souls.*

The most difficult thing about having a second baby is the necessary "desertion" of the first one. I have had mothers tell me about
their second pregnancy with tears in their eyes. When I congratulated them and seemed glad, they reproached me. I have increasing
respect for the power of the ties to the older children and how hard it
is for a mother to conceive of diluting them by bringing a second baby
into the home. It is as if she were indeed deserting the older child
and were endangering his or her future with the new pregnancy.
Why do mothers feel so deeply about this? I think it is because no
mother dares to believe that she will have enough nurturance to go
around. She has made it with the first child, and she has felt the
solidity of that relationship. Perhaps she daren't face the prospect of
diluting that relationship, of losing the intensity of it, for a new and
unknown one. Certainly it is a universal fear, that the older child will
suffer and be damaged by the rivalry he will feel for the new baby.
The truth is that most children profit enormously by having to share,
by having to learn to adjust to a sibling. And no family is likely to be
less enriched for having two children instead of one.

And yet the fear of deserting the present child is based somewhat in reality. For just as a pregnant woman withdraws from her
husband, her friends, and her older family into herself in the earliest
part of her pregnancy, so will she turn inward and very subtly withdraw from her other children at such a time. She will do so unconsciously and will be surprised when the older child minds it.

Even small children recognize changes in their mother that start in pregnancy.

I shall never forget Leslie, who was in my office for a checkup when he was two. As I talked with his mother about him, he played around the office. Every time he leaned over to pick up a toy or squatted down to the floor, he let out a soft grunt. He didn't appear to be in any pain, nor did he limp or seem to be guarding himself as he played. But the grunt was regular every time he squatted or bent over. I palpated his abdomen carefully, felt each hip and his spine, and he did not wince. I could find no reason for his grunting. Perplexed and feeling rather desperate as I groped for a reason for Leslie's grunting, I finally asked his mother if she was pregnant. She said, "Why, no, I certainly am not," and they left. She called me two days later to congratulate me on my correct diagnosis. She said, "How in the world did you know I was pregnant? I certainly didn't think I was." I told her that I'd been groping for a reason why Leslie would be grunting as he bent over until I noticed that she did too. This was a completely unconscious response to her new, unrecognized pregnancy. Leslie had picked up on and identified with the changes in her even before she recognized them herself.

This kind of experience has led me to feel that an older child does notice the changes in his mother. If she can be open with him, he will begin to adjust to the new baby long before this baby is actually born. As his mother turns inward, the older child will be pressed to turn outward for nurturing. The nicest thing about my wife's pregnancies was that the older children turned to me when she was less available. Given the chance to turn to their fathers or to their grandparents or to siblings, most children will begin to work on the coming separation. When the baby comes, the older child will be ready to share. If his mother is upset by the impending separation, she may easily overprotect or hover over the older child, so that he has less chance to find other resources.

So I wondered with Mrs. Clark about why she was so mad. She told me that she'd never had such a rewarding time in her life as she'd had these past two years with Alice, and she could see that this was the beginning of the end of their nice time together. "Already," she said, "Alice is being negative with me and pulling away." Alice was sitting in her lap by now, leaning back soberly against her mother.

I tried to assure her that Alice's negativism was a normal two-year-old's pulling away. If she saw it as bad, how could Alice ever become independent? Mrs. Clark barely heard me, so mournful was she. I wondered again why she was so upset by this coming event. Finally she blurted out, "I've barely learned to mother Alice. How can I ever be a mother to two children? I'm afraid I'll desert one in order to mother the other. I've never been any good at sharing relationships."

I assured her that she could and would, and I also tried to reassure her that Alice would, indeed, profit from this adjustment in the long run. As we talked, Alice let me know that my remarks were hitting home. For she began to relax and climbed out of her mother's lap, walking sturdily back to the toys to begin playing again. Mrs. Clark watched her go, brightened up, and said, "You have really helped me."

Her next question really surprised me. "When should I tell Alice that we're going to have another baby?" After the demonstration we'd just been through, I was able to tell Mrs. Clark that I was pretty sure Alice knew something was up already.

If she meant by her question when should she discuss leaving her to deliver the baby, I felt that could wait till the end of her pregnancy, but meanwhile, Alice would be reassured by their talking freely and openly about what was happening. Trying to hide it or save it for a big confrontation would only frighten her, for she needed now to understand her mother's quick and rather unpredictable changes of moods. I did feel that maybe Mrs. Clark could talk to her husband and her own parents more about some of her reluctant feelings, for I felt Alice had a rather burdened look on her face when her mother began to expose her stronger feelings about "leaving Alice" for this baby. And I felt Alice would be likely to take such a statement literally and be frightened by it. Working her feelings out with others might free Mrs. Clark to act more normal with Alice.

Parents ask me when they should tell the older child about the new baby. I feel that it is artificial and even frightening if "telling him" is saved as an event for late in pregnancy. I feel that their reluctance to treat it normally stems from their reluctance to give up the previous relationship with the older child and the fear that they will not be able to make it with two children. Hence the sooner parents accept the reality of the new baby, the sooner the child can. And then the mother can be freer to think about and relate to her fetus. Since the older child is likely to sense that things around him are tense and changing, it would be wise to give him the reason. Hence I would advise talking about the baby's coming from the first as if it were the natural event it is and part of the family's development. Hiding it from the older child will only serve to heighten his anxiety. However, there can also be a tendency to overdo the talk about the baby in one's own excitement about the coming event.

> *I learned this from a three-year-old named Joe, a chubby, out-going little boy who always spoke what was on his mind. His mother was a child developmentalist and endeavored to talk everything out with Joe, often pressing him into corners by her eagerness to inform him about coming events. All during her pregnancy she talked to Joe about "the baby," asking him how he felt, warning him about how he might feel. Toward the end of this interminable nine months and after another speech about prep-aration by his mother, Joe blurted out one day, "Is it a boy? Is it a girl? What is a baby?"*

Joe had gotten sick of "being prepared" and no longer could be-lieve there was any end in sight. You can overdo the preparation.

If the baby is talked about naturally, an older child can partici-pate in the preparations. The older child can help with preparing the baby's room and in this way feel a sense of participation and a reason for relinquishing some attention to the new baby.

Later on in pregnancy he can participate in all the preparations for the baby, and the family can "get ready" together. For example, a father and his older child can listen to and feel the baby's move-ments. They can feel shut out together and can establish links with each other in imagining what the baby is doing and what he is like. They can be jealous of the baby inside the mother and of the mother's exciting condition. I have rarely seen a toddler who doesn't begin to walk with his abdomen pushed forward like his mother's in imitation of her.

> *"What will I do to prepare her?" asked Mrs. Clark. "When must I tell her about leaving her? Who shall I leave with her? My mother will take her to her house, or can she stay at home with*

her father? All of these questions are already boiling around in my mind."

Preparation for leaving the older child is the most difficult but important part of planning for him. If it is at all possible, he will be better off in his familiar surroundings, with his own toys and own bed—and with his own father to come home to him. If grandparents or relatives or sitters can come to him at home, he will adjust more easily. The separation from his mother is the one that he will need to adjust to. This separation will crown the beginnings of separation that have taken place during pregnancy and will culminate symbolically as well as literally in his having to give her up to the hospital for a few days.

Not having to leave the older child is one of the arguments for a home delivery. It is true that when a woman delivers at home, she doesn't actually leave the older child. But the actuality doesn't hide the fact that she must and should turn away to the new baby. No one can hide that fact from the older child. One cannot protect the older child from having to adjust to this, but one can mitigate it and help him over this adjustment. The best prospect is that of being able to turn to his father at such a time. Hence he should be at home and near his father's comings and goings if at all possible. Introducing him to the sitter or reviving his knowledge of his grandparents before she leaves to go to have the baby gives him the mother's assurance that she is turning him over to them only temporarily. And he needs to hear repeatedly that she'll *come back*. For a small child one or two days of separation is an eternity. A separation is endless until it stops. Reminding him that she'll be home soon and letting him telephone her and visit her in the hospital all keep the faith in return alive. But he will still need to adjust after she returns. The understanding and support he gets from all of those around him can certainly mitigate the pain and can lead him to make an adjustment that will serve him for the rest of his life.

At the end of Alice's checkup, I wondered why Mrs. Clark had brought all these questions to me so early in her pregnancy. I was glad she had, for I felt she and Alice were relieved by the chance to get them out and talk about them. I was pretty sure that we'd done Alice a service by exposing them now. Mrs. Clark was likely to be freer with Alice and seemed to feel less torn about her pregnancy. The other reason she wanted to expose her questions didn't occur to me until later. She needed to be given permission to start attaching to the new baby. And she needed this permission from Alice's advocate, her physician. When I gave her permission and reassured her that Alice was competent and would even profit from this, she took courage. And with that, she could begin to feel free to attach to the new baby, to see her job as that of mothering two babies instead of one. It is easier the second and third times, but there are important adjustments that are distinct to each new addition to a family. Mrs. Clark was on her way. She would have sorted out some of the division of her own attachment to the two by the time the baby arrived. Hence it is important to expect to work out this turmoil even with a second or third infant and to be given the chance to do so.

What about Mr. Clark? Will he have an opportunity to do his work of dividing his affection for Alice and for the new baby? He is already trying—by planning or wishing for a boy. But we have no institutionalized way to help him work out his concerns. It might help him to talk to someone, and I wish more fathers would come to my office to ask their questions.

2

Delivery:
Separation and Bonding

PREPARATION FOR CHILDBIRTH

Mrs. Johnson's labor started at 2:00 A.M., about four hours after she'd gone to bed. Her husband first became aware of her discomfort when she involuntarily began to grip the squeaky bedsides. Her pains were strong from the first, and she began to remember all that she'd learned in childbirth education courses. "Short, shallow breaths, concentrate on something out there, don't try to hold back, and don't worry—it won't last forever." All of this came flooding back and reassured her. What it really meant to her now was that many, many people had been through this before and had come out all right. She knew she could too. She had toned up her muscles; she had rehearsed and rehearsed for this. She had learned all the stages—when to push, how to breathe, and when to relax. She knew about the purpose of the first stages, and when she found a bloody mucous plug in the toilet water after her pains began, she knew her cervix was dilating and she was "on her way." All of this pointed to an exciting adventure, even if it was to be a painful one.

The importance of intellectual preparation cannot be overestimated. Before Dr. Grantly Dick-Read in England in the 1940s and Dr. Fernand Lamaze in France in the 1950s began their pioneering inroads on medication that affected our obstetrical approaches here, labor and delivery were still treated as if they were illnesses. Women were not asked, "Do you want medication and anesthesia?" but always, "What anesthesia do you want?" Even after the push toward "natural" childbirth was begun by the International Childbirth Education Association (ICEA) in the mid-1950s in the United States, obstetricians and hospitals took decades to catch up.

Over the years the public pressure from women who demanded to be awake, to participate in their own deliveries, and to be treated more humanely in the process has gathered steam under the umbrella of the ICEA and sister organizations (Lamaze, La Leche League, and so on). There is still a tendency to treat labor and delivery as if they were medical problems rather than exciting developmental achievements, but that attitude is changing rapidly now.

The work of Dr. Marshall H. Klaus and Dr. John Kennell (1976, 1982) demonstrating the powerful effect of an alert infant on the early bonding process between parents and babies gave a further reason to question the use of heavy pain medication or anesthesia in delivery. Their current work (1991) on the effect of labor support, of the presence of an experienced woman called a doula, on both the length of labor and the number of Caesareans is of great interest for expectant parents as well as childbirth professionals.

Birthing room settings, where parents can have privacy and where a hospital atmosphere is avoided, are now popular and have done much to dispel the medical image of childbirth. In many maternity centers parents are invited to familiarize themselves with the birth setting as well as the staff that will be in attendance.

HOME DELIVERY

Those who choose home delivery must recognize the element of risk. In many parts of the world home delivery is the only way. In our society we have the capacity to protect mother and infant with advanced medical resources. The goal of birthing room settings is to monitor out the risks to both mother and baby and still maintain a homelike, humanized atmosphere. The training of nurse-midwives for home deliveries has a similar goal. They can and do decide which mothers are at risk and must be in the care of a hospital. But there will still be unpredictable events when rapid transport to a hospital is needed. Homelike birthing rooms under the umbrella of a hospital, where deliveries can be nurtured and assisted by midwives, supervised by obstetrical teams, and made quickly accessible to intensive care units for baby and mother if necessary, seem to be the best we have to offer today.

I have seen and participated in home deliveries, and they are not always relaxed events. Everyone is aware of the dangers, bravado is in the air, and things can easily go wrong. If they do, there is no recourse for the family but to blame themselves. With optimal care available, any compromise deliberately made becomes the burden of those who make it. I remember the baby of a young couple who had a home delivery, supervised by an excellent midwife. Everything went well, and the baby was fine. He cried immediately, went to breast, and suckled well. The mother recovered quickly. But the baby had a very minor anomaly, in that his urethral opening was placed on an unusually high part of his penis. This is not an uncommon anomaly and has nothing to do with labor or delivery because whatever caused it happened during pregnancy. Its occurrence is unrelated to anything the mother could have done. However, because she felt responsible, as *all* mothers do, for this very minor defect, and because she had hidden her concern about her role in flouting the system to have a home delivery, she blamed the delivery for his penile anomaly. Although she is a very intelligent woman, she continued to blame herself and the delivery for this over the next year despite my constant explanations and reassurances. To me, her distortion represented an example of the powerful forces of guilt ready to take over and burden young parents for anything that might go wrong. I feel we in the medical profession should do more to help parents sort out real responsibility from unnecessary guilt. We can and must improve our system so that parents don't need to run away from it. The autonomy, warm atmosphere, and chance to make choices that young parents are looking for by delivering at home can be provided in a hospital setting as well.

ANXIETY AND EXCITEMENT

As soon as he realized that this was really it, Mr. Johnson was as excited as his wife. He wanted to phone everyone—the obstetrician, the pediatrician, his parents, her parents, the childbirth educator, all the other parents in their class.

The importance of the group as a support system for parents-to-be is enormous. The families that go through these classes together turn to one another before and after the delivery to share experiences. They often form important support groups afterward for sharing and comparing child-rearing concerns. They are a kind of peer-group substitute for the old extended-family supports.

His wife reminded him that it was early in the morning and reassured him that they could handle this themselves. As she anchored him down, he laughed to realize that she was supporting him, and he began to turn his excitement into more productive channels. He packed her bag for her. He helped her around the house. He began to read out loud their notes and instructions from the classes, and with that he began to calm down — to count, to time her labor pains, and to prepare himself for being a support to her.

The anxiety that young husbands have around a delivery certainly floods back to me as I write. I worried irrationally all through my wife's labors. I worried about whether she'd survive. If she did, would she be intact or would the baby have damaged her? My anxiety was for her and covered the guilt I felt about having produced this situation. With our first babies there was nothing for me to do but "turn it over to the medical profession." That was the hardest of all — the feeling of being useless and helpless — and I went home miserable, while my wife did all the work. Including the father in labor is certainly a major step. He can be useful, he can be a part of it, and he's bound to feel tremendous pride in his wife after it's accomplished. All of his anxiety can be directed and utilized in the direction of the baby and of cementing the family at such a time.

As her labor progressed, they found themselves getting more and more excited and more and more involved in concentrating on her labor. The "pains" were not really painful, and they seemed to be leading toward a goal as they gradually became closer together, and more and more regular, more prolonged. After a few hours, in which Mr. Johnson had read out loud to her, her waters broke with a gush, and it was time to call her physician. He could barely control his voice as he reached the answering service. When Dr. Thompson called back after what seemed an interminable wait (actually it was fifteen minutes), Mr. Johnson proudly announced "their" symptoms and progress. Dr. Thompson had been awakened from a deep sleep and found it difficult to match the excitement in Mr. Johnson's voice. He ascertained that labor was indeed going along and that labor pains were regular and getting harder. Mr. Johnson was pressing to get his wife to the hospital and under medical protection. Dr. Thompson's nonchalant suggestion that they wait at home until the pains were only five minutes apart irritated him. But the doctor promised to notify the hospital to be ready for them and said that he'd see them there soon.

There are at least two reasons why a physician suggests doing a certain amount of laboring at home. Braxton-Hicks contractions, or "false labor," can mimic the real thing, but those pains don't get regular or stronger over time, and parents can avoid an unnecessary hospitalization if they wait to see that the pains are really leading to delivery. Braxton-Hicks contractions can and do occur several days before real labor begins. The second reason is that unless labor is really instituted and going along well with hard pains, the transfer to the hospital and the relief of being supervised can slow down and even stop the laboring uterus. Since this is counterproductive, it is better for a mother to stay at home and build up her labor there. In Mrs. Johnson's case the fact that her waters had broken would already make it important to go to the hospital. If the waters are broken, the seal of protection against an infection's reaching the baby in the uterus is gone, and for medical reasons we feel that twenty-four hours is the critical cutoff beyond which it is not safe any longer to assume that the baby won't be infected. So she will need to be there.

Mr. Johnson realized that if he calmed himself down, he could be of more support to his wife. So far she had been stoic and apparently unconcerned. When he calmed down and tried to reassure her, she began to cry softly on his shoulder. She admitted that she was frightened and let him know how much she needed him. He became a new person.

In the next hour he alerted her parents. Her mother came over in time to see her off to the hospital. Her labor pains were building up now, and so was her strength. Her weeping period had relieved her, and she felt ready for the rest of the day.

THE QUESTION OF MEDICATION

As they entered the hospital, they felt a combination of relief at getting there and a curious feeling of impersonality. Everyone on the floor was busy with early-morning chores. No one treated them and their arrival as anything but routine. They were one more admission to be attended to. The nurses were pleasant and comforting, but not cozy. A nurse walked in briskly and asked, "When do you want your medication?" Mr. Johnson quickly told her that they did not want medication. The nurse ignored him and continued to press Mrs. Johnson. Mrs. Johnson's pains were strong, and she was tired from the drive in. She rather weakly refused the offer. She had to remind herself that they'd decided to postpone any medication or anesthesia as long as possible. It already seemed like a very seductive offer.

Unless the resolve to go through labor naturally and without medication is firm, it becomes pretty difficult to refuse it at times when a woman is tired and worried. The comfort that medical people get out of doing something and preventing pain does not escape her, and she has been properly reared to try to please people in authority. But it is time for her to think of herself first and of her goal—of being awake for the birth and of having an alert baby. The first shot of medication dulls a woman's resolve, and from then on it's downhill. In former days, when premedication during labor was routine, the striking aspect of all labor and delivery rooms was the lack of control of the medicated women. Hence a woman must constantly remind herself that she is resolved to go as far as she can without medication.

From a pediatrician's standpoint the less medication that reaches the baby through the mother's bloodstream the better, for the medication comes across the placenta into the infant's circulation, depressing his nervous system. We have known for some time that the effects on the baby of prolonged and big doses of premedication given to the mother can affect his behavior for as much as seven days after delivery (Brazelton, 1963). Even more prolonged effects on problem-solving behavior, effects lasting as long as four to eight months, have been observed in infants whose mothers have been significantly medicated during labor (Brackbill, 1974). Certainly the effects on babies directly after birth are significant and observable, and as we pointed out earlier they affect their parents' impression of them. Even if medication becomes necessary later on in labor, the longer a mother can postpone it, the better it will be for the baby and for her and for their recovery afterward. Each hour without it is a step in the right direction.

INDIVIDUAL CHOICES IN DELIVERY

After she was in bed and at rest, her labor slowed down briefly. Her husband reminded her that she should get up to walk around. This induced the regular pains again, and by the time Dr. Thompson came to examine her, she was in good, hard labor again.

As he examined her, he reviewed her history and went over their plans for delivery. The Johnsons had searched for a physician who was recognized for his willingness to go along with the choices of his patients. There were several obstetricians in town who professed an interest in natural childbirth and in husband participation but who were not prepared to back a couple if there were any problems during labor. They resorted all too quickly to medications and anesthesia. Dr. Thompson had the reputation of being committed to the patient's choices and was willing to work to achieve them.

Since this is an opportunity for us in the medical profession to reinforce the parents in feeling important to their babies, it seems critical to me to back them up as decision makers. There are now many choices available for different kinds of delivery, and parents-to-be should be well enough informed to be involved in making one of

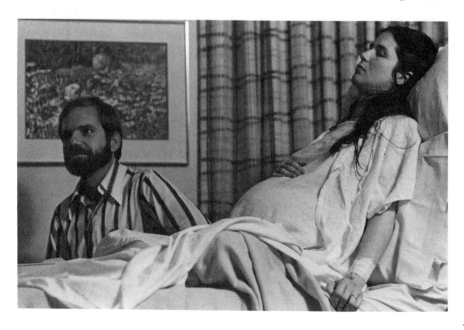

the following choices: (a) unmedicated childbirth; (b) techniques of delivery in different positions and in a quiet, semilit room; (c) local anesthesia, such as spinal or epidural, which does not reach the infant but does block out the most severe labor pains at the end and the pain of an episiotomy, when that is necessary; (d) small doses of premedication toward the end of a long, difficult labor to relax the cervix and the muscular tension that may be building up to interfere with relaxation and delivery; (e) a repeat or elective Caesarean section for pelvic disproportion, dystocia (cessation of labor) of the uterus, and fetal distress. All of these can be discussed and agreed upon ahead of time with a sympathetic physician. Each type of delivery can be planned to minimize the effects on the baby's behavior and to enhance the mother's participation as much as possible in her own labor and delivery. This participation is critical to her feelings of competence. Giving her the information and options necessary to make informed choices about delivery seems to be a critical aspect of backing her up as a decision-making adult at this important time. Now that parents have choices and are participants in their deliveries, the difference in them after delivery shows up in their self-confidence as they handle their babies. Without such choices parents come away from a hospital experience feeling devalued and depersonalized. This has changed in most parts of the country. I would urge parents to find a responsive physician to work with and a hospital setting where this change has come about.

> *The Johnsons reminded him that they'd like to make it as far as they could without any medication or anesthesia. He acknowledged this and told them that he'd have his nurse supervise any medication that they requested to be sure it seemed necessary. He'd be in from time to time to check Mrs. Johnson's progress. He asked Mr. Johnson whether he felt competent to monitor his wife's pains and to stay with her and reassured him that he would be necessary and welcome in the delivery room. They settled down to the next period of labor.*
>
> *Her labor seemed to go on and on. After six hours they both were exhausted and welcomed the boost that each visit from the doctor and the nurse gave them. Each visit and check on Mrs. Johnson's progress also raised their anxiety, for there was always the gnawing concern that things might not be right. However, labor seemed to proceed uneventfully.*
>
> *At one point Dr. Thompson's nurse suggested speeding up*

the labor with a shot of Pitocin (trade name for a hormone called oxytocin), which reinforces uterine contractions. There was a real urge on both their parts to comply with this. Mrs. Johnson was getting pretty exhausted, and Mr. Johnson wanted to save her as much discomfort as was feasible. But they remembered the warnings that they had learned in their classes about any unnecessary interference and resolved to continue as they were. When they asked the nurse whether the Pitocin was really needed, she assured them that the only advantage was in speeding up labor. So there was no harm in deciding to wait it out.

Although Pitocin in the hands of experts probably does not present any danger to the fetus or to the mother, there are advantages in postponing it, too, until it is necessary or unequivocally indicated. If anything should happen to the baby by such a choice, the parents would feel endlessly responsible. When the uterus contracts normally, there is a slowing down of fetal heart rate, and the pressure on the fetus's head to mold itself to the pelvis is increased. Presumably a slower process makes this molding easier on the baby's brain (Rosen and Rosen, 1975). Any unnatural reinforcement of the strength of the uterine contractions might push the baby beyond his limits of adjusting, and hence the longer, slower labor pains are serving a purpose. Mothers who know this can tolerate them better, toward the goal of an intact baby.

THE FETAL MONITOR

At another visit Dr. Thompson suggested that they could begin to monitor the baby's condition with a fetal monitor—electro-encephalographic electrodes applied to the baby's scalp via the cervix. Since he did not seem to feel it was necessary, the Johnsons pressed him to elaborate on why he'd suggested it. He said that it was a procedure that was easily available in the hospital, often used to be certain of the status of the fetus in hard labor. When they pressed him further, he assured them that in his judgment the baby was doing fine, and it was usual for a primipara to have a long labor. He felt quite secure in following the baby's progress without a monitor but also felt he should offer it to them since it was available. They refused it but assured him that if he felt it to be necessary at any time, they'd certainly agree.

There is often no reason for high-powered equipment to replace clinical judgment. There are times when we need it to confirm our clinical decisions, but to use an intrusive device such as the monitor as a routine or for a clinician such as Dr. Thompson to feel pressured to suggest it in order to clear himself of the suggestion of not having done "everything he should" is too bad. Certainly he must be trusted to be in charge, and the Johnsons must be ready to accept that. The threat of malpractice hangs over all of us. But it mustn't endanger medical relationships and judgment to that extent. The intrusive, anxiety-producing aspect of a device such as a monitor is considerable for the laboring parents. The overinterpretation of electroencephalographic records that has gone on in the past makes it critical that we reevaluate the indications for its use, as well as those for its interpretation. Caesarean section rates have nearly doubled in many hospitals as a direct result of monitoring and of the overinterpretation of fetal distress from them. (It is important to put this in context and to remember that the advent of Caesarean sections brought a real decline in the incidence of brain damage in the infant.) While the Johnsons were right to push Dr. Thompson to postpone use of the monitor in favor of his clinical judgment, if it were indicated, the monitor is an excellent backup for deciding whether the baby is in real distress and needs to be delivered. Much central nervous system damage has been averted by appropriate use of fetal monitoring (Rosen and Rosen, 1975).

THE FETUS DURING LABOR

As labor continued, the maneuvers taught in the childbirth education classes of panting, relaxing between contractions, and pushing during a labor pain became automatic. One of the fears that had plagued Mrs. Johnson initially was that labor pains would get worse over time. She found to her relief that they didn't. After they reached a regular interval, the painful aspect of them reached a plateau, and they just became regular, hard work. Having her husband there, as well as the visits of Dr. Thompson and the nurse, made it tolerable. She needed to remind herself from time to time of the baby. For the fetus had virtually stopped moving; no longer did he kick or move about. With the onset of a contraction she could imagine that the baby's little movements ceased entirely, and he seemed to stiffen out. She prayed that he was all right and felt very close to him in his plight.

Actually the spontaneous movements of the baby are markedly reduced in labor. This would certainly be expected, for the laboring uterus is in contraction, and all extra space is taken up. The cushioning waters are gone, and the baby is being squeezed out. He does undoubtedly twist and turn a bit, adjusting his position to fit the contracting uterus. His reflexes (Moro reflex, tonic neck reflex, and stretching reflex—see next chapter) may serve to help him writhe along through the birth canal. His head must get molded, the small bones overlapping to reduce its circumference by an inch or more to be able to get through the pelvic outlet. There has been some work to show that the threshold for tactile sensitivity, for pressure and for pain, goes up considerably in the ninth month, as if nature were preparing the baby for delivery. The habituation mechanisms we shall talk about in the next chapter also serve him well. Evidence from fetal monitoring of heart rate and the central nervous system shows that there is a protective slowing of the heart and of the electrical activity of the brain that accompanies each contraction, with a speeding up and revitalization afterward. All of this not only protects the fetus in labor but serves to prepare him for the major adjustment at delivery of taking over his own breathing and cardiac controls. Whereas he has been parasitic, depending upon the placenta and maternal circulation, within minutes he must become independent. Labor and its repeated stimuli may well serve to prepare him for this transition. We have observed in the past that babies who were delivered without labor and by Caesarean section needed more stimulation in order to cry at birth and needed to be watched and stimulated from time to time to make this necessary adjustment. This is probably not true with the infants born with normal, vaginal delivery. They handle the adjustment themselves. The circulating blood gases stimulate the baby's brain to make the necessary respiratory and cardiac efforts without any help from the outside.

MORE CHOICES

After two more hours Mrs. Johnson's labor pains were much closer, the contractions seemed to last a long time, and she could feel their effectiveness increasing. She could even imagine that she felt the baby's head pressing equally between her legs and into the pelvic opening between contractions. The increase in labor became more painful, but the pain was balanced for her by the feeling of effectiveness. She and her husband were renewed by anticipation that they might be nearing the end. The nurse assured her that she was now "getting somewhere" and began to prepare her for her move to the delivery room. Her pubic hair had been shaved off (an optional procedure in some hospitals), and she was ready to go to the delivery room. She found her heart pounding, and she squeezed her husband's hand hard now with each contraction. Thank goodness he could go with her for this next stage.

In the delivery room everything was bustling. She was moved abruptly from her bed to the table. Her legs were put up into stirrups, and she was "prepped" all over again with a cold antiseptic solution. As she looked around at the businesslike nursing staff with their masks on, all ignored her as they went about their clattering business of getting the instruments ready. Mr. Johnson was almost breathless with excitement. Although he felt as if he had extra feet that were always being tripped over by some efficient person, he also knew that his wife needed him even more as all the impersonal hustle increased. Her pains were longer and stronger now, and she had to squeeze him hard in order not to cry out. He continued to instruct her as he had been taught with each labor pain. As her pains grew stronger, she seemed to latch on to him with her eyes and listened to his instructions with a kind of avidity that made him feel really useful. The activity in the delivery room and the constant checking of her abdomen to monitor the baby's heart rate increased. The anesthetist arrived and began to quiz her as to her need for an anesthetic. When he asked whether she could continue without an epidural or a cervical block (anesthesia injected locally to ease the local pains of the cervix stretching), she asked him what the arguments against them were. He told her that she was so close to the end that little of it would reach the baby, and it might make the last bit easier for her. It would be particularly easier if she had to have an episiotomy. But, he added, the anesthetic might slow labor down a bit.

This latter information is rarely shared with patients, and it might make their choice clearer. Most women are eager to get to the end of this stage and would be willing to finish without anything if they were given such a choice. An episiotomy (an incision of the perineum) for a primiparous delivery is almost routine, and the argument is that it prevents a more dangerous kind of tearing of the perineum at the end of a delivery. It also serves to speed up the delivery of the baby's head. However, an episiotomy means more pain for the mother after delivery, and I've been told that a little more patience on the part of everyone concerned can pay off in reducing needless episiotomies. If so, it is worth the extra effort.

Mrs. Johnson looked at her husband pleadingly as if he should make the choice. Since they had made it this far, he wanted desperately for her to hold out. He asked whether they could postpone the decision even longer and decide for a local anesthetic if it looked as if his wife would need an episiotomy. Dr. Thompson arrived at this time and backed up this approach. He scrubbed quickly and took his place at the delivering end of the table. As she had a long contraction, he asked the anesthetist to raise the end of the table by her head so that she could push more effectively. Even a ten-degree rise made a real difference in her comfort and in her ability to press down with each contraction.

As long as her blood pressure was being monitored and there was someone (the anesthetist) to watch her condition, there seemed to be no reason not to have her more upright. She was in little danger of having her blood pressure drop abruptly. In countries where babies are delivered more naturally, women sit or squat in an upright position for the delivery of the baby, and it certainly seems more effective, as well as more comfortable. The reason we keep women flat is to prevent their blood pressure from dropping, because their blood concentrates in their laboring uterus and they get less circulation to the brain. In most cases this is not a problem. Mothers certainly can be more comfortable and can assist more effectively in the delivery when they are more upright.

THE MOMENT OF BIRTH

Her labor reached a peak. She was panting, pushing, trying not to cry out, but gripping her husband's arm and hands with each prolonged pain. At last it looked as if she were ready to deliver the baby. Her cervix was dilating successfully, and on one particularly long and difficult contraction a tuft of black hair showed in the mirror that had been set up for the Johnsons to look into. This little bit of baby revived both of them, and Mrs. Johnson began to feel that it was all worth it. She had an almost uncontrollable urge to cry out, "It's really going to be a baby!" As she pressed down, uncontrolled, with the next long pain, Dr. Thompson said, "Pant, breathe rapidly, but don't push," as he gently held the baby's head back to keep it from tearing her perineum. She cried out when this pain was over, and her husband felt her nails digging into his palms. With the next contraction, Dr. Thompson encouraging her, she felt the baby's head slide out slowly but surely. He called out, "Great! You've done it," and began to aspirate the mucus from the baby's mouth and nose, to clear his nasopharynx before the first breath. Even before the next contraction, which would push out his shoulders and trunk, the baby had begun to gasp and made a slight gurgling noise. She felt elated, and when the next contraction followed almost immediately, she felt herself pushing the whole baby out. Dr. Thompson was pulling gently on the baby, freeing his shoulders and then his extremities, but the rest of the push was easy! She had delivered a healthy, active, well-developed eight-pound baby boy! Mr. Johnson was so giddy and so caught up in the process that he almost forgot his wife. He reached for the baby even before the cord was severed. Mrs. Johnson was sobbing for joy and with relief. They both watched every move that the baby made—as he was suctioned, as he opened his eyes to look gingerly around, as he reacted with startles and began to cry. His color changed from a puffy, dusky blue to pale ivory, and within three gasping cries—to pink. He was a wriggling, crying person! And they had done it.

The elation that follows such a massive effort is in proportion to the anxiety and the hard work that have preceded it. No wonder parents are high after such a multihour effort. The excitement, the fear, the relief, the anxiety, and the elation generate a kind of availability on the parents' part that makes them ready for almost anything. Even a flattened nose, pushed-away ears, a slightly bluish, puffy face, arms and legs that flail, a piercing cry, a distorted-looking head, skin covered with a thick, waxy vernix—all of these look as wonderful to parents in the delivery room as the picture-book baby they've had in their minds all through pregnancy. It's only later, as they begin to come down off their high, that they begin to count toes, to study the face to see whom the baby looks like, to notice the flattened nose and ears and the molded head that comes to a point. Only later do they begin to care that it was a boy—and not a girl. Or a girl and not a boy. The reality of not having the perfection one has dreamed of doesn't come until several hours later. The feelings that are at a peak are relief at having made it, gratitude that it's a baby at all, ecstasy that it's normal, and an overwhelming feeling of wanting to hold and nurture that tiny, dependent creature.

BIRTH OF A FAMILY

Dr. Thompson's routine after delivery was simple, partly based on Dr. Frederick Leboyer's suggestions. He wrapped the baby loosely and handed him to Mr. Johnson. Mr. Johnson nearly dropped him in his excitement. All he could do was look down at the baby's face, saying, "You're here! You're here! We did it!" Dr. Thompson broke through gently, saying, "Don't you think you should share him with your wife?" Mr. Johnson pulled himself together and handed the baby over to his wife, saying, "Here's

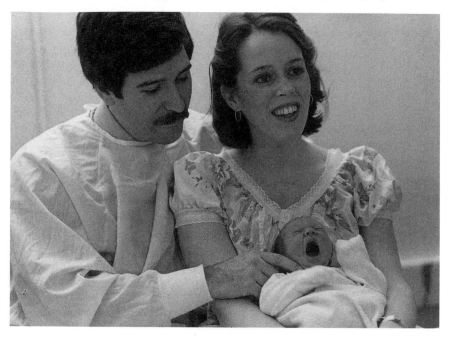

your baby." She looked down at the baby, murmuring, "Our baby."

The baby was put to her breast. He suckled once or twice as expected, then looked halfheartedly around him, shut his eyes against the too bright lights in the operating room, and seemed to fall quietly asleep inside his wrappings.

Dr. Leboyer has suggested that less brightly lit, less noisy, less cold delivery rooms are more appropriate if we want babies who are alert enough after birth to bond successfully to their new parents. Drs. Marshall Klaus and John Kennell are the major proponents in this country of giving baby and parents a comfortable interval together so that bonding can take place at this important, sensitive time. Their work, as summarized in their excellent book *Parent-Infant Bonding* (1982), demonstrates the importance of cementing the triad together at this time. They encourage delivering the baby without medication so that he is alert and responsive and so that the mother is alert and able to see and touch and suckle him. With the father present, the couple will have a significantly better chance of becoming a family and of rearing this baby in a more nurturing way.

Since it is easy to see that new, young, insecure parents will be reinforced by such efforts on the part of the medical personnel at delivery, it is an easy step to believe that they will thereby feel more important to their baby. After such a rewarding experience they are also likely to pass this feeling of increased self-value on to the baby. I am convinced that this is a rare, actually unique opportunity for us in medicine to influence the future course of family life. We can support parents in such a way that they learn to value themselves as parents and to value their baby as an exciting human being. All new parents have the potential for not trusting themselves. All new parents question their competence. How much more they will be able to give to the new relationship if they feel as excited and as rewarded and as competent as the Johnsons must feel after such an ideal experience. The more oppressed and the more at risk new parents are, the more important it is to offer them this kind of supportive experience. For I do feel (perhaps romantically) that anyone can identify with the future potential of a healthy newborn infant and can feel stirred by the exciting new life ahead. No matter how pressured they may be by their own lives, I believe that new parents, with the right support, can rise to such an occasion and become committed to making a good life for this child. It is time we in medicine seized such opportunities to help on this level—they are rare enough.

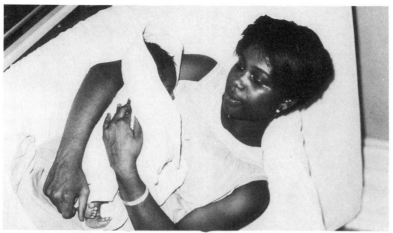

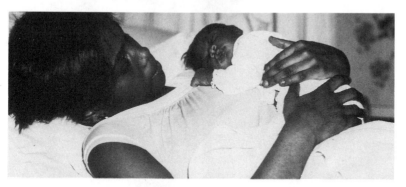

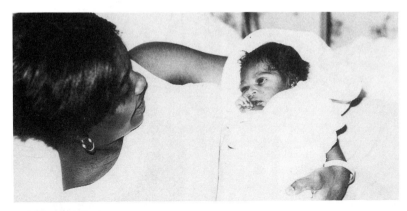

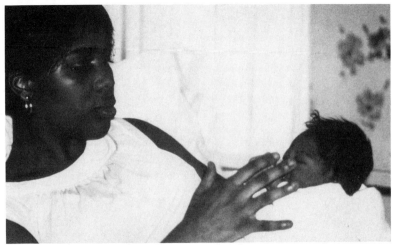

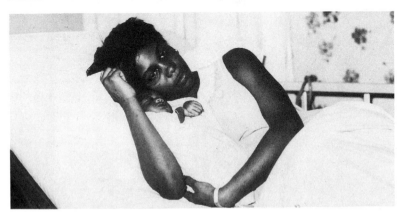

On Becoming a Family

3

Prematurity and Attachment

W hat about the less than ideal delivery that many people must experience? If one cannot produce a baby in optimal circumstances, will that baby's future be endangered? Will the heavily anesthetized mother, or the mother who has a premature delivery, be any less attached to her baby? Is she likely to feel less than elated after delivery? The development of attachment is less smooth, but there is no reason that the eventual outcome cannot be as rewarding. In fact, the effort to overcome such difficulties can be a strong force in attachment.

> *Bonnie Campbell delivered an infant eight weeks early in a small suburban hospital. The premature baby, who weighed less than three pounds, was noted to be in respiratory distress from the beginning. He was rushed off by ambulance to the Children's Hospital Medical Center, where he was hospitalized for the next six weeks in intensive care.*
>
> *Mrs. Campbell was a nineteen-year-old mother who had not had an easy life. Her own mother lived in the Midwest, and they had been alienated from each other. Mrs. Campbell had been on and off hard drugs for several years and had "been around." Her wanderings had brought her to the East Coast, and she had had several rather intense affairs before she met the father of her child. They began living together, and she became lax about her contraceptive precautions. When she found she was pregnant, she was not too surprised. The question of an abortion was*

raised, but both she and her boyfriend kept putting the idea off. Mrs. Campbell began to be careful about drug taking, cutting out all hard drugs, and even reduced the amount of marijuana she smoked. She cut back to half a pack of cigarettes within the first weeks after she realized she was pregnant.

The influences on the developing fetus are additive. Probably a single toxin, such as nicotine or marijuana in low doses, wouldn't affect a developing fetus, for the effect is related to several variables: (a) the stage of fetal development (the younger the fetus, the more vulnerable); (b) the blood level of circulating toxin in the mother; and (c) the mother's tissue sensitivity (that is, how much of the toxin she absorbs, thereby protecting the fetus). In the case of several such toxins, not only are they likely to be additive, but they may even reinforce each other's effects. If undernutrition is present in the mother, the effect on the fetus of such drugs, of nicotine, of alcohol may be increased, for the mother's tissues may not be as capable of absorbing the toxins. They will then be transmitted to the fetus, who is rendered more susceptible by his own poor nutritional status. Undernutrition in the fetus has two effects: (a) It can cut down on the effectiveness of the liver and kidneys, which have the job of detoxification; and (b) it renders the possibly already reduced number of brain cells more susceptible to toxins. If an unpredictable event, such as a short period of hypoxia (lack of oxygen), occurs, the baby who is exposed to drugs is more vulnerable to brain damage. Hence Mrs. Campbell's protective action of cutting down on all of her habits is well founded and is a reflection of how much she wanted this baby. Cutting them out entirely would be ideal.

A GROWING COMMITMENT

Although they continued to debate about whether to abort the baby or not, they had both made up their minds. Mr. Campbell had a job as a helper in a boat building establishment and had been working part-time "when it pleased him." Once on the job, however, he was a hard worker, so when he asked for a full-time job, the head foreman looked at him in surprise but took him on. He laughingly chided Mr. Campbell, "What are you doing, getting square or something?" Above his rich red beard, Mr. Campbell's face turned red. He began to take better care of himself too.

He began to wash his clothes and even took baths twice a week. He began to fix breakfast for both of them. She in turn began to have a regular supper for them when he came home from his job. They straightened up the two rooms they shared, and they talked of getting some "furniture." When they realized that each of them was talking about a crib and baby furniture, they laughed at themselves. All of this miraculous change in attitude had taken place in the three weeks after she'd missed her first period. She had felt different, her breasts were tender, her bladder was more active, and she felt slightly nauseated in the morning, but she'd been so ready that she'd recognized these immediately as symptoms of pregnancy. Each symptom added to her warm glow. She began to realize that she treasured this condition and felt more complete. When the two young people realized that they both wanted the baby and were already planning for it, they began to plan to marry. Marriage was a real step for each of them. It meant that they must make all sorts of concessions and commitments—commitment to each other, willingness to join the establishment to the extent of being married and settling down in a regular job and home, and, above all, acceptance of responsibility for the baby.

When Mrs. Campbell-to-be went to the clinic to confirm her suspicion of pregnancy, the nurse in charge, who had known her over the past year and had detoxified her on two occasions after indulgence in LSD, asked her when she was going to have her abortion. Mrs. Campbell found herself stiffening with anger. "I'm going to have my baby!"

As her pregnancy progressed, she returned to the clinic for advice about her pregnancy—even though it meant facing the nurses and physician, who could hardly hide their disapproval. She could feel their critical eyes on her as they weighed her, evaluated her, and took a routine history.

Our hospitals and outreach programs are set up for the strong and the middle class. The disapproving attitudes of the staff toward anything less than the conventional implicitly condemn those who are less than strong and unblemished. So good are we at labeling and identifying all the failures and all the weaknesses in our patients that we pass our disapproval on to them unconsciously. As a result, they are made more aware of themselves as weak, as poor, as failures. And in a curious way they are likely to live up to those images. Our attitudes are likely to create a Rosenthal effect. Rosenthal (1969) conducted in the 1960s an experiment in which he assigned a random group of first graders to one teacher and labeled them as having low IQs (around 90). To another he assigned a group that he labeled as having above-average IQs (around 110). At the end of the year each teacher had produced the expected performance in each group. The children had lived up to their labels.

I think that we in medicine are likely to have very critical eyes and expectations, and we unconsciously pass our doubts on to our patients. They, in turn, will tend to present their weaker sides to us, hiding their strengths. It takes a determined and strong-minded patient to face the barrage of accusing eyes that met Mrs. Campbell as she sought advice about her pregnancy. No wonder our medical system is so poor at reaching out to those who need us most.

At the fifth month, when her baby began to move, Mrs. Campbell began to feel like a new person. She had gradually become more and more committed to her new life. She and her husband ate better, they smoked less, they drank less, and they dreamed together of their future with the "squirt." They even put a picture of a baby on the wall next to one of a rock star. After the baby began to be more active, Mrs. Campbell decided to tell her mother. Mr. Campbell had taken her to meet his parents soon after they were married, and she found she liked them. They were a serious, hardworking couple on a farm in Maine. Having raised their four children, they were now alone and struggling to keep the farm going. They were glad to have one of these children marry and begin a home of his own, so they welcomed Bonnie with warm affection. She felt herself wishing they could let themselves accept the older Campbells' offer of a home for the three of them.

When she reached her own mother on the long-distance phone, her mother's voice hardened. "I wondered when I'd ever hear from you again. I guess you're in some sort of trouble." Bonnie found it difficult to go on. When she told her mother that she was married and was having a baby that they both very much wanted, she expected another blast from her mother. Instead, there was silence at the other end. Bonnie was frightened by it and called out to her mother. Her mother's voice was teary as she replied, "Bonnie, I'm so glad for you. Can't you come home now and let me help you?" Bonnie began to feel surrounded by caring people.

EARLY WARNINGS

Her visits to the clinic became more regular, and it wasn't until the sixth month of her pregnancy that she began to have a sense of trouble. She experienced a steady rise in blood pressure, plus swelling of her hands and feet at night. She was placed on a low-salt diet and finally on diuretic drugs to try to counteract the fluid retention. She found herself forgetting to take the medication and forgetting her appointments at the clinic. As her swelling increased, her fingers became too swollen for her rings, her feet too swollen for her shoes. She became frightened and, too late, began to conform to all of the clinic's admonitions. She was put to bed, and Mr. Campbell was instructed about taking care of her and keeping her off her feet. He realized that he'd have to give up his job if he stayed at home to care for her, and they needed the money desperately. They were caught in a bind and had to decide what to do. They had friends who took welfare checks for unemployment, but they hated to get into that "racket," to cross that line. They thought of their own parents, but they wanted to do this on their own. Finally Mr. Campbell arranged with his employer to be able to work for two hours at a stretch, then space a break in between each two hours of work in order to rush home at his coffee, lunch, and afternoon breaks. He worked even harder to make up for this arrangement. His wife lay in bed all day, miserable and rebellious but dreaming of her baby. She was now completely committed to this baby.

At thirty-two weeks she began to feel contractions and produced a bloody "show." As if she knew the significance of this immediately, for she'd not been warned or given instructions about such an event, she called Mr. Campbell at his work, urging him to rush home to take her to the clinic. Her faint contractions were accompanied by an ominous quieting of the fetus. Having been in bed so long, she had become acutely attuned to its every movement. She knew when it was likely to kick hard, when it might move more slowly, when it liked to "turn over" or seemed to be listening to her radio. She knew it as well as she possibly could and was in tune with every signal it could give her. So when it became quiet, she knew that something was wrong. She could barely endure the wait for her husband for fear that something would happen before he arrived. It never occurred to her to call the clinic for advice or to summon the emergency team's car to take her there.

So poor had been her relationship with the clinic that she still couldn't feel protected by its staff in an emergency. She needed the protection of her husband to face them with this new "failure." Unconsciously, as we have seen before, a mother blames herself when something begins to go wrong. Mrs. Campbell was already going over and over all of the things she might have done to bring on the contractions and what she knew was happening — a premature delivery.

THREATS TO ATTACHMENT

By the time they reached the clinic, she knew she was in hard labor, and the nurses rushed her by ambulance to the nearby hospital. The baby, a well-formed but tiny (1.3 kilograms, about 2.8 pounds) boy, was delivered almost immediately and suctioned, wrapped, and rushed off to the premature nursery. Mr. Campbell had been kept outside the delivery room by the emergency personnel, and he saw the incubator rush past him, pushed by an anxious-looking nurse. He was not able to see the baby inside his wrappings. Mrs. Campbell was completely spent emotionally and physically, almost in shock, and she didn't see or hear her baby immediately after he was born. It had all happened so fast that she could barely keep herself conscious; certainly she had no memory of anything but the emergency aspects of her delivery. Personnel were urgently called; they in turn called for "Suction! Oxygen! Emergency to the nursery! Call Children's Hospital in Boston to send out the ambulance and the special incubator for this baby — if he survives!" All of this went on around her, yet her senses were so dulled by the experience, by the feelings of having failed her baby, that she lay in a semicoma. She was too weak and too overwhelmed even to ask to see the baby, and no one remembered to show him to her. After he had been wheeled away, all she could remember was the feeling of him in her belly, how exciting it was when he had moved. Now she was empty.

In the face of the emergencies she has been through, it will be very difficult for someone like Mrs. Campbell to maintain her attachment to this baby. She must defend herself from the overwhelming questions about her baby's survival and the equally overwhelming but inexpressible feelings of guilt in having brought him to this dangerous situation. It is no wonder a mother might want to flee or hide or go into a protective state of depression—or to detach herself in self-protective ways from caring about this baby. These are *expectable* responses to such an experience; they are *not* abnormal ones. The remarkable thing to me is not that many mothers and fathers are overwhelmed and must defend themselves but that mothers and fathers can overcome these feelings and begin all over again to become attached to the baby they feel they've endangered.

The baby was rushed in oxygen to Children's Hospital, where he received optimal medical care. He had severe respiratory distress—a condition common in premature infants, which results from their lungs' inability to absorb oxygen properly and to discharge the carbon dioxide they manufacture. As their lungs mature over time, the condition improves slowly, although there may be some residual damage to the lungs from the high oxygen levels that must be maintained during the initial period, oxygen that is pumped into them under pressure for the first few weeks. On the sixth day, because he was being kept alive with extreme difficulty, he had what turned out to be an intracranial hemorrhage and barely survived. This "stroke" left him with a paralysis of most of his left side. His face drooped, his left leg and arm became flaccid, and his survival hung in the balance for the next week. Meanwhile, he had a tube in his nose, an oxygen mask over his face with a respirator going, monitors of his heart rate and respiration attached by electrodes to his tiny chest, and two intravenous lines dripping slowly at the side of his incubator, one into his scalp and one into his leg. He was bruised in several places from unsuccessful attempts to find his veins. His poor bluish color was visible in only a few uncovered spots. What one could see of his face was that of an exhausted, unresponsive, wizened premature who looked barely alive. No spontaneous movement was visible, and the heaving of his fragile chest was obviously being brought about by the instruments above him. His incubator was in the most intensely active room of the premature nursery, brightly lit and with the constant noise of the apparatus of fifteen or twenty other such incubators.

The bustling of the nursing and physician personnel is constant and necessary to the tenuous survival of these infants. We have made remarkable technical progress, and we can assure survival for an increasing number of babies (from less than one pound upward). The last figure we now have shows that well above half of babies under two pounds will survive. We can also reassure parents with increasing confidence that their premature infant has a normal brain. Lack of brain damage depends on size, the stage of maturity, the condition of the baby before its premature delivery (caused in turn by nutrition, the effect of drugs and maternal conditions, and so on), and then the rapidity with which he is gotten into therapeutic balance after delivery and on how well that balance can be maintained. We are finding that more than three-fourths of all prematures will have normal brains.

We are now in a position to worry about the quality of life, the emotional climate around the baby after survival. Most severely premature infants will have been through the experiences I am describing, and their parents will have been scarred by experiences similar to those of the Campbells.

> *Mrs. Campbell was returned to her room after her baby had gone. She had not needed an episiotomy, nor had she lost much blood. Her blood pressure and her edema began to subside rapidly after the baby and the placenta were delivered. Within two days she was physically able to get around, and in three she was discharged. Mr. Campbell had been frightened for his wife throughout the emergency of the delivery and discovered how much he cared for her—more than he had realized. As she recovered, he transferred his concerns and caring to the baby. At the end of the second day he took a bus into Boston and found his way by subway to the hospital. Gingerly he asked at the front desk to see his new son. As in most hospitals, the first line of defense is the receptionist. As in most hospitals, people in this job become bored and are not aware of the importance of their role. The woman who greeted him looked up his name in the card index, and, not finding it, announced casually, "Sorry, but there's no one here by that name." His heart stopped, and he immediately thought that the baby must have died. But he knew they'd have been notified. Then he asked her again, telling her that the baby had been brought in by ambulance last night. She rallied, saying, "Oh, then we just haven't gotten his card down yet. Let me call up the special-care nursery." When she got the go-ahead from it, she rather reluctantly directed him to the special nursery.*

THE PREMATURE NURSERY

The nurses in our premature nurseries are trained to help parents with the adjustments they must make to the baby's condition. As soon as the head nurse realized which baby he was here to see, she took him in tow. Meanwhile, he had had a chance to look through the large plate glass windows at the incubators lined up side by side, with a veritable maze of wires, tubes, and complex monitors coming from each one.

One's first look at a nursery such as this makes one wonder how any tiny baby can have the resistance to survive being hooked up to all the overwhelming machinery. Watching an expert nurse or neonatologist put an intravenous line or a nasogastric tube in place is like observing an expert watchmaker at work. The delicacy, the artistry that are demanded by the technical side necessary to the baby's survival give one an uneasy feeling of how tenuous it is at any moment.

When the head nurse took Mr. Campbell into this jungle of equipment and hovered with him over a few tiny, almost indistinguishable bodies, he felt as if he might faint. The smells of alcohol and of disinfectant, the noises of monitors clicking in all directions, the tension in the air, coupled with his own anxiety about his baby, made him feel helpless and terrified. Could any

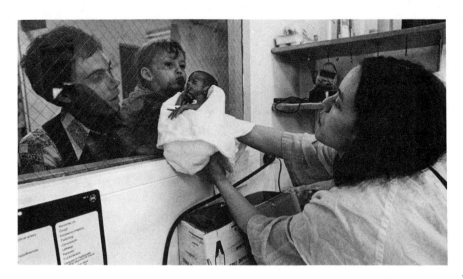

baby be normal after such an experience, after all the manipulation necessary to keep him alive?

He was finally led to his own baby. The square card on his incubator was the most personal thing about the setup, for it announced, "It's a boy! Boy Campbell. Birth weight 2¾ lb. Birth date 10-10-78." The parents' names had been left blank, and he hastily told them that his was Tom and his wife's was Bonnie. The tiny piece of instrumented flesh was indeed difficult to make out or to relate to as a person. He stood numbly over the incubator for thirty minutes, watching this tiny lump in an effort to feel something about his baby. The nurse uttered a few soothing remarks, but when he said nothing in response, she left him to take in what he could. He knew he should feel frightened or glad, but all he could do was wonder why. "Why were they working so hard to save these babies? Why did it happen? Why did it happen to us? Why can't I feel anything?" And, of course, lurking in the back of his consciousness was: "What if he makes it—will he ever, ever be okay?" He daren't let himself begin to care about this tiny creature who seemed to have so little chance.

After thirty minutes of watching, he had tried to feel all he could and was still numb. He was glad his wife hadn't been able to come in. It would frighten her to death, and he hoped he could prepare her a little before she came. How could she stand it? He had to take deep breaths himself in order not to run out of there, never to return. As he left the nursery, the head nurse asked him to sit down and gently tried to tell him a little bit about his baby. She asked him about his wife, about himself, about how they would manage to get in to see the baby. She asked whether his wife would like to be able to call in twice a day to find out about the baby. She gave Mr. Campbell a photograph of the baby that was taken as he was brought in and before he was placed in his incubator, before he was surrounded with all of his equipment. In the photograph he almost looked like a baby—a tiny, frighteningly fragile one, but a baby at least. Mr. Campbell stared hard at the picture, trying to believe in it. He startled when the nurse asked him what the baby's name was. "We haven't named him yet. We weren't sure he'd live, but let me call him Tony until I talk with my wife." The nurse smiled and said, "We like to be able to call him something besides Baby Boy Campbell. They become people to us, and they make us feel like they will live when they're named."

The climate of premature nurseries has changed dramatically all over the country, since Klaus and Kennell's (1970, 1976, 1982) and Leiderman's (1973) work demonstrated to the world of neonatologists how critical it was to bring the parents into the high-risk nurseries, in order to give them a chance to touch and grieve over their fragile babies under the cover of the nursery, to work out their anxiety, and to get to know their premature infants before they took them home. They demonstrated that parents would grieve more openly and adjust better if they were allowed to see, touch, and relate to a baby, even if he had to die later. If he lived, they could begin to work on their natural grief at having such a baby and their inevitable guilt at having brought him into the world as a "premie" before they took him home. Afterward they could relate more easily to him as a person and could nurture him with significantly more confidence. The future development of such babies was clearly enhanced if their parents were allowed to get to know them in the nursery. These important studies have revolutionized nurseries all over the world. Our nurseries are concerned about helping create strong bonds between these parents and their infants, for they have seen that if they don't, the parents are likely to continue to treat them as if they were at risk for years afterward. When the babies are treated as vulnerable and overprotected, the quality of their lives as well as their potential for developing autonomy may be seriously affected.

One important spin-off of this movement to help parents with their adjustment has been that we have brought more humanity into the nurseries. In bringing in the parents, we have looked freshly at the inhuman aspects of the nurseries and have begun to try to humanize them. All cribs are likely to have a mobile over them and a bright picture where the infant can see it. The nurses are encouraged to be more human and to play more with each baby. In the process they have allowed themselves to become attached to the babies they are caring for. And that isn't always easy. The personal anguish a nurse must go through when she's attached to a baby and must lose it—either by death or by sharing it with the parents—is not often understood. But it is an occupational hazard of working with these delicate babies. As the baby begins to respond, to become more of a person, his nurses feel a tremendous investment in him. It is no wonder they are competitive when his parents want to take him over. Klaus and Kennell's work has shown that the nurse in a high-risk nursery must have a double goal: not only to help the fragile baby survive but also to develop empathy for the parents, to help them bond to that baby. In neonatal intensive care units nurses are as much social workers for the parents as nurses for the babies.

> *Mr. Campbell left the nursery feeling cared for. He couldn't wait to take the picture of "Tony" to his wife.*
>
> *Mrs. Campbell greeted him eagerly when he returned. She wanted to know every detail he could give her. She hung on to the photograph as if it were the baby himself. She asked him to repeat all the nurse's comments. She seemed to be clinging to the baby through him. He tried to hide his own fears and his own sadness from her. Indeed, she seemed so hungry for any contact with the baby that he promised to borrow a car to take her to the hospital as soon as she was able. He hadn't the heart to tell her how devastating it was to see the baby as he really was. He just hoped that if the baby lived, he'd already be better by the time she arrived to see him. He asked her what she'd like to name him. Her face went blank, and she said, "I hadn't even thought of that. He doesn't seem like a person to me at all. You'd better name him." So Tony it was.*
>
> *After her own discharge from the hospital she was able to go to Boston to Children's Hospital, and she went through the same shocked feelings that had overwhelmed her husband—feelings of numbness, of disbelief, of feeling that Tony was not a real person, of not daring to think he'd ever live. The nurses in charge of Tony were eager to see Mrs. Campbell, and they called his doctor in to see both of the parents. Mr. Campbell listened to him and tried to take in all that the young physician was trying to tell them. Mrs. Campbell seemed dazed and dutifully repeated a few words from the doctor's message, but it was apparent that she couldn't take any of it in. Mr. Campbell found that he could understand very little of it, but he groped for a few facts, such as how much oxygen Tony needed, how his lungs were behaving, and what his blood gases demonstrated. What he could grasp were the more personal descriptions of how Tony tried to squirm and move when they had to give him a needle or of how he responded when they fed him by his tube. None of the technical information meant very much, and he was happy to turn the responsibility for Tony over to the hospital.*

STEPS TOWARD ATTACHMENT

We are in the process of studying the "stages" that parents must go through as they form an attachment to such a baby. In the first place they are working against a "grief reaction" (first described by Erich Lindemann in relatives and friends of young people killed unexpectedly in a nightclub fire in 1945). Grieving after a premature birth is inevitable. Not only do parents grieve for the loss of the perfect baby they'd anticipated and grieve over the defects in the one they've produced, but they blame themselves, whether consciously or unconsciously. They feel guilty for the baby's condition, whether there is reason or not. Although Mr. and Mrs. Campbell might have found reason more easily because of their recent life-style and of their guilty feelings about it, they would have felt guilty about Tony's condition in any event. Even under the most blameless conditions, parents feel implicated by having produced a premature baby. In order to overcome these feelings, it takes time and hard personal work. Although going to see the baby helps them do this work, it still takes time.

We see parents go through at least five stages before they can finally see the baby as theirs and can trust themselves to work with and relate to him. The five stages that we see are the following:

1. Parents relate to the baby through the information about body chemistry, oxygen, blood gases that they hear about from the medical team. They take heart as these indications of improvement go up and feel devastated as they go down. Their tenuous relationship to the baby hinges on the medical lab reports.

2. Parents observe and take courage from the reflex, automatic behavior that they see when a nurse or doctor disturbs the baby. "He can move!" Any movement at all becomes a big thing, but the parents do not try to produce it themselves.

3. The more responsive movements of the baby are noted. For example, if he turns to a nurse's voice or responds by grasping a doctor's finger, they see him becoming a person. But these responses are seen only when someone *else* elicits them. The parents still don't dare to produce them themselves.

4. The next stage begins when they do dare try to produce responsive movements themselves. It is the real beginning of their seeing *themselves* as the parents of this baby. When they touch him, he moves away or toward them. When they speak to him, he turns toward their voices. When they stroke him, he quiets down. Now they can see themselves as responsible for his responses.

5. The fifth and final stage we see in the nursery occurs when

the parents really dare to pick him up and hold him, to rock him or even feed him. At this point parents have achieved an attachment. Before this they have seen him as a terrifying, fragile object and themselves as dangerous to him. When they can begin to see that he won't break and that they can comfort him and treat him as a person, they are ready to take him home, ready to nurture him.

We are trying to delay the discharge of premature infants until we know that parents are ready, for they do quite a different job of parenting if they have made it through these stages before discharge. To expect them to be able to attach to such a baby without this kind of work seems absurd. And it may be destructive to press them too hard and too fast because they will try to live up to expectations in order to prove themselves. They will be readier if they've had time and support to do this "grief work."

Each time the Campbells returned, they found they were better able to take in the situation. After a few days they could understand that Tony had "stabilized" and that everyone hoped he'd start getting better. He looked the same to them. But each day seemed like a miraculous gift, and they began to feel he might make it. They almost didn't dare wish for it.

When Tony had the cerebral hemorrhage on the seventh day, it was as if they were being punished for beginning to hope. They had been urged to touch him and begin to relate to him. Mrs. Campbell wondered whether they had in some way damaged him by their ineptness.

The vulnerability of the parents of premature infants to feeling responsible for everything that goes wrong remains right at the surface. Of course, they haven't hurt him, and these setbacks are too often a part of the course for such a baby. But it is a setback for the parents too. There are some normal, predictable events that appear as crises to the parents of a premature baby. His first bowel movement is one. His reorganizing to breathe for himself, the beginning of his desire to suck, and his fighting of the gavage feeding tube are others. There are many expectable hurdles for the baby that appear as setbacks to those around him. They often precede a stage of reorganization and progress.

*By the time Tony finally began to recover from his cerebral hem-
orrhage a week later, the Campbells had begun to pull away
again. They had telephoned each day but had not driven in to
see him. Not only was it too painful to see how ill he was, but
they couldn't feel that their visits made any difference. So they
stayed home and worried. Mrs. Campbell felt depressed and unable to function. She felt as if she'd been hit on the head by all of
this. Mr. Campbell tried to get back into his job, but he could
function only at half speed. His boss appreciated what he was
going through.*

*When they telephoned, they were given reports on his med-
ical condition. Only part of the language meant anything to
them at all. They began to be familiar with such terms as* critical
oxygen levels, motor patterns of recovery, lung compliance, *for
this became a language in which to understand their baby. But
what they really wanted to know was: "Has he opened his eyes?
Does he know you're there when he's fed or changed?" or even
"Has he had a bowel movement like a normal baby?" Any of these
things might have helped them make him into a person. And they
were trying desperately to hang on to him as a person.*

The nurses and doctors who are the most successful in communication are the ones who realize what grieving parents secretly
need; they try to give them this information in the process of convey-
ing observations of the baby's behavior. Parents then feel that such
practitioners see their baby as a person, not just an illness.

A REAL BABY

*When they saw him about ten days after his setback, he was
being gavage-fed (by a tube through his nose into his stomach).
As he was fed, he lazily opened one eye and closed his right fist
to bring it weakly up to his face. Since these were the first movements they had seen him make, they felt as if they'd seen a miracle. Their hopes began to return. They began to come in every
few days, and Mrs. Campbell found she was looking forward to
each visit. They had to borrow a car or else come in by bus and
subway, and either mode was difficult for them. But she needed
to see Tony, and Mr. Campbell felt left out if he couldn't go in.*

Tony's steady improvement over the next three weeks en-

*couraged them, and they gradually began to feel again. It was
slow, and each bit of improvement seemed to take forever. But
each time Tony's oxygen could be reduced or his gavage feeding
could be increased or the motor patterns on his weak side made
a bit of improvement, their hopes soared, and they felt as if
they'd been given a gift. They had been in touch with both of
their families all along, and they couldn't resist spending more
than they could afford to call long-distance with each bit of
news. When they sat by his incubator, they watched him for any
evidence of recovery. When he moved at all, they chortled and
pointed it out to each other. At last they dared to put their hands
in to touch him, the first day with a gentle poke. The second day
they dared to put a hand on him, and by the end of a week they'd
found they could even stroke him gently. When they did, he began to open his eyes in a half-alert way. They got themselves into
all sorts of contorted positions in an attempt to line up their
faces with his and to catch his eye.*

Klaus has recorded a predictable sequence of behaviors that the
parents of such a premature infant will follow as they try to make
contact with him over time (1976). As they become more coura-
geous, they will try to engage him in *en face*, eye-to-eye, contact. At
this point they feel they are really in touch with him as a person.

*As Tony began to gain weight and needed fewer tubes, fewer mon-
itors, and less equipment generally, the nurses urged them to
pick him up inside the incubator. He was so weak, so floppy that
they felt at first that he might break. After they got used to his
fragility, they began to feel responsive movements, and their
feeling of closeness to him redoubled.*

*By the time he was able to be out of the incubator and off
oxygen, he already seemed like a miracle to them. He was so big,
so strong, so responsive. Although his left arm and leg were still
weak, they had seen him respond to the physiotherapist with
some movement, and they watched what she did in order to be
able to reproduce it themselves at home. Already they were beginning to prepare themselves for the rather dreaded step of taking him home and becoming responsible for him.*

*Up to this point they had never dared to bring out into the
open their fears about his being brain-damaged by his cerebral
hemorrhage, or "stroke." That was submerged in their struggle*

to keep up with his step-by-step survival and their step-by-step attempts to relate to him—to personify him in their minds.

A LITTLE AT A TIME

When they were able to see him out of an incubator and hold him in their arms, they felt as if he were a real baby. Mrs. Campbell wanted to rock him, to sing to him, to stroke him—all at once. But each of these seemed to overwhelm him, and she found he was all too quickly exhausted by her attempts to mother him.

After being premature and ill and after being in such a totally nonstimulating environment as an incubator, babies are easily exhausted even by attractive or positive stimuli. Their thresholds for letting in stimuli are so underdeveloped and are so easily overwhelmed that they are at the mercy of everything that happens around them. They startle or blink at every sound. They withdraw from every touch. They must sleep in order to shut out the unremitting nursery lights, and they are unused to looking at attractive stimuli. Learning how to adapt to the world around them takes time after they come out into a crib. A mother or a nurse must be aware of how raw these babies' nervous systems are. They can afford to take in only a little stimulation at a time, and in only one sphere—hearing *or* touch *or* vision. Gradually and over days they will get better at it, so that they can afford to take in two modalities at once. They can be rocked *and* sung to at the same time. Finally they can afford to look at a face *and* be talked to *and* be held. At that point all the costly learning they have been through begins to pay off, and they are on their way to becoming social beings.

At first the Campbells felt that they were too much for Tony. He always appeared to be exhausted near the end of their visit. But as they understood that he was following a normal course of slowed-down development in adjusting to the world, they could adapt to it and work with it. They had to realize his hypersensitivity to any of their approaches, for everything they did seemed to be too much for him. A nurse showed them how much more alert he was if they handled him very gently or sang to him very softly or let him look at them at a distance rather than close to his face.

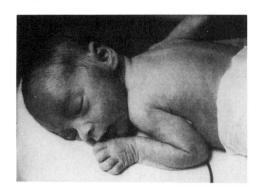 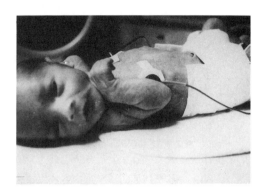

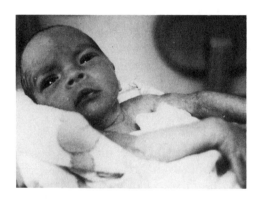 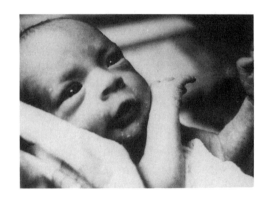

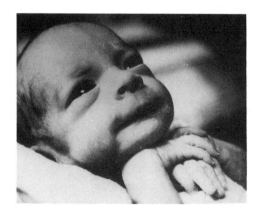 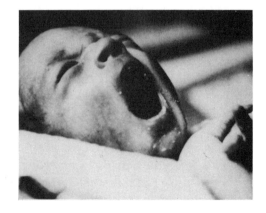

We have found that eye-to-eye contact is a threatening mode of communication for small premature babies. Not only do they prefer you at a distance until their visual threshold has increased, but they will actually turn pale or withdraw if you insist on engaging them in eye-to-eye contact and are too close to them. To me this confirms the importance of the visual mode of communication between mothers, fathers, and babies (see next chapter). The sensory stimuli to which Tony is most sensitive are the ones most important to his future development.

The hypersensitive reactions of prematures and babies who have been ill can make parents feel "turned off" by their baby. Just as he is recovering and they are eager to get close to him, they tend to overwhelm him with social stimuli. When they do, he will greet them with a negative response. Their vulnerability in having failed him before is revived, and they feel as if they not only don't know him but are failures as well. It would be well for us in nurseries to warn parents about this necessary sequence of the baby's recovery so that they do not feel it is their failure in reaching out to him.

His weakness, alternating with startling and jittery movements of his arms and legs, bothered them as he made progress, and they began to face the prospect of taking him home. At last they got up the courage to ask Tony's doctors their question about his brain. "Has he got brain damage from his stroke?" The doctor was quite honest in telling them that he didn't know the answer to that but that Tony had recovered remarkably well already, and if his progress continued, he would give him a very good prognosis for future development. He urged them to believe in Tony and work on his weak leg and arm. He didn't need to press this couple. They were committed to Tony completely by now.

We have found that the best way to instill hope in parents who, like the Campbells, have been through a devastating time with a sick baby is to play with the baby with them. If he can produce some alerting responses to your voice and your face, if he can quiet down when you talk to him, if he can nestle when you cuddle him, they can begin to see him as a total person—not just as a sick baby (see the next chapter for those responses in normal babies).

Parmelee and his group in Los Angeles (1975) conducted a two-year follow-up study of high-risk premature and sick babies. They reported that one cannot make predictions about a later outcome, even on the basis of known neurological damage in the newborn period. There is often surprising recovery of function. What does constitute a factor for prediction is the capacity of the parents to relate to the baby and work for this recovery. A second source of prediction is found in the infant himself. If he can respond visually and auditorily to a caretaker by one month of age, you can bet that he will improve, even if he has neurological deficits. In other words, even a damaged infant has marvelously unexpected capacities to recover if appropriately nurturing social interactions are started when he is small. A caring, sensitive environment can bring about improvement that professionals acquainted with his illness would not have expected.

Work lies ahead for the Campbells to get Tony going. They will have to take an entirely different track from the Johnsons. They represent to me an example of how difficulties and the effort to surmount them can cement a family. Overcoming problems can be a strong force for attachment. The work ahead will be enhanced by the strengthening of family ties that comes from sharing difficulties. The parents have learned a great deal about Tony and about themselves over this period. All of this will help them in many of the stressful times ahead. For Tony's progress won't be easy, and it won't be straightforward. Premature infants remain complicated, and raising one is a demanding process for a long time. (See Chapter 7.) But the Campbells have invested a great deal in Tony's recovery. This certainly makes them feel responsible in part for that recovery and can be used as fuel to keep them going. If they'd been left to wallow in their guilty, depressed feelings about having damaged him, it would have been much more difficult for them to take pride in his success. By encouraging them to participate in his care before discharge, the nurses and doctors not only have helped them recover from their own depression but have also reinforced their feelings of competence in helping Tony through this crisis. I would urge all parents of prematures to fight to get into the nursery and to get to know the baby before discharge and under supervision. Most hospitals today are ready for this, but if not, it is time they were. Often, determined parent groups can do more to change the medical system from the outside than we as professionals can do from the inside. The very quality of Tony's future life was at risk. Now one would predict that he and his family will develop stronger and stronger attachments to each other—and the accident of his premature birth will serve to enhance the quality of their family life.

4

Forced Separation: A Caesarean Delivery

Lucy Thomas had just delivered her second baby, a much-wanted girl. She and her husband had worked hard and long—both before labor began and during a prolonged eighteen-hour labor—to have this baby naturally and without medication. Her first baby, Danny, had been delivered three years before in a hospital that still used a lot of premedication and spinal anesthesia. She had been drugged and had had a spinal headache for most of the week after Dan was born. He, too, had been so sleepy that she remembered their experience in the hospital as almost a nightmare of ineffectuality. It took her a month afterward to feel really "normal" again and to have a sense that she was on her way with Dan. This time she wanted a better experience and a chance to get to know her baby in the hospital. The Thomases attended childbirth education classes, practiced exercises together, and learned all the breathing cues, the time to push, and the ways to support each other. So they felt ready to sail through labor and delivery.

A BABY IN DISTRESS

It was not to be. This baby's head presented as a brow presentation (baby facing toward front of mother), and labor could not progress. Hard labor began after a few hours, and although Mrs. Thomas pushed, Mr. Thomas helped her pant, and Dr. Fen-

*ton tried to manipulate the baby's position, the baby's head was
stuck against the pelvis, and each contraction made her arch
away from the cervical opening in an ineffectual way. After
many hours of this, fetal monitors were applied to the bit of
scalp that was presented, and the tracing demonstrated what
both the parents and Dr. Fenton had come to accept: that the
baby, too, was fatigued and might be getting into trouble as the
result of low oxygen levels.*

Fetal monitoring has become more and more common. While
there is disagreement on whether it should be a routine part of delivery, it is vital in situations like this, where the baby's condition may
be worsening. Severe fetal distress, with low levels of oxygen circulating to the baby's brain, can be identified by tracings on the monitors so that steps can be taken to hasten delivery. We have made a
giant step toward preventing brain damage in prolonged or complicated labors by being able to detect the danger point for the baby. We
are reducing to a dramatic extent unnecessary brain damage of
stressed infants. This means more Caesarean sections, but it also
means that we can almost always assure parents of an intact baby if
we pick up the stress early. So one would hardly dare object to such
a procedure if the baby is clearly at risk.

At the same time there are reasons for reevaluating the potential
overuse of fetal monitors. We have been so impressed with their value
in identifying stress and preventing any damage to the infant's vulnerable central nervous system that we may be going overboard in
using them. When physicians substitute instrumental recording for
clinical judgment, that is not good. If the fetal monitor is used to
detect suspected stress, then it is certainly worth it every time. For it
offers important confirmation of suspected imminent damage. So far
we are not at the point of being able to detect fetal distress accurately
enough without invading the amniotic sac to apply these monitors,
for they must be applied directly to the fetal scalp. This introduces a
slight possibility of infection and can also speed up labor. We also
need more experience, for we have not yet reached the level of so-
phistication that would allow us to ignore less acute signs of distress
in order to avoid unnecessary Caesarean deliveries. If we must indeed
resort to them in order to protect the baby, then we cannot argue
about them. But they certainly constitute a difficult hurdle for parents to overcome in the process of getting started with a new infant.
I shall be glad when measured clinical judgment catches up with the

instrumentation. The major advance with both the fetal monitor and the Caesarean is that parents can be assured of a normal baby. As I said earlier, the incidence of brain damage in these situations has dropped dramatically.

In Mrs. Thomas's case, after many hours of hard, ineffectual labor and a fetal electroencephalogram (brain wave) that showed beginning signs of distress with each contraction, it seemed evident that Dr. Fenton would section her. The disappointment was somewhat balanced by the relief at finding a solution to the ineffectual, hard labor pains that had gone on for nearly eight hours. Mrs. Thomas was exhausted, and Mr. Thomas was frightened for her. He didn't see how she could last much longer. So for the moment they both welcomed the decision.

Even when the decision seems obvious and the criteria are as clear-cut as they were for the Thomases, the self-recriminations, the feelings of failure and of having lost a major opportunity can be great. There are helpful books on the subject, and some childbirth preparation classes offer preparation for a possible Caesarean section, including films. Mothers who have undergone sections can help one another.

When the reasons for the decision are less clear-cut, parents feel a real sense of anger, of being manipulated. There is a continuing protest today over the misuse of Caesarean sections. The rapid rise in incidence makes thoughtful obstetricians wary. It certainly behooves an obstetrician to present the parents with as much information as possible and to take them into his or her confidence in weighing the decision. Otherwise, he or she will be in for their inevitable questions afterward about the necessity of such a move.

How much can and should parents protest? This is almost impossible to answer, for each case should be individualized. The parents dare not risk the baby's brain or his well-being if the obstetrician says there is danger. Hence it is critical for them to have chosen an obstetrician or midwife in whom they have real confidence and who will share everything about the decision with them. Only in this way can they feel comfortable in accepting and participating in this radically different course of events.

All parents hope for a normal and rewarding delivery. If they have participated in childbirth education courses and practiced techniques of delivering the baby naturally, they will be even more determined in their expectations. Hence the blow of not being able to proceed without such major interference will be especially disappointing. Not only will it inevitably be seen as some sort of failure on their part, but even the danger to the baby that makes such a step necessary will be felt as their responsibility. Just as with the parents of a premature, they will face a kind of grief reaction about the disappointment that will make them feel overwhelmingly guilty. As part of this guilt, and in order to handle it, they will question and even blame the decision to interfere. This is all part of a defense against these feelings of failure. The defense is called projection—placing the blame on someone else. In this case it is likely to be the medical personnel. Since projection is a normal, even a healthy mechanism, it will serve the parents in the critical adjustment to the unexpected and will eventually help them get over their disappointment and move on to attaching to the baby. So it behooves the maternity staff to be ready for such a reaction and not angered by it. All those caring for the parents must realize that a Caesarean is going to cost parents a good deal in the way of disappointment. The decision must be medically justified and not made lightly. The Thomases are lucky in one way, for they have understood the reason for the operation, and that will help them get on with the new job of adjusting to the baby.

A FATHER'S ROLE

The section was performed quickly and without event. Mr. Thomas was allowed into the delivery room and held his wife's hand throughout the procedure. He and the anesthetist sat at her head and behind a sheet, which shielded the operative field. He was glad not to have to watch the procedure itself, but being there, he felt himself to be a real part of the delivery. He and his wife shared their relief at the decision and at placing responsibility for the baby in Dr. Fenton's hands. They talked in low tones to each other as the operation proceeded.

A spinal anesthetic allows the mother to be awake and to participate in the delivery. She can be alert when the baby arrives. The anesthetic agents used for spinals do not get absorbed quickly enough to reach the mother's bloodstream in significant levels and affect the baby after delivery, as do many other premedication drugs.

Allowing fathers to participate is still not universal. There are all sorts of taboos and reasons still given. "Fathers carry infections." Do they any more than any of the operative personnel if they are appropriately scrubbed and gowned? "Fathers are likely to faint and become third patients—and we already have our hands full with the mother and baby." This seems a spurious reason to me. Few fathers are likely to faint if they are given a job to do—that of comforting and supporting their wives and of being available when the new baby arrives. If they are worried about the procedure, shield them from watching it. I think such an excuse may be used as a resistance against having to think abut one more person and his role. Surgeons traditionally have wanted the freedom from being observed as they operate, so that if things go wrong, the observer's concern won't add to the general tension. In a case like this the gains for the future of the family of having the father involved must be balanced against the inconvenience of having another person present. I think fathers (and their wives) should be given a choice. In making the choice, they can weigh for

themselves the responsibility, the opportunity, and their roles in the delivery room. If things go wrong, they must be prepared for the crisis. Many men will choose—appropriately—not to be there. But for those who elect to be there, it will be a rewarding way of participating in the important event. Giving the father this choice implies that he *is* important to his wife and to the baby. Hence he deserves the choice.

> *When the baby came, a perfect eight-pound baby girl, she was handed to Mr. Thomas to hold, and then she was placed by him across his wife's chest, so that she, too, could hold her. They were both elated and relieved at how active, how perfect, how alert this baby was. Their anxiety about her now took the form of relief and exhilaration. With a heater placed over Mrs. Thomas's head, they were allowed to hold the baby undressed while the umbilical cord was tied and cut. Neither of them moved as they leaned together, relieved at the end of such an ordeal.*

THE FIRST SEPARATION

> *A nurse then took the baby—Andrea—away to clean her up, to wrap her, and to give her the medications which are required by law (silver nitrate or an antibiotic ointment for the eyes and an injection of vitamin K or an analogue, which interferes with a newborn's tendency to bleed). Mrs. Thomas felt an emptiness she couldn't describe. She wished that they had left the baby with her while they sutured up her wound. For now, without the baby, she began to feel a kind of depression. Mr. Thomas had followed the baby to the nursery and planned to call their parents to spread the word about her. The anesthetist noticed a drop in Mrs. Thomas's blood pressure and a slight slowing of her pulse. When she asked her to respond, Mrs. Thomas looked up at her with sad eyes and began to cry softly. With the activity of crying, her pulse and blood pressure returned to normal, and the anesthetist resumed her routine monitoring. The rest of the procedure went on uneventfully for the operating team.*

But not so for Mrs. Thomas. The act of separating a mother from her new baby has more significance than we have paid attention to in the past. Psychoanalysts have written of the feelings of loss that mothers experience when the baby is finally born (Deutsch, Bibring et al., 1961). Klaus and Kennell (1976, 1982) have made a dramatic point of this in their work on the bonding process. They cite animal research in which monkeys, either feral (reared in the wild) or laboratory reared, were surgically delivered and then separated from their infants for a few hours. The feral monkeys took a period (one or two days) to accept their babies after such a delivery and separation, but the laboratory-reared monkeys still hadn't accepted their babies by the third day. The implication of this is that under the added stress of a surgical delivery, separation from the new baby at this critical period interferes with the attachment process, especially if the mother has not had a good experience with other attachments in her life. It is always dangerous to apply animal research unquestioningly to human behavior. Humans appear to be more plastic, and the damage left by early experience is not comparable with that of laboratory-reared animals except in extreme cases. But the animal reactions may suggest tendencies also found in humans. Animal behavior should make us wonder and look beyond the overt human reactions to the underlying psychology.

Separation from the baby after a Caesarean birth must be more dramatic in mothers' minds. Feelings of loss occur even in an optimal delivery. After a Caesarean, a mother must feel even more torn away from her baby, and her baby torn away from her. Not only has her own body been violated surgically, but she must worry even more about her role both in endangering the baby and in letting her go to any other person. She will yearn to take care of this endangered baby, yet she is bound to feel (at least unconsciously) that *maybe* the baby is better off without her. She will hear something along these lines from the medical personnel: "It's lucky we got her out when we did, for she might have been damaged had we left her." What does this mean to a caring mother—that she was bad for her baby? So she must balance her natural wishes against the "better" care for her baby in the nursery. She will resent it but also feel she deserves it. By this "wrenching away" of the baby after a Caesarean birth, without giving the mother a chance to see and hold the baby and resolve her questions about the baby and about herself, the medical staff risks weakening her feelings of attachment for the baby. Such rigid routines surrounding delivery must be reconsidered.

As for Mrs. Thomas, she felt unreasonably sad and deserted. Although there were at least six people paying close attention to her, and although she had come through a potentially dangerous situation and was in expert hands, she felt a sense of failure. Her empty feeling of having given up her baby to someone else, of having failed to produce her normally, as well as the underlying fears of having damaged her, all began to plague Mrs. Thomas while she lay being sutured. She tried to repress these feelings, and after a few sobs she mastered her weeping. She felt foolish and ungrateful and murmured to the nurse-anesthetist, "I don't know why I'm being so silly. I am really happy—and very grateful." The anesthetist patted her cheek and told her that she was "a good girl." This well-intentioned gesture made her feel even more devalued, and she turned her head away. Dr. Fenton spoke cheerily to her about the baby—how perfect she was, how they had gotten her out at the right time—and about herself—how healthy her tissues were, how well her ovaries looked, and how he had snipped out her appendix while he was there to "save her future trouble." Despite his efforts at cheering her up—and she certainly heard and appreciated them—she continued to have a sense of loss.

This sense of loss, which occurs in all women after all kinds of deliveries, is the aftermath of the really gratifying period of carrying a baby. The lovely locked-in responsiveness that we talked about in Chapter 1 becomes so gratifying to the mother that it is hard to give it up. These feelings exist in spite of the burden of carrying a heavy baby, of being uncomfortable and out of balance physically and psychologically, and in spite of the relief that it is over at last. Even though labor and its attendant discomfort make the final effort and delivery of the baby such a euphoric event, there does follow a short period of a sense of loss and separation from a very much beloved part of one's body. Important events and powerful emotions can be seen as a set of balances. If one reaches a crescendo, there is an inevitable letdown or dip in emotion to balance the preceding "high." One without the other would not be tolerable psychologically, nor would either be as meaningful or as intensely felt. Hence the dip or depression Mrs. Thomas is experiencing will serve as a precursor, a period of recovery and of gathering steam, for the next burst of energy and emotion, when she is reunited with her baby.

Apart from this natural sense of loss, however, are the feelings about being forcibly separated from one's baby by hospital personnel. Many thoughtful investigators today feel that this separation—baby to nursery, mother to recovery room—not only is unnecessary but can be destructive. I agree and see that in home deliveries or in hospitals where alternatives are offered, babies can remain safely and productively with their mothers right through what Klaus and Kennell call the "sensitive period for bonding." My only objection to this thinking is the idea of its being absolutely critical or necessary. I worry about the mothers who can't be with their babies at this time and who feel they have missed out and that all their future relations are therefore critically endangered. They need our reassurance that they can make up for this period of separation. These feelings of loss and of separation will be there in any case and will surface as the mother allows time for her own recovery as well as a rest period for the baby. The critical issue may be whether an enlightened hospital staff or the midwife team in home deliveries supports the mother as being important to her baby. This factor may be more crucial than the actual timing or duration of togetherness in cementing the bond between mother and baby. I am all for revising our delivery practices and early care of mothers and babies (as well as fathers) to include this kind of attention to cementing family bonds.

In Mrs. Thomas's case it would have been good if her husband had remained with her to help her with these feelings. The operating-room personnel cannot be expected to play psychotherapist, but they can and should offer the reassurance that most women feel this way right after a section and that it will pass. Mrs. Thomas knew this herself, but she felt unreasonably weak and disintegrated after the lengthy ordeal.

Wheeled into her room to recover, she half dozed from the medication they had given her "to quiet her after her tears."

Any show of emotion is likely to be interpreted as dangerous at such a time. I wonder what the danger is? "Will she get too emotional? Will she get out of control?" At any rate it doesn't seem to be acceptable, and I know of no medical reason why the expression of a new mother's feelings would be anything but a relief to her and, hence, therapeutic.

Mr. Thomas returned from the phone calls he had made to announce the "great news." When he saw his wife so quiet, he tiptoed toward the door. She struggled through her fuzzy feelings to make a sound. It came out as a moan. This made him feel even more like an intruder, and he hurried out.

Instead of the joyful reunion as a family if everything had gone well, she will now be treated as an invalid. The surgical nature of Caesarean delivery puts all the focus on the mother's physiological recovery. Instead of being free to rejoice in the baby and the event, each participant must consider the mother's health and recovery first. This is surely important, and it will indeed be harder for Mrs. Thomas to get her strength and energy back after the Caesarean, but a little more attention to the joy of having a new baby would make recovery less like work. Mr. Thomas was, of course, in awe of the clinical atmosphere that is inevitably engendered around any operation. Mrs. Thomas felt let down and alone all over again.

She resigned herself to waiting and dozing, gradually more and more aware of the aching of her abdominal wall as the anesthesia wore off.

As a nurse looked in to check on her, she made a massive effort to uncloud her mind and her speech. She struggled to turn over; the nurse patted her to be quiet. She roused herself to call out, "Please!" The nurse patted her forehead soothingly. "Don't try to talk." She struggled with the fuzz in her mouth, the cloud in her eyes, the ringing in her ears, and finally said, "My baby!" The nurse said soothingly, "She is just fine! She is being taken care of in the nursery, and she is great. When you get more wide-awake, we'll bring her in to you. Meanwhile, just rest and get well in a hurry. Now, that's a good girl." Mrs. Thomas made one more massive effort to express her wandering thought that she needed her baby, but she couldn't quite get it formulated. The nurse silently wheeled out, as if on roller skates.

As the door closed, Mrs. Thomas set her mind to the job of overcoming the medication and the feelings of being out of her own control. She wanted so desperately to get to the wide-awake state that would allow her to see her baby. She tried to count. She held up her fingers, waving them to see whether she could stop the double vision that came and went. After a few more minutes, which seemed like years, she was able to concentrate on them. She could wave them, she could count them, she could make a duck's beak out of the first two, and she chuckled softly to herself as she became more and more in control. The effort wore her out, and she dozed again. Each time she dozed, she counteracted it with a massive attempt to stay awake, fearful that she would miss the nurse's next visit and an opportunity to close the gap between her and her baby.

*As her abdomen became more sensitive, she also felt the loss
more keenly, and she welcomed the dull aching in a curious way.
She saw it as a stimulus for getting her awake and near her
baby. By the time she became alert enough and active enough to
convince the nursing staff that she was "competent," she was
feeling pretty desperate about her baby. Was she all right? Were
they just using excuses for not bringing her out? What did she
look like? Was the baby deformed in any way? She blamed herself
for not having examined the baby more minutely when she had
had a chance in the delivery room. Would they bring her the right
one? She thought she had heard of mix-ups in the hospital.*

The tags on babies and mothers make a mix-up virtually impossible today. But the fantasy is so great and such a universal one that
all mothers express it and all hospitals are alert to it now. The one
instance that was ever documented, of course, made the newspapers,
for it is a threatening possibility to all parents. Mrs. Thomas's feelings
are raw and heightened right now. Worries about mix-ups and a damaged baby are just a part of her overall sensitivity.

COMPLETE AGAIN

*When Andrea was brought in, she was whimpering in her crib.
Mrs. Thomas was ecstatic that she was alive and could cry, and
she felt ever afterward that this cry was indelibly imprinted on
her brain.*

Each signal like this is endowed with such importance as a tie
to the baby that it does take on the attributes of an "imprinting" stimulus. Imprinting in animals has a specific meaning—that is, a built-
in or "instinctive" reaction gets set in action by an appropriate stimulus presented at a critical period. Thus Konrad Lorenz was imprinted on goslings by nodding to them and making appropriate
noises at the time of hatching. From then on they saw him as the
nurturing figure and followed him thereafter. In animals the appropriateness of the stimulus and the timing of it are critical to the setting of these patterns. In the human the range of appropriateness
and the timing seem to be much more flexible. But the underlying
need for attachment between parent and child is still there, and this
creates a sensitivity to all means of communication. In the case of

the baby's cry, mothers can differentiate their own baby from others in the nursery after a few days. Within a very few weeks they are able to differentiate with reliability the reasons for crying. Within a week after birth they can listen to a tape and distinguish a cry of pain from a fussy one. The cry is a significant form of communication from the very first.

The nurse took ages to get Mrs. Thomas propped up in bed. When she was finally set up, she leaned over to soothe Andrea, and as she took her out of her crib, the baby quieted. When she handed her to her mother, Mrs. Thomas felt a surge of emotion. At last she really had her baby. She began to examine and to touch each part of her: her soft, rounded face with the little pouting mouth; the fine, soft hair that framed her face; the perfect little ears with almost imperceptible fuzz on them. She longed to uncover her and look her over more completely. But the nurse had slipped out, and she was too uncomfortable to move around in bed. She wished for her husband. She had to be content with her bundled-up, now-sleeping baby. She, too, fell asleep with her baby in her arms, soothed by the feeling of completeness that holding Andrea brought her.

After they had dozed for a while, Mr. Thomas came in. Seeing Andrea in her arms, he almost forgot to greet his wife. He was overcome with excitement at seeing the baby. He went through the same inventory of her features that Mrs. Thomas

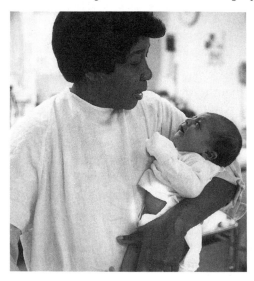
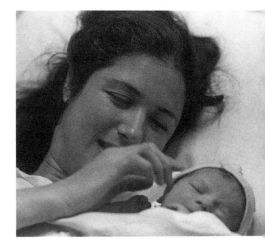

*had made. When he got to her mouth, he gently stroked it, and
of course, Andrea followed his stroking finger to root toward it.
This first movement made them brave, and they began to un-
dress her. They felt guilty about it, feeling as if there were something sacred about her wrappings. They felt like children who
were stealing cookies.*

The hospital setting is likely to engender this feeling of "lending
the baby to the parents." Any spontaneous feeling or response to the
baby is inhibited. Parents do not trust themselves and worry that they
might harm their baby. The wrappings are for two purposes—to help
the baby keep warm at a time when loss of body heat would be one
more adjustment for him, and to keep him still, not at the mercy of
the jerky startles that get set off easily when a newborn is not restrained. A brief period without wrappings will hardly endanger the
baby, and parents should feel free to unwrap and investigate. I have
seen a well-meaning nurse admonish a new mother about unwrap-
ping her baby as if it were dangerous. If, instead, she showed her
how to keep the baby warm and under control, by heaping the blan-
kets around her on each side, a mother could feel free to examine
her new baby. This kind of prohibition only adds to her feelings of
inadequacy.

*When the Thomases unwrapped Andrea, they watched each ex-
tremity as if it were magical. The tiny, delicate fingers that
moved independently and the feet and legs waving in the air all
were wondrous. They lifted her shirt to look at the already
slightly dry skin and her belly with the stump of the cord attached. As her abdomen pumped up and down with each breath,
they became fascinated by her breathing. They didn't dare undo
her diaper or turn her over, although each of them secretly
longed to see her in the nude. They reminded themselves that
they had had her nude in their arms earlier, and would again.*

*As they watched her, she began to wake up, and gradually
her eyes, swollen from the silver nitrate drops, began to crack
open slightly. She looked sleepily out of one eye. Mrs. Thomas
tried to engage her by presenting her face. As she talked to her,
Andrea's face brightened, and her eyes widened a bit more as if
she really saw her mother. Mr. Thomas saw it, and it was all he
could do not to shove his wife away so that he could try the same
maneuver.*

The competition for the baby starts early. It is largely unconscious, is present in any caring adult, and shouldn't be allowed to come between new parents. *Of course,* both parents want to get as close to this baby as they can. The forces of caring should be treasured, not seen as a threat to the future intactness of the family.

Mrs. Thomas was so touched by Andrea's response that she picked Andrea up to cuddle her. When she lifted her up, her eyes came open even more, and as she put Andrea on her shoulder, Mr. Thomas was able to engage his by now wide-awake baby in eye-to-eye contact. They both felt she was theirs at last.

Eye-to-eye contact is terribly important to us in our culture. I have studied babies and child rearing in cultures where the fears of the evil eye prohibit this kind of eye-to-eye contact. In Kenya, for instance, the fear is that you may reveal how much you care and how proud you are by looking too hard at your baby. As a result, either the gods will take him away to punish you for your pride or you will damage him by your unintentionally evil eye. In a culture where infant mortality is high, this is a way of guarding oneself against caring too much in case you lose him. To me, this kind of old wives' tale expresses the importance of eye-to-eye contact in the growth of attachment to a baby.

As soon as she established this important visual bond and held Andrea, Mrs. Thomas felt complete again. Now she could rest. Mr. Thomas took Andrea from her mother, felt her all over to see that she was intact, wrapped her up again, and placed her back in her crib. He subsided into an armchair, and they all settled back to sleep.

The recovery period from labor, delivery, and the new adjustments will be great for each of them. I think it always surprises mothers that they are as depleted as they are after a delivery. With a Caesarean section it probably is more expected. But nearly all mothers experience a combination of elation and depression for at least a week and often two or three weeks after delivery. It is certainly one good reason why rest and recovery have been institutionalized over the centuries. We hear about cultures where "strong" women go on working right after new babies. And now that we are shortening the hospital stay after a delivery and are experiencing more home deliveries, we may be pressing mothers to feel that they *should* be back on their feet soon. I feel it is critical to the baby's future and the mother's feeling of competence to care for the baby that we respect and even foster this need for physical recovery. Otherwise, the euphoria that is a natural sequel to "having made it" may press a mother beyond her limits.

In Mayan Mexico the extended family takes over for a mother, and she, too, is wrapped up, next to her baby and treated like a baby by the other women in the family for several weeks after delivery. That would be intolerable in the United States today, but a mother should respect her body's need for physical recovery. A part of this is hormonal readjustment. The hormonal imbalance that follows delivery and is further upset by lactation is undoubtedly a component in postpartum depression. If a new mother can give her body a chance for this to proceed without more than the necessary stress, the hormones will seek their own balance. I realize that there are many readjustments to be made in this period, such as a desire for independence, the need to feel one's competence—and these may be equally important to the physiological and psychological adjustment. Hence each mother must find her own level of activity, but a warning against too much activity is surely in order. I can predict from my own experience in following many new mothers that the more elated one gets and the more activity one takes on in the few days after delivery, the lower one feels after these first days as a result. A lot of this is simply physical fatigue, as well as an aftermath of the euphoric excitement of having made it successfully.

ROOMING-IN

Over the next few days Mrs. Thomas had a chance to get to know Andrea better and better. She was caught between her own problems in recovering from the Caesarean—gas pains, the inevitable stitch problems, the sore abdomen—and her desire to have Andrea with her all the time. When Mr. Thomas could be there to help, it seemed ideal to have her in the room. When he was not, she spent a lot of time wondering whether she could move fast enough to deal with an emergency if it arose. She listened to Andrea's breathing as if it were a lifeline. Whenever the baby gasped or choked or just fell into an irregular pattern (called Cheyne-Stokes—a few deep breaths, then a pause for twenty to

thirty seconds before resuming the deep-breathing pattern),
Mrs. Thomas startled, her heart raced, and she prepared herself
for an emergency. So at first she slept or rested very little when
Andrea was there. As time went on, she got more used to these
irregular breathing patterns and rested better.

Her anxiety is normal, but the great attention given to sudden infant death syndrome (SIDS) further burdens new parents. All of our very fragile clues about the causes of it are given much publicity, and any irregular behavior is suspected as a precursor of SIDS. Irregular breathing and apneic spells (periods of cessation of breathing) are being implicated. For new parents, who are ready to be anxious about almost anything, the publicity given to the as yet speculative theories about and medical investigations into the causes of SIDS is making for more insecurity and anxiety than these parents need to have. My own feeling is that by our uncertain efforts at prevention, we may be contributing to a general overconcern that is damaging to the many, many infants it will affect. The incidence of SIDS is very, very low, and this kind of general concern affects everyone. So far our success in identifying ways of predicting it does not seem to me to warrant the generalized publicity it has received.

Fortunately the hospital had instituted a relaxed policy for
rooming-in. Mrs. Thomas could have her baby when she wanted
her and could leave her in the nursery for care when she was
exhausted. The policy also allowed her husband and immediate
family members to be present if they wore gowns and washed
beforehand.

These policies are certainly supportive for new families. To let the mother decide when she wants her baby and when she needs time for herself places the proper emphasis on both sides of her needs; a mother wants free access to her baby, but she also needs time for recovery and the rest that recovery implies. To include the father is a further step toward cementing and emphasizing the importance of the family. Not all hospitals, so far, include siblings and grandparents, but this will certainly increase in the future, for the more emphasis that is placed on the extended family, the more support parents can count on at such a critical time.

Siblings have been excluded until now because they "carry germs," and indeed, children's germs are more virulent and children do carry more pathogens than do already immune adults. But with proper precautions, hospital staff can show siblings how to wash and gown and then can allow them to participate in the family excitement around a new baby. What a step! Mothers are a bit more likely to tire themselves when siblings are present, but to balance this, the chance to let the older children see that Mother is still alive and well and that there has been a reason for her absence in the form of a new baby seems well worth it. The sooner they can participate, the more positively involved they are likely to be.

Mrs. Thomas found that rooming-in with her baby gave her a chance to get to know her in all sorts of unexpected ways. Not only did she begin to recognize the important signals of hunger, of general fussiness, of wanting to be played with, but she began to recognize Andrea's sleeping-waking patterns. At first these were unpredictable in their timing and were difficult for Mrs. Thomas to read. She couldn't tell whether a bit of fussing presaged a sleep period or whether it meant she was building up to hunger. At first she put her to breast at each fuss. But her nipples began to be sensitive, and she realized that she was using them too much. In addition, Andrea refused the nipple more often that she wanted to suck. Mrs. Thomas began to watch her for other cues and to realize that she could tell a great deal about her if she looked. If Andrea was fussing and rooting around for her fist or rooted toward an offered finger, it was more likely that she'd be hungry. If, in addition, Mrs. Thomas let her build up for five or ten minutes until she was really awake and fussing, the signals would get clearer. Also, she realized that if Andrea had time to build up to a wide-awake state, she was more proficient at sucking when she finally got to the breast. Letting her fuss was hard, but it certainly seemed to make the feedings more effective. When she watched Andrea, she began to see that the short fussy period helped the baby play out an indeterminate waking-up state and move into either a clear waking or a clear sleeping state. For just as many of these fussy periods ended in sleep or a wide-awake state as they did in sucking and feeding. Allowing Andrea to sort them out rather than trying to do it for her seemed to cut down on the time spent fussing. Early interference seemed to confuse her and prolong the indeterminate, fussy states.

One of the most important aspects of behavior that must mature over time is that of "state control" (see next chapter). An immature baby has fewer clear states, and they will get clearer as his central nervous system matures over time. I am convinced that we can push this maturity a bit by allowing the baby time and space to sort out his states (as did Mrs. Thomas). We can also reinforce the end state when he gets there, by playing with him in an alert state, leaving him to sleep, or feeding him promptly and effectively when he is ready and awake. For the baby this sense of control is a developmental step that brings with it its own rewards. Isn't this a precursor of other kinds of autonomy?

In the original rooming-in studies in New Haven in the 1950s, Dr. Edith Jackson and her coworkers found that babies and mothers alike slept better if they were separated at night. In a nursery off the mother's room the baby's stirring and whimpering, which were a normal part of REM sleep, were ignored, and the baby began to stretch out his periods of deep sleep. Over time the duration of deep-sleep cycles would increase, and light sleep would decrease. If they can hear every sound, parents of a new baby find it very hard not to respond each time.

The literature on crying and fussing is confusing. There is very little in the way of theory or research that backs up parents' desire to allow a little fussing and wait for clearer evidence, as I have just suggested. On the contrary, some experimental literature speaks of how a baby will cut down on his crying if the parents respond to it immediately. This literature maintains that a response contingent on the crying "teaches" the baby that he will be responded to and that therefore, his need for crying to summon help drops out over time. Another group of investigators have taken issue with this position, and their data seem to prove the opposite: that a baby will cry just for an adult response (Gewirtz and Boyd, 1977). Neither of these positions is quite enough to satisfy me. Any single approach would be likely to be too simplistic and would not really contribute to the baby's learning about himself and his environment in any satisfactory way. I think that there are times when a baby's cry should be responded to as soon as possible (contingently), and there are other times when his crying may serve as a way of letting off steam or of getting himself under control before the next state of consciousness. If I am right, and clinical experience has led me to this complex approach (see the section on crying in Chapter 7), then it is up to the mother to decide which condition it is. For a new, inexperienced mother, this amounts to indecision much of the time at first. But as she learns more about her baby and finds the solutions that work for her *over time,* she is bound to feel closer to her son or daughter, to feel that she is getting to understand her baby, and to feel more competent as a mother. Thus crying and a new mother's attempts to understand it become a learning opportunity like everything else in the baby's day.

DISORGANIZATION AND DEPRESSION

Rooming-in seemed to provide Mrs. Thomas with a chance to feed Andrea more often, and as a result, her breast milk began to come in earlier than it might have otherwise. She nursed the baby for short periods but frequently. By the fourth day her nipples were tingling and sore, and her breasts were beginning to engorge. Everyone had warned her that it might be as long as five or six days after a Caesarean section before she got milk, so it was a great event when she began to feel these new sensations. The baby, too, was waking up more and more. Each day she seemed more responsive. On the second and third days, when she was losing weight and was not getting fluids, her skin began to dry out, her mouth looked slightly blistered, and her eyes had become a bit sunken. By the third and fourth day she had developed a golden color (of physiological jaundice). With these changes her behavior changed too. She was difficult to rouse on the second day, and when she was awakened, she startled. Her extremities were jittery, and there was often tension in her legs and arms, which came and went as she was handled. When she was played with, she finally began to respond, but after a few minutes, by the fourth day, she cried almost all of the time she was awake. Her jittery, startling behavior seemed to upset her, and it was all her mother could do to keep her under control. She tried to swaddle her and to nurse her frequently. She placed her on her abdomen and found that she was quieter this way. She tried water and sugar water to calm her down and found that they did quiet her briefly. The baby sucked on them avidly as if she were starving—and indeed, Mrs. Thomas feared that she was. She would easily have given up on the breast feeding because she felt as if she were cheating the baby while waiting for her milk to come in, but everyone assured her that all breast-fed babies went through this waiting period. So she persisted, but uneasily.

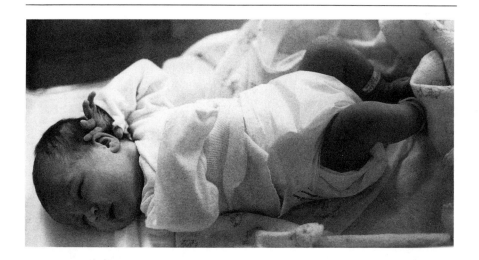

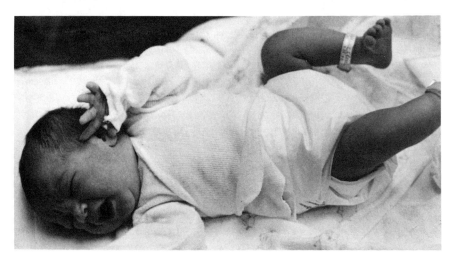

This jittery, disorganized period, when the baby is hard to rouse and overreacts with startles and excessive crying, can be expected between the second and fourth days. Certainly the drying out and the mild weight loss do represent an imbalance in the baby in terms of his stores of salt and calcium. The jaundice, which occurs in most normal babies—caused by extra blood breakdown after delivery and immature liver clearance of the bilirubin breakdown products—is a temporary irritant and slight depressant to the baby's nervous system. All of this is transient and does no damage except in extreme cases. As soon as fluid begins to get to the baby, as soon as his mother's milk is coming in, all of this corrects itself. By the fifth day the balance is usually corrected, and the baby becomes a different, well-put-together person.

Even this period of disorganization seems to me to serve a kind of purpose in the attachment process. When the baby begins to get rehydrated after this period and settles down, the mother can see clearly that her milk and her nurturance are working. After this period of stress a mother must feel a sense of relief and competence when she gets her baby reorganized and into a consistent pattern. If she is breast feeding, she can see that her milk is doing its job for the baby. Once again, the stress can motivate learning and help build the relationship.

From the infant's standpoint, this period of disorganization follows a rather depressed, overwhelmed period right after delivery. After a half hour of being quite alert after labor and delivery, the new baby seems to become quiet, sleepy, and relatively unresponsive over the first day or two. This is a response to being exhausted by labor, delivery, and the demands of the new environment (light, noise, temperature change, handling—all of which are new to him). A state of jittery disorganization then follows. The baby must reach a new physiological balance. This disorganized period ends in a kind of reorganization, and the baby becomes alert and responsive to the environment. Does he learn from these stages? I would like to think so. At least at some level he must be aware of the relief at being organized rather than disorganized. After each period of disruption or disorganization the resultant homeostasis (balance) becomes a sort of goal. At a physiological level the immature infant's whole body begins to learn about homeostasis. At the same time the baby is beginning to learn about his own inner control systems. We see this as a baby tries to calm himself down by sucking his own thumb.

> *In the first few days Mrs. Thomas felt quite depressed, and she worried alternately about herself and about the baby. In a curious way it was a blessing to have a quiet baby. But on the fourth frantic day she really hit bottom. She cried right along with the baby. Whenever the baby whimpered, so did she. When her husband asked her a question, she sobbed. He was frightened and tried to find out what was wrong. She assured him between her low sobs that nothing was really wrong. She felt achy and tired, her breasts were engorged, but it wasn't really this minor pain that was making her feel bad. What she really had was a sort of postpartum depression. The postoperative effects from the section didn't help, but she might have hit bottom in any event.*

What does this do to the burgeoning parent-child relationship? My own feeling is that although it places a temporary strain on it, the mother should know that it is part of her recovery. Hitting bottom is like hitting oneself on the head: It feels so good when it is over. In this case, once the bottom of the depression is over, the recovery phase must seem that much better. And from this time on all of the cementing of the mother-infant relationship may profit by contrast.

A positive side of this period is that in the hypersensitivity that comes with this depression, the mother will usually search for cues to help her understand the baby. Almost as if it were a solace to her own feelings of disorganization, she will seek organized behavior in the baby. When I go to visit mothers in the immediate postpartum period, they are likely to tell me about their observations. One mother described how she had learned that if she talked to her baby in a rapid, high-pitched, strident voice, he would always turn away from her, shut his eyes tightly, and start to breathe deeply and rapidly, as if he were shutting her out. As if with a magnet, she could gradually change the pace and tonality of her voice to draw the baby out of this shut-out state and lead him to turn to her voice. As he gradually turned and relaxed, he would look up into her face and would follow it as she moved it. If she kept on talking in a slow, rhythmic way, she could keep him moving to follow her. If she stopped talking abruptly, became too monotonous, or stopped moving her face as she talked, the baby would register this change in auditory and visual input within a few seconds. With a startled look of surprise and concern, he would turn his face away. He would then refuse to look back again for a period afterward. In this kind of observation, which came from working with him for many of his alert periods, this mother had learned that (a) her baby had a very finely tuned decision-making process for choosing auditory signals; (b) when he shut out the unpleasant ones, he still kept the channels open for picking up those he was looking for; (c) his responsive behavior to the appropriate auditory signals was rich and expressive; (d) he used auditory cues to enhance his visual responsiveness; (e) there was a fine line between what was appropriate to keep this complex responsiveness coming and what wasn't; (f) she had already found behavioral responses that told her when she was successful with her baby and when she was not. The adaptive aspect both of his behavioral repertoire and of her own finely tuned sensitivity to it is obvious. Perhaps a mother's postpartum depression helps accelerate her withdrawal from her old world—to give her the time to develop this kind of sensitivity and responsiveness to her baby.

CEMENTING THE BOND

As she began to pile up experience with Andrea, Mrs. Thomas found she felt more and more sure of herself. She no longer dreaded Andrea's whimpering, for she knew that if she spoke to her in a certain way, Andrea would quiet down to attend to her mother's voice. This was such a thrill that it felt like a recharging of her batteries. As her mother changed her diaper, Andrea would become jerky and startled and begin to cry. Mrs. Thomas had learned that if she held down her arm or even a leg while she undressed her, she could stop Andrea from startling. She recognized the cycle that began when Andrea was unrestrained: She began to move slowly at first; as her movements met with no restraint, she began to flail; then came startles of her arms and legs; and finally her whole body was accompanied by crying and disintegration. As she cried, she flailed and startled again. This in turn reinforced her crying, and the whole situation deteriorated into a kind of helpless disintegration. If a part of her body was held down, this cycle was broken, and Andrea could gradually get herself under control in order to quiet down. Mrs. Thomas began to experiment with other techniques: holding Andrea's attention with an insistent voice, turning her on one side or on her abdomen, or wrapping her arms in a diaper while she changed the diaper on the lower part of her body. All of these worked at certain stages and failed at others. The tuning up of her own antennae to see whether she could predict which technique might work for Andrea made it an event to have to change or to bathe her. She found she was obsessed with watching Andrea, trying to figure out what was going on inside her mind and how she could fit into it. She wanted to exclude the rest of the world as she turned to her baby. Even her husband had to fight his way into this closed circle.

This is the beginning of the work of attachment to a new baby. It appears obsessive when you read about it or watch it, but it serves a major purpose for each of the participants—the mother and the baby. They are learning about each other rapidly—learning the important things about each other. Thoman (1975) showed that primiparas spent significantly more time at each feeding with their first baby than did a multipara or an experienced nurse. This says two things to me: that a primipara is learning all the nuances of a baby in that extra time and that she is learning about herself as she reacts to them. By the second or third baby the value of experience is beginning to show, and one has only to learn about that particular baby, as is Mrs. Thomas. In other words, learning the language of attachment is learning about yourself as well as about the other.

What if this important period is not protected, not nurtured in the beginning? Won't it be that much harder to make the attachment work? Can one ever make up for lost time? Many hospitals in our country are not set up to allow the freedom of rooming-in or of having the father and the extended family in at will. Some hospitals are still using excessive medication and anesthesia and are not geared to the mother's real needs. Can a parent still establish an attachment with his or her baby in the face of these odds? The answer must be obvious, for most of the current generation of young parents were born under such conditions, and we must assume that their parents found ways of making it. However, I am fervent in wanting to see our hospitals offer optimum support to new parents because an insensitive atmosphere does set up unnecessary hurdles. And parents-to-be today are besieged by new pressures around them that interfere with the time and energy necessary to develop the capacity to believe in themselves and for deep attachment to grow.

5

The Vital Strengths of the Newborn Baby

The newborn baby brings with him to this life the pervasive quality that insures what is waiting for him (and relying *on* him) in the needs and drives of individual women, in the tradition of generations of mothers, and in universal institutions of motherhood.

—Erik Erikson, *Insight and Responsibility*

While anyone writing about babies today would want to add fathers to this equation, Erikson's words convey a sense of the imposing strengths lying ready and waiting both in new babies and in new parents. The work of attachment does not have to be carried out single-handedly by parents: the newborn is programmed with a great variety of abilities and responses that reach out to his mother and father. He meets them at least halfway.

If new parents are to understand the job of parenting, they must be able first to understand the baby and this extraordinary endowment that he brings with him at birth.

UNDERSTANDING THE BABY'S BEHAVIOR

Rewarding communication between a baby and his parents is critical to his development. Every new parent both realizes this and is overwhelmed by it. Few parents are fully aware of the baby's role in communication. The responsibility of wondering at each turn whether they have made a mistake or not weighs parents down, so that there is too little joy in parenting a first baby. No wonder most first children are so serious!

When I discharge teenagers from my practice to an "adult" doctor as they reach seventeen or eighteen, I always sit down with them to say good-bye. As part of our leave-taking I ask them what they remember about being small children. I have their records in front of me, and they know it. They know I have all the "important" information, like how many times they spit up, how their bowel movements were, how many illnesses they had, and so on. They don't always know that I also have notes about what kinds of children they were and how their parents reacted to them. But because of our past years together, they try very hard to remember and to tell me what their impressions were. Almost universally they tell me that they remember their childhood as being very serious business: "No one ever smiled." If I ask them, "Why not? Was it because your parents didn't care for you?" they say, "Oh, no! They cared too much. They were always wondering whether they'd done the right thing by me or not. And it made them very serious." These were intensely caring parents, and it seems too bad that this is what they are remembered for. This observation from my grown-up patients has led me to want to help parents understand their babies' reactions so that they don't get caught up in anxious wondering and in too-careful decision making. I feel that if parents understand what their baby is going through, if they understand the nonverbal responsive "language" of a baby's behavior, they will have an easier time making appropriate decisions and will enjoy their baby more.

No longer can we look upon a newborn as a lump of clay ready to be shaped by his environment. This concept came from the days when he was thought of as neurologically inadequate, functioning without the use of his brain's cortex. William James called a newborn a "blooming buzzing confusion, a blank slate to be written on by his world." These descriptions do not fit a baby with predictable, directed responses, the kind one sees when a newborn is reacting to auditory or visual stimulus. Even in the delivery room, when positive stimuli are offered, the newly born infant will demonstrate his amazing capacity for becoming alert and attending to them. He suppresses interfering motor activity in order to attend. In the very first minutes of life he shows predictable, orderly behavior and begins to interact with his environment. In other words, he is equipped with a set of responses, as well as the capacity to shut some out in order to produce

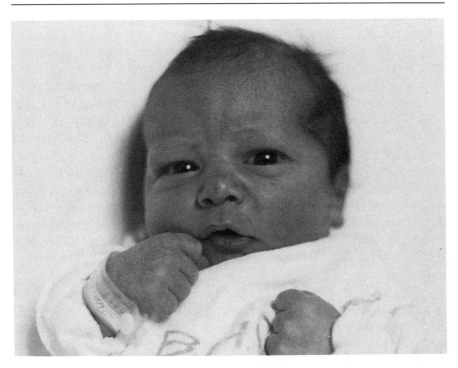

others. These responses are organized and ready to go at birth. Of course, they have been developing in the uterus, and of course, they have already been fed appropriate information to ready them for the external world. The marvelous thing is how complex they already are, how little information they need to set them off, and how, when they are set off and in motion, the baby seems to be entirely absorbed in them. Not only does the baby respond, but he seems to be actively learning from the feedback from his own responses. Learning and storing away what is learned undoubtedly begin before birth. One can see the pleasure of achievement on the face of a newborn, as if he were already set up with recognizable goals from his intrauterine experiences.

FUEL FOR DEVELOPMENT

There are two sources of energy for development that are apparent in the small baby. One source comes from within, a kind of feedback that occurs with the completion of any goal. Babies practice behaviors as if they wanted to get them under control and as if they were gaining a kind of energy from each completed act. The more important the goal may be and the more practice it takes, the more this "sense of competence," mentioned earlier, is realized. A dramatic example of this cycle can be seen in the twelve-month-old baby who has been pulling himself up on furniture for several months, cruising along the edge of tables, and holding on to his parents' fingers to practice walking. When he finally takes off *alone* and staggers forward, arms up to balance him, legs wide apart, propelled forward and unable to stop except by crashing, his face is alight. He staggers around as if he could go on and on forever, as if he were *there* at last. He chortles with inner excitement and strives to get your attention, to show you how great he is and to get your approval of his massive achievement. The effort to get there has been great, but getting there fuels him, and he is ready to charge on to the next stage of development. The same cycle takes place in the newborn infant, but it is far subtler to see and to believe in.

The second source of energy comes from outside. The newborn is fueled by external stimuli for which he is programmed. As he registers responses from people around him and is responsive to them, each new stimulus temporarily upsets the balance he may have achieved previously. Achieving his balance again becomes a new source of internal satisfaction. The cycle of disruption and correction is complete. Somewhere he registers that he can achieve homeostasis and reorganization after responding to an outside stimulus. He is beginning to build up an active coping system and to be aware of his control of it. This cycle—that of receiving, registering, being upset by a signal, and then achieving a new balance—becomes a very important basis for his future development. Stimuli from his caretakers, from nonsocial events and objects, are more than just information, since they challenge the infant to achieve this balance. Each becomes more attractive to the infant because of the internalized feeling of having exercised the control that goes with each response and its aftermath. Thus the baby's future cognitive development is tied inexorably to his social development and his sense of self.

The two sources of energy can be seen in many segments of the newborn's behavior. When a sleeping newborn begins to wake up, he will probably begin to cry if left alone. But often he can be seen to make rather massive efforts to get into a position where he can manage to turn his head to one side. What enables him to do so is the motor behavior he is programmed with called the tonic neck reflex. This reflex sets off a fencing position of the whole body: The arm and leg on the face side extend outward, the trunk arches away from the

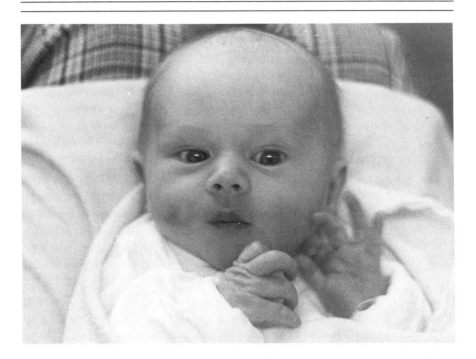

face, and the arm and leg on the opposite side flex at the elbow and knee. Thus he looks as if he were fencing whenever his head is turned to one side. Next he makes efforts to overcome this set of reflex movements, to bend his arm and bring his hand in front of his face up to his mouth. As his hand gets there, his mouth begins to root against it. When he is finally able to insert a thumb or finger into his mouth, he sighs, quiets down, and begins to look around. His expression seems to say, "Now I've done it! I'm under control, and I can pay attention and listen." Such behavior demonstrates that a newly born infant will make real efforts to get and keep himself under control *in order to* reach out for the sights and sounds in the world around him. This programming is one more indication that the human organism is hungry for stimuli from the very first. Watching a baby pull off this series of entirely independent behaviors makes one realize how elaborately he is already programmed—to complete inner feedback cycles and to search for stimuli in the world around him.

Besides fueling the baby, these programs serve another very important purpose: they attach his caregivers to him. The human infant has the longest period of dependency of any of the mammals. In order to survive, he must learn all about himself as well as the important messages and patterns that will help him adapt to his world—

his family, culture, and society. He needs to be nurtured in a way that will encourage this learning process. Sustenance alone will not do it. We have seen from work with institutionalized infants that food and maintenance are not enough. Provence and Lipton (1962) studied a group of babies in an orphanage who were fed every four hours and cared for in a routine, apparently adequate fashion. These infants survived well enough physically, but they didn't develop in many other ways. They were delayed in motor milestones and seemed to prefer to lie in bed all day, watching their hands or a mobile overhead. They could not sit or stand and showed little interest when helped to do so. They did not initiate responses from adults around them, and they were flat in their responses when they were picked up or held. They withdrew to hide behind their open, outstretched hands if one tried to talk to or play with them. As they grew, they developed stereotyped, unexcited, and unexciting responses and motor behavior up to about the age of four or five months. After that, their development lagged, and most of them began to regress. Their flattened emotional responses to outside stimulation were accompanied by a lack of drive to go on developing achievements of their own. These babies ultimately became withdrawn, retarded in appearance, and delayed in all behavioral achievements. To me this study showed that there is enough internal drive for the baby to go on for a few months, but without interpersonal and environmental stimuli the fuel for further development runs out after about four to five months.

APPEARANCE

The newborn baby is equipped with configurations in his appearance that are designed to capture adults around him. The soft cheeks, the roundness of his face, the size of his head relative to the rest of his body that renders it too heavy and floppy for him to maintain alone are all markers of immaturity. Work with other mammals has demonstrated that even adolescent male monkeys (which might not yet be hormonally equipped to nurture) are attracted by the relatively large size of an infant monkey's head and its smaller body. They become gentler in their behavior, cooing and behaving in a nurturing way toward a small animal or toy equipped with such configurations. In humans we all are aware of our responses to a helpless-looking baby. The fine hair on his scalp, the softness of his skin, even the peach-fuzz hair, or lanugo, over his face, shoulders, and extremities are each "attachers" for us. The soft spot of his scalp makes us want to protect his head. The rounded soft belly produces another kind of protective response. And his relatively floppy, undirected muscular behavior produces an "instinctive" feeling in us of wanting to cuddle, shape, or teach him. These have been called imprinters by ethologists, who attempt to relate the triggers for animal responses to those of humans. In other words, adult humans may well be equipped with inborn responses that are triggered by certain features of the immature members of our species.

ROOTING AND SUCKING

The strong rooting reflexes of the newborn show up when the cheek around his mouth is stroked. He turns toward the stroking finger, grasps it with his mouth, and starts sucking on it. The strength of his suck will inevitably produce a sensation of real excitement in the adult.

With a finger in place in his mouth, one can feel separate responses that go off independently. There is a chomping from the anterior part of the tongue, a rhythmical milking movement from the back of the tongue, and suction from the muscles of the esophagus. All of these can be felt on different parts of the inserted finger. They start off as independent, segmented movements and come together after a few moments, quickly producing a very strong, unified pull on the finger. Together, these three ingredients of the suck reflex create an effective sucking mechanism.

In babies with brain damage these separate responses take a longer time to become organized. In premature infants they do not become effective until a certain level of maturational development is reached. An experienced nurse can tell by the way the premie sucks on the gavage tube when this suck is effective enough for him to start on a bottle or breast. The maneuver of her finger in a baby's mouth can tell her even more clearly when the baby is ready to do his own sucking. For a mother who is breast feeding, the jump from the initial chewing in the front of the mouth to the integration of these three segments of sucking is critical and a relief. When he first produces an effective pull on her nipple, the pull produces a letdown reflex in her breasts, and her milk begins to flow. The spasm she feels initially is relieved as the more effective suck begins to draw out her milk. Very quickly over the first few days the newborn baby learns to shorten the time it takes to get it all together, and by the third day he can suck effectively in a few seconds at most.

A baby's sucking behavior can also demonstrate to us his ability to make very fine choices. Lipsitt and his colleagues at Brown University (1963) demonstrated that a baby sucks more effectively for sweetened fluids than he will for fluids that are less sweet. He can detect very subtle changes. In fact, he can tell the difference between 5 percent sugar water and 10 percent (one versus two teaspoons sugar per pint) within two to three sucks! His preference for sugar water over unsweetened water becomes obvious as he refuses the plain water with a frown and spits out the nipple. If formula is being delivered to a new baby by nipple and he is sucking contentedly and breast milk is then substituted, he will demonstrate a marked increase in the rate and effectiveness of his sucking. If a change back to formula occurs, the baby will stop sucking within two to three sucks. He will register his disapproval of the change by an initial frown, a gasp, and a period of choking.

Using this sucking behavior, the same investigators have demonstrated a baby's awareness of human signals as opposed to non-human stimuli. While their experimental baby was sucking peacefully on a pacifier, they presented him with a nonhuman sound. He stopped sucking in response to it, then went on with his sucking. When they substituted an exact replication of the stimulus but made by a human voice, he not only stopped sucking but, when he resumed, continued in a pattern of bursts and pauses. In other words, he gave a few sucks, then paused at regular intervals as if he were waiting for the next human sound. It was as if he had saved the burst-pause pattern of responsiveness for the more interesting human stimulus.

The burst-pause pattern is built into the baby's repertoire at birth. The pauses seem to me to be used by the baby to elicit responses from the adult who is feeding him. A hungry baby will start out sucking on the breast or bottle with a steady series of sucks. After he is initially satiated, he will fall into a pattern of bursts of sucks (ten to twenty) and pauses (for a few seconds). The adult who is feeding him will jiggle him when he pauses or will move the bottle nipple or the breast up and down in his mouth "to get him going again." She will look down at the baby at this point to talk to him or to stroke his cheek, or she will hold him closer. Although she will say that she is doing this to start him sucking and to make the feeding more effective, the results do not bear this out. Kenneth Kaye and I (1974) studied the duration of these pauses when the mother responded and when she didn't. When she did not respond to the pause, it was shorter than when she did. The pauses seemed to be actively prolonged by the infant when she responded, as if he were more eager for her social response than he was for the milk. We felt that the baby seemed to be programmed to elicit responses from his caregiver during a feeding by the use of this burst-pause pattern.

HAND-TO-MOUTH BEHAVIOR

When the baby first brings his hand to his mouth, it is part of a reflex cycle. If one strokes his cheek, the hand will form a fist on the same side, and he will gradually bring it to his mouth. If one inserts a finger in one hand, as he closes on the finger in a grasp, he will bring the whole fist up to his mouth. In other words, the hand and mouth are linked together neurologically, as if there were a purpose for thumb sucking from the first. The Babkin reflex is present at birth. In fact, thumb sucking can be seen in fetuses as early as twenty-four weeks. Our research team once observed a twenty-four-week-old fetus by the technique of ultrasound visualization. He was swimming around actively, kicking his feet and turning over and over. Lying on the table, his mother said, "He's always active when I first lie down. But then he quiets down and seems to listen to me when I talk to him." As she began talking, he curled up in a little ball and brought his arms up to his face. At this point Dr. Birnholz, the X-ray physician experienced in ultrasound techniques, said, "He just put his thumb in his mouth, and now watch him suck on it!" As we watched the face and the barely visible jawbones, we could indeed see them moving rhythmically up and down, the arm still and the finger apparently inserted. He seemed indeed to be still and listening.

A newborn has therefore had practice in sucking on his fingers before birth, and he uses it from the first to keep himself calm. As a new mother watches this, she can see her newborn baby's ability to keep himself under control and even to comfort himself. She can also see how he will use sucking as an important source of gratification and control in the future. If she understands this, she may be more tolerant of his thumb sucking later, rather than see it as a habit or as a problem.

STANDING AND SITTING

As a new baby is held standing up, he will stiffen his legs and trunk in an attempt to support himself. His head is likely to bobble after an initial period, but his trunk and legs will be as strong as he can make them to support himself. The vigor and excitement that a newborn demonstrates as he is brought to stand are remarkable. There are strong individual and genetic differences in this response around the world. As we played with black newborn babies in eastern Africa and pulled them up to sit by their fists and extended arms, they invariably seemed to come right on up to standing. As they did, their faces brightened as if to say, "WOW! I'm here!" It made one feel that the new baby was programmed for an upright posture and was excited by it. No wonder mothers in Zambia and Kenya responded by carrying their babies upright on their hips from the very first day. From birth onward they played with them by bouncing the babies on their feet in front of them. The baby seemed excited by it, and of course, the mother did. As a result, their trunks and legs became stronger very quickly. Motor milestones such as standing and sitting were achieved several months ahead of norms in our country. Super (1980) has attributed this motor precocity to the early and consistent stimulation they received from their caregivers. The newborn babies, in turn, fueled the caregivers to play with them this way by their excited and vigorous responses to such play.

An excited, vigorous response to sitting is built in for the baby as well. As a newborn is pulled up by his hands and extended arms, his entire shoulder girdle responds with an increase in tone. His head may lag, but he will attempt to right it when he gets to a sitting position. As he sits, he will attempt to right his head in the midline position and will fight to bring it up several times in succession if it falls backward or forward. Babies are programmed toward the goals of sitting and standing. A parent will see and feel this drive to get upright and will automatically begin to encourage the baby to work toward these goals in play periods.

EYE REFLEXES

As a newborn is brought to an upright position, his eyes widen and he becomes more alert. Korner and Thoman (1970) have demonstrated that the newborn becomes more visually responsive as he is moved to a semiupright position. Movement of his head stimulates the fluid in the vestibular canals located in his inner ear, and the vestibular nerves set off reflexes that control eye opening. As his eyes open, they are centered on the midline, and he is alerted and ready to start interacting visually. In order to alert a newborn to respond visually, one can rock him gently up and down and to each side. A sleeping baby will gradually awaken and begin to open his eyes to look at the person rocking him. A mother or father learns quickly that rocking can be alerting as well as soothing.

REFLEX MOVEMENT PATTERNS

Held in a standing position, a newborn has two motor patterns that are exciting to produce—exciting to him and to the adult who produces them. In order to elicit the first reflex pattern, the infant must be supported standing and slightly bent forward over one's hand, the soles of his feet flattened and pressed down against the bed. In this position he will gradually pick one foot up in the air, then put it down again to lift the other foot. He will alternate back and forth, walking in a rhythmic patterned reflex. He can be made to walk across the bed. This reflex walking response is a precursor of the voluntary walking pattern that he will develop much later in the year. Before he is ready to walk voluntarily, he will lose this automatic pattern. It will go underground as the more voluntary patterning of walking and standing surfaces in the fifth and sixth months.

To produce the second pattern, the baby is held upright in one's arms, and the upper part of his foot is stroked. The leg will flex at the hip, the toes will fan out, and the foot will come up to reach forward. A curling grasp of the toes and foot ends the motor sequence. This reach and grasp of the leg mimic the reach and grasp of the arms in older infants. Even in the newborn one can produce a similar fanning of the fingers and an effective grasp of the hand by stroking or tapping the outside of the hand. These reflexes in the newborn infant are called placing reflexes, and they serve our monkey relatives well. As they fall through the trees and as an extremity touches a limb of the tree, this reflex results in an automatic grasp of the tree limb. Thus they are able to break the fall.

FINE MOTOR MOVEMENTS

The lovely, delicate movements of a small baby's fingers as he waves his hands in the air presage the precision movements of later infancy. The strong automatic flexion grasp from his fingers and his toes may come as a surprise when one places a finger in his palm or on the upper part of the sole of the foot next to his toes. A baby monkey's whole foot and leg can be picked up by one finger as he flexes and grasps it with his toes. One can see that these reflexes become the basis for more complex hand and foot behavior later on. They serve no similar purpose in the human newborn, but the pattern they represent may become part of reaching and grasping later on as the baby begins to discover toys.

MORO, OR STARTLE, REFLEX

Another remnant of our heritage in the form of a primitive reflex is called the Moro reflex, named for an Italian neurologist who identified it a hundred years ago. It is set off whenever the baby's head drops backward suddenly. As part of a massive startle, the baby will throw out his arms and legs in extension, then follow with a hugging movement, flexing them back to his torso. This startle is easily set off by an active, fussing baby. When he startles, it upsets him even more, and he prolongs the vicious cycle by crying, startling, crying from the startle, and so on.

In monkeys the Moro reflex serves a more useful purpose. In a film by Irving deVore of Harvard, taken in the Gamba reserve in Kenya, a mother chimpanzee is feeding in the jungle, with her new baby playing beside her on the ground. She hears a predator, and without looking at the baby or without attempting to pick him up, she claps the baby chimp on the back. He responds with a Moro reflex, throwing out his arms to clutch her fur, then bringing his arms together to hug himself to her chest, and they are off into the trees. In one split second, by setting off this reflex behavior, she can bring him to her more effectively than she could do in any other way.

I have seen a tragic instance where the Moro did have value in the mother-infant interaction. I watched the mother of a brain-damaged infant who was hungry for responses. She hugged the unresponsive baby to her, clapping him on the back to produce his Moro reflex and the hugging response that was part of it. She seemed capable of getting satisfaction from this very primitive reflex, although he had little else to offer her in the way of responsive behavior.

PROTECTIVE MECHANISMS

When a cloth is placed over a newborn's eyes, nose, and mouth, he will first begin to root with his mouth and then turn his head from side to side. If he cannot dislodge the offending cloth, he will toss his head up and down in an effort to throw it off, to free his nose and his airway. If these thrashing maneuvers are unsuccessful, he will bring up one arm after the other, and with a swiping motion directed at the cloth, he will repeatedly attempt to push it away from his face. The determined activity in this response shows how hard he would fight before smothering.

As he is turned over onto his abdomen into a prone position, he will automatically lift his head and turn it to one side to free his face from bedclothes. While he lies there, he will make alternating movements of his legs in a reflex pattern of crawling. These are the precursors of the voluntary crawling patterns that will become effective when he is seven to eight months old. In this primitive crawling effort he may even propel himself across the bed to end up in a corner. He may scrabble among the bedclothes until he finds a "nest" for himself, to quiet down as if to go sleep. Nesting behavior is present from the first in a newly born baby. A new mother who sees it comes away with respect for her baby's competence.

All of the foregoing motor patterns, present from birth, give a parent indications of the programs for future motor development, and indeed, the baby's later behavior is built on these reflex patterns. When one plays with a baby to produce them, the gratification that appears subtly on the baby's face or in his whole body as he performs can give one the feeling that he is already learning about himself. As he grows over the next few months, he will practice them over and over again, learning to master them.

STATES OF CONSCIOUSNESS

Most important for parents to understand as they try to elicit responses from their baby are the various states of consciousness (see Chapter 1, page 20). In each state the baby is likely to respond differently to a stimulus. If parents expect a sleeping baby to respond immediately to a voice, of course, they will be disappointed. If the baby is in light (or REM) sleep, they may well receive a response, such as an "angel's smile"—a sort of reflex smile that is likely to occur in response to internal or external stimuli. A brief description may help parents recognize these states for themselves.

Deep sleep. In deep sleep a newborn's breathing is regular and deep, his eyes are tightly shut, and at fairly regular intervals he has a brief startling movement of a part of his body, accompanied by a shudder of his body and a brief cessation of regular breathing. Then, as if uninterrupted, his deep, regular breathing goes on, and the original position is resumed. His hands lie beside his face, fingers jerking a bit at times. In deep sleep noise and light changes don't seem to disturb him. If he is handled abruptly, he may respond with a startle of the entire body. If he is gently moved or if he is spoken to softly, he may not respond at all. If a bright light or a sharp noise like a rattle is presented to him in deep sleep and it successfully intrudes on this state, he will blink, startle slightly, but return to the sleeping state without rousing. Although the period between the stimulus and the response is only a matter of seconds, it is long in comparison with the span of time in a more awake state. This period is called the latency to response.

In deep or regular sleep the baby is essentially able to shut out the world around him. After a disturbance his respirations will get deeper and more regular, he will shut his eyes more tightly, his body will be held more stiffly as if he were trying not to move, his face will wrinkle as if he were determined not to respond. When I observe a baby doing this, I feel that this is an active state of shutting out, used for self-protection. This state of sleep can be confirmed by "sleep spindles" (which look like sharp spikes) on an electroencephalographic tracing. A mature baby has relatively longer and more stable periods of deep sleep, whereas a premature baby or an infant who has been stressed during delivery will have shorter, less stable periods of deep sleep. More-fragile babies are less able to shut out the stimuli around them in this state and are more at the mercy of the environment. Loud noises, changes in light, or movements of the bed will disturb them each time, producing a startle and often a change to another state of consciousness in the baby. For practical purposes, this means that the parents of a normal full-term baby needn't worry so much about isolating him in a quiet, dark room, for he can probably manage to stay asleep despite an active world around him. A premature or sick baby, however, would profit from a quieter situation for sleeping.

Light sleep. As the same baby begins to wake up, he goes into a period of light or irregular sleep. In this state his breathing is irregular, alternating between jagged and smooth bursts of respirations. He makes little bursts of sucking motions. His eyelids flutter, and if one looks at his eyeballs under the lids, they are moving rapidly up and down or from side to side in bursts. Hence this sleep state is called rapid eye movement, or REM, sleep. The baby startles more frequently in this state. Each startle ends with a smooth movement of the extremity that has just startled. In this state he can and often does move around with slowed writhing movements of his trunk. The more awake he is, the smoother are his movements.

If one talks softly to him or touches him gently as he lies in bed in light sleep, he is likely to come to a more awake state. If he is rocked or sung to, he will begin to rouse. Attractive stimuli tend to alert him, and this light sleep state is often a precursor to a more responsive awake state. It is seen at regular intervals throughout the night, a transitional state interspersed between periods of deep sleep.

If presented with a series of negative stimuli—loud noises or bright lights—the baby will appear to go back into deep sleep. In other words, he can go either way from this transitional state. Left to his own, he will move in a regular way through deep sleep, light sleep, and alert states throughout a twenty-four-hour period in a regular, predictable cycle. These cycles are most important for parents to understand if they are trying to predict their baby's behavior for the purpose of having some effect on entraining him and shaping him to their own day (see Chapters 4 and 6).

Alert states. As the baby comes to a more alert state, he passes first through a semiawake, semidozing state. In this he may try fitfully to whimper, to squirm, to shut out things around him, but in general he is on his way somewhere else. This is not a stable state of consciousness. He can be pushed either way—either to more alertness or back into sleep, depending on the kinds of stimuli he receives. If the stimuli are attractive, they will draw him out; if they are intrusive or negative, he will try to defend himself by going to sleep. Crying or fussing may become a forceful way of managing the inde-

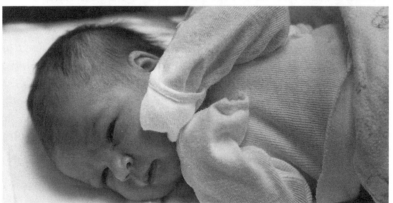

cision that is engendered by stimuli that are not clear in their message to him. Crying serves many purposes. It helps him shut out the world around him and serves a protective purpose. Also, it calls for more definite responses from those who care for him. They must respond in an effective way, or his crying will continue. If he is managing alone, crying can serve the further purpose of organization. As an important discharge of activity and stored-up energy, it helps him manage the transition from being semiawake to going back to sleep. Crying discharges the energy that could otherwise lead to disorganized and disturbing responses. Fussing or crying can lead into an alert, wide-awake state as well. We see babies who are more solidly alert and responsive after they have had a crying episode—as if it were some sort of catharsis. If parents can successfully soothe their baby in a fussy state, they will be able to produce the most gratifying state of all—wide-awake alertness. In this state babies will demonstrate the amazing responses described throughout this chapter.

To maintain this alert state in a newborn baby, the parent or adult observer plays a critical role. So fragile is this state that any overwhelming motor response will throw the baby out of it into a fussy state. As he gets involved with an exciting stimulus—whether visual, auditory, or kinesthetic—he is likely to respond with an excited motor response that will break his concentration. The adult must be there to calm him, so that he can continue in this responsive state. A hand on his extremities, a soothing voice, or gentle rocking are each ways the adult can do this. We have seen babies with cardiac problems who have gotten so excited by watching an exciting toy or responding to an adult's talking to them that they threw themselves into a kind of cardiac overload and momentary collapse. These infants needed the constant soothing containment of an adult in order to be able to pay prolonged attention to any set of interesting stimuli. As a result, I think that a nurturing adult's first role in responding to this state in a small baby is to hold him gently or to provide a low-keyed soothing background that will allow him to respond to and become engaged by stimuli but not be overwhelmed by them. As the nurturing adult learns how to contain him in this way, he or she teaches him, in turn, how to contain himself. Over time he will learn the maneuvers necessary to gain mastery over interference from his own responses that might otherwise throw him out of this state.

This role is a natural one for most parents when they have an easy baby. With a hypersensitive infant, who responds to almost any stimulus with a rapid, overactive response, it becomes a more difficult job. I can identify such babies in the newborn nursery. As you stand over them, they seem to sense your presence and respond with a startle. If you speak or if a nurse rustles by without even touching the crib, such an infant will startle, start thrashing, and go quickly on to crying. He seems to shoot from a sleep state to an overwhelmed crying state, with no transition time during which an adult can have the chance to contain him. His hypersensitivity and hyperactivity extend to all stimuli—movement, noise, visual stimuli—and adults wonder what they can do to reach such a baby. Premature infants are likely to go through a period of such hypersensitivity (see Chapter 3), and this becomes the most difficult adjustment for a parent in handling such an infant. There are many full-term, normal infants who are like this at birth as well.

There is another group of infants who are somewhat depleted at birth; they are called "small-for-dates," or small for gestational age. (See photos on following page.) They are slightly dry, with peeling skin and long, skinny legs and arms, and they frown a lot as they lie in their cribs, staring off into the distance. They are likely to be over-responsive and have difficulty maintaining an alert state. The parents of such infants need to be as gentle and as patient in communicating with their babies as the parents of premature infants do. Their hypersensitivity makes them either sleep a lot or cry for long periods—as if to shut out stimuli from the outside. Parents of these babies tend to feel that the crying is their fault, but it may not be. As these babies get older and better able to shut out stimuli from the outside, they become easier to live with.

Habituation. Important to a baby's survival is the capacity he shows to defend himself from stimuli that might otherwise force responses from him that would make excessive demands on his immature physiological systems. When a bright light is flashed into a new baby's eyes, not only do his pupils constrict, but he blinks and withdraws his head by arching his body, setting off a startle as he withdraws. With the startle his heart rate increases and his breathing speeds up. His skin color may change if the bright flashes are continued. After a few startles his capacity to shut out the stimuli begins to appear, his startles cease, the rate of his heart and breathing decreases, and he goes into a fixed state of unresponsiveness, as if he were asleep. His eyes are tightly shut, arms and legs pulled into him, his body curled up, and he breathes in a deep, regular way. At first he appears to be working hard to maintain this shutting out state of

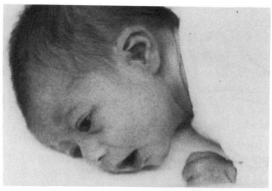

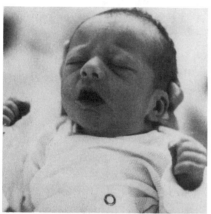
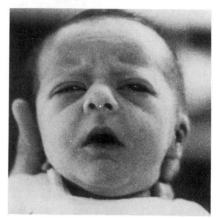

"sleep." If one continues with the intrusive stimulus, he will eventually relax and look as if he were in a real sleep state. In other words, he has been able to gain control over his responses to the disturbing stimuli and finally to put himself into an unavailable state of sleep.

This capacity to shut out is called habituation in the psychological literature and serves as a major source of protection. As we saw in Chapter 1, fetuses can demonstrate this in utero, but it becomes even more necessary in the outside world. When one thinks of the too brightly lit delivery rooms and newborn nurseries, one can see how critical this mechanism is to a new baby. Babies in newborn nurseries spend a lot of their time in this "defensive" sleep state, and one wonders at what cost to them. Certainly a baby who is delivered with Dr. Leboyer's techniques in a quieter, darker delivery room can afford to be more alert at birth and remains so for a significantly longer period. The same observation can be made of a baby in a rooming-in situation. As it is darker and quieter than the regular nursery, he will spend more of his day in both alert states and in a more peaceful sleep.

The ability of the two- or three-day-old to manage the world around him by this mechanism of habituation is awesome. Because of this capacity to shut out what he doesn't want to attend to, he has the freedom to choose what he does want to respond to.

SENSORY CAPACITIES

When a sensitive adult can act as a sort of containing envelope, the newborn baby demonstrates remarkable capacities to take in and respond to the world around him. Why have we insisted that a newborn doesn't see for several weeks after birth? Why have we claimed that he can't hear for the first few days? In a noisy, overlit nursery it may well seem as though he can't respond, for he is in a habituated state in order to protect himself. But if an adult gradually rouses him, containing and soothing him as she does so, he will demonstrate remarkable responses from birth.

Vision. The newborn is equipped with the capacity to process visual information and to respond differentially to stimuli at birth. For example, Robert Fantz and his coworkers (1963) found that newborns show a clear preference for certain kinds of complex visual stimuli. They propped a newborn up in a reclining infant seat in a darkened box. Then they presented him with a pair of visual objects matched for light intensity and size. They were able to measure how long he looked at each of the paired visual stimuli, assuming that preference would be demonstrated by more prolonged looking. They found that patterns with sharply contrasting colors, large squares, and medium brightly lit shiny objects are more appealing to the newborn. Using the same technique, they and others found that the newborn much prefers an ovoid object in the shape of a human face. Stechler (1966) demonstrated that a new baby would stare at a schematic face for as long as twenty minutes without turning away. When a real face was presented, the newborn looked at it, appeared surprised, then returned to the schematic face, frowned, and looked away in order to return to the real face by preference. While he looked at the three-dimensional face, his eyes widened, his eyebrows went up, his mouth opened, and his whole face seemed to say, "Come on, talk to me, play with me!" In other words, at birth the infant is programmed to search for and respond with excitement to a human face in preference to other objects. In the experiment, when the adult continued to stare fixedly and unresponsively at the newborn, he began to look worried, frowned, and then turned away. He checked back once or twice, then actively averted his eyes for good. Genevieve Carpenter (1970) used similar experimental techniques to show not only that at one month a baby recognizes his mother's face in preference to other adults, but that if she is unresponsive to him, he is much more upset by her lack of response. In other words even at birth the newborn seems to have an expectation for interaction with a human face. A real three-dimensional face attracts him, but it also turns him off when this expectation is not met (see Chapter 6). The nonhuman or schematic face attracts the baby but does not carry this kind of expectation with it, and he will stare at it for longer periods. He already has the capacity to differentiate an unresponsive object from a potentially responsive one.

Goren (1975) demonstrated that even in the delivery room a newborn not only would fix on a schematic face but would follow it for complete 180-degrees arcs, eyes and head turning to follow it. If the drawing of the face was scrambled, he would still fix on contrasting areas of the drawing, but he would follow for only half as far and with only half the degree of head turning. In order to assess newborns' depth perception, Gorman, Cogan, and Gellis (1957) placed them inside a lined drum that moved slowly across their field of vision. As their eyes caught and automatically followed the lines, one could test for visual acuity by changing the visual arcs of the lines. The newborns seemed to have 20/150 vision when tested in this apparatus.

In our laboratory Adamson (1981) demonstrated the importance of vision to the newborn by covering an alert baby's eyes with an opaque shield. The baby swiped at it and attempted to remove it just as he would a cloth placed over his face, building up to frantic activity as he did so and quieting down when it was removed. When a clear shield was substituted for the opaque one, he calmed down and looked through it with interest. Being able to see seemed to *be enough* to compensate for the intrusiveness of having his face covered.

Salapatek and Kessen (1973) studied the newborn in an attempt to map out what he saw. They found that he concentrated on the contrasting edges of an object or on the shiny eyes of the face or on the bright red mouth. Moving objects were more attractive than still ones. Moving eyes and the mouth of a face became much the most preferred foci for the baby's attention. When the face was very still, he tended to look to the sides of the face or at the hairline and would scan the whole face during a period of alertness.

If a newborn baby is propped up at a 30-degree angle in a reclining chair or on one's lap and rocked slowly, his eyes will open and he will come into a more responsive state. He begins to scan the environment with a dull look, his pupils widen, and his eyes move in rather jerky side-to-side movements. When a bright, shiny red ball is brought into his field of vision at about ten inches in front of him and is moved slowly up and down to attract his attention, his eyes brighten and his pupils contract. If the ball is moved slowly from side to side, his eyes will widen and follow it, and his whole face will brighten, his body becoming still. He seems to work to maintain his still posture in order to attend to the ball. At first he tracks it in small arcs, and he loses it repeatedly by overshooting, but as he gets more invested, his eye movements get smoother. Thus he can finally move his head to follow in a full 180-degree arc. If a face is substituted for the ball, the baby appears to become even more fascinated and will follow the face for 120 degrees to either side, having to turn his head and to arch as he keeps it in sight. He will arch his head up as much as 30 degrees to follow the face upward or downward. If one talks softly to him as he follows the face, he will blink at the sound of the examiner's voice, but then he will appear even more intense in his efforts to follow the face and voice. His face will remain alert, his body still, as he stays intensely involved for several minutes at a time. Finally all this effort will overload his system, and he will either startle or close his eyes or even cry with exhaustion. The intensity of his response, his ability to maintain an alert state of consciousness at such a cost, the involvement of the motor pathways of his head and eyes, coupled with his ability to suppress other interfering motor activity, certainly point to the marvelous capacity for attention that is already present in the newborn. These responses also seem programmed to capture a mother or a father and to say to her or to him, "You're the most important thing in my universe!"

Visual responsiveness is of enormous significance to new parents. Right after delivery, when I have examined the baby, they first ask me, "Is my baby all right?" The second thing they ask is: "Is it a boy or a girl?" And the third thing is: "Are his (her) eyes all right?" As Klaus and Kennell (1976, 1982) demonstrated in the interactional patterns of parents and premature and sick babies, the attempt to engage them in eye-to-eye contact becomes an early and critical way for parents to establish that "this baby is really mine." When a newborn looks up at his parents, fixes on their faces, and brightens, this opens up one of the most important systems of communication between them. When I point out this behavior to mothers, they always say, "I thought he could see!" and they take my sanction as permission to believe in it. Why can't they believe in it themselves without sanction? My own guess is that it must be such an important mode of communication for them that they almost dare not believe in it without permission from outside.

I experienced an interesting example of this. I was demonstrating for a film crew some of these responses and their significance to a mother in preparation for a national television show. As I wheeled a three-day-old baby named Laura down the hall, her mother told me about how she had seen her watching the light reflection on the side of her crib and how excited by it the baby had become. When we started playing with Laura, she watched my face to follow it, and she began to be more and more excited by it. As her mother saw this, she said, "I didn't *know* she could really see!" I replied, "But you just told me she could see." "But I mean that she can see *important* things." "What important things?" I asked. With this, the mother blushed and said softly, "Like *my* face." To me this represented the deep importance to the mother of this ability in the baby and her need to hide it, even from herself. As we played the game of letting Laura choose between our voices, Laura turned quickly and repeatedly to her mother's voice in preference to mine. Each time her mother's arms came out automatically as if she wanted to take her. As I turned her over to her mother, she looked down tenderly at Laura and said, "You know *my* voice, don't you?"

I played one last game with this excitingly alert baby. As I got her wide-awake by rocking her in a semiupright position, I began to stick out my tongue at her. Her eyes widened, and she gradually opened her mouth, to stick out her own tongue. I was so surprised by what appeared to be her imitation of me that I shook her gently, got her alert again, then repeated my gesture, twice this time. Laura's face softened, her mouth opened, and she stuck out her own tongue twice—in what appeared to be direct imitation of my behavior. At this her mother gasped and said, "She knows more than I realized!" I asked her what it means to her to have seen this behavior in her baby. She responded quickly, "I'll treat her like a *her* rather than an *it*." This mother's honest response is typical of many mothers—sophisticated as well as naïve ones—who seem to be surprised and delighted when they are shown their newborns' responsive capacities. Most of them say, "I didn't know they could do that." They probably did, but they didn't trust themselves to believe in these responses. After seeing it with me, they could utilize them as confirmation of the presence of strength and personality in their babies. Many of them say that they will behave entirely differently with them after they have been freed to be aware of these responses. They say, "You've just shown me what I *need* to know to mother my baby." This is hard for me to believe, for I think parents must already know that this behavior is there—but they need to know that they can trust their observations.

Hearing. The complex behavioral responses to auditory signals that a newborn baby demonstrates are as exciting as his visual responses are. For the newborn not only hears but has a complex set of behavioral reactions to confirm this fact. Young physicians in medical schools are still being taught that babies don't see or hear until they are several weeks of age, "until their ear canals have cleared of debris from the amniotic sac." I have wondered why this myth still prevails. I can only assume that it has been easier for physicians to think of newborns as insensitive if they must hurt them when they are ill or if they must study them in order to gain the marvelous advances we have made in neonatal medicine. Perhaps also, hearing tests have been performed in noisy neonatal nurseries, and many of the neonates are in a habituated state, protecting themselves from the noise around them.

The newborn has the same capacity to shut down on and adapt to repeated noise as he does to visual stimuli. He will startle with the first few stimuli, but he will quickly quiet down, and his heart rate and respirations will adapt as they do with repeated visual stimulation. He can and does manage in a noisy environment.

Even with a deeply sleeping baby, one may see a slight stir to a quiet voice near his ear. His breathing pattern will change, his eyes will open slightly, and he may even produce a slight smile in response. If the soft-spoken voice continues, he will gradually begin to stir and to awaken. Except when he is in a deep or exhausted sleep period after a feeding or play period, or after a trauma, one can rely on his awakening. As he awakens, he begins to look around interestedly as if he were searching for the source of the sound. When he finds it, he will stop and look at it, and his face will register his interest.

As we saw in Chapter 1, if you hold a baby up in the air facing

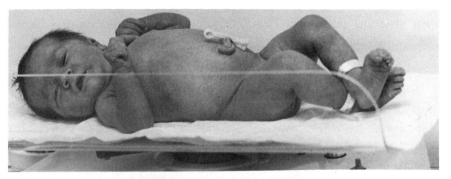

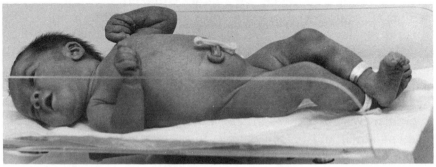

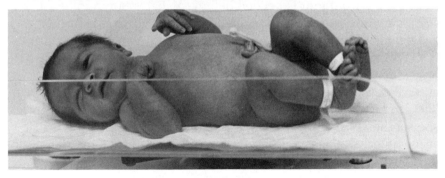

the ceiling, his head resting on one of your palms, his buttocks resting on the other, and speak softly but insistently to him, he will startle slightly. Then he will quiet down, begin to look more and more alert, and turn his head in the direction of your voice. When his head is fully turned, he will begin to search for the source. As he catches your face and moving lips with his eyes, his whole face will brighten as if to say, "There you are." Now, if you give him a choice between a male voice and a female voice of equal intensity—one standing on each side of him—he will turn to the female voice. This preference for the high-pitched voice is clear, and he will repeat this behavior over and over again. Undoubtedly this reflects prenatal experience with his mother's voice. This preference for certain auditory bands was confirmed by the work of Rita Eisenberg (1964).

Smell. The newborn has a refined sense of smell at birth. For example, he acts as if he were offended by acetic acid, asafetida, or even alcohol. He screws up his face and turns away abruptly. On the other hand, he will rapidly turn toward a milk or sugar solution if it is offered to him. A mother who is breast feeding will find that the baby will refuse a bottle after a few weeks, turning to the smell of her breast in strong preference. Yet a father can feed the same baby the formula. I would recommend introducing a bottle of formula every two or three days so that a breast-fed baby will not get too "stuck."

MacFarlane has shown (1975) that seven-day-old infants will turn reliably to their own mother's breast pads if they are offered a matched pad from another mother who is at the same stage of nursing. A two-day-old baby has not yet learned the smells and will choose at random which pad to turn to. But by seven days he knows his mother's smell and responds to it. In other words, the capacity for such a discrimination is probably available at birth, but information from the environment is needed before the baby can manifest it. It is surprising how quickly this happens and how obvious is his behavior as he makes the choice.

The sensitivity of the infant to being handled is apparent. He quiets down from one kind of touch, and he gets stimulated by another. From the first a mother is sensitive to this. She gears her handling to be appropriate to his state of consciousness. If he is upset, she soothes him with a slow, gentle, patting rhythm. If he is asleep or too quiet, she uses a different touch to alert him, more of a rapid, intrusive stimulus. Fathers are more likely to tap or poke a baby as if they saw their goal as that of energizing him to play. Fathers and mothers are significantly different in this respect from the outset (Dixon 1980). These different approaches give the baby a chance to learn about the important people around him.

THE IMPORTANCE OF SENSORY AND SOCIAL STIMULI FOR THE NEW BABY

This richness of the baby's repertoire offers his parents many different ways to know him. If they are unable to reach him with one set of stimuli, there are many others. Each baby has individualized sensitivities. Each baby responds differently to various stimuli. Parents have a whole spectrum of opportunities for communicating with their baby. When they discover the appropriate ones, the baby will learn from a few experiences and will develop expectations surprisingly quickly. His preferred stimuli seem to trigger already mapped-out responses. As these responses are completed the baby's inner satisfaction fuels him to repeat them. Each time he stores up a memory of the experience. This feedback after each cycle, in turn, sets up clearer and clearer expectations. Each time these are fulfilled, the baby feels a sense of gratification.

The baby starts learning about himself and his world in the uterus and gathers speed rapidly after birth. The first job of parents in the newborn period is to discover their baby's particular sensitivities. They must also learn to calm and contain him so that he can find out about his own control systems. With their help he can learn how to move from one state to another, allowing time to take in information, how to maintain a balance between shutting out disturbing stimuli and paying attention to attractive ones, and how to focus and maintain his attention on important messages from his environment. All of this is as critical to his development as is proper feeding and other physical care.

There is now available a body of research that gives graphic confirmation of these responses in a newborn baby by registering the heart rate as the baby responds. When the newborn baby is interested in a new stimulus, he is likely to quiet down, and his heart rate decelerates. When it is an unpleasant or a nonsignificant stimulus to him, his heart rate will accelerate, and he may or may not startle. This research has been used with sick or premature babies to determine how intact their brains are even when they may be too weak to move. It also shows us the cost to the baby of a negative or intrusive stimulus and the calming, reorganizing effect of a positive or appropriate stimulus. Gerald Lucey's research with prematures who are attached to oxygen monitors placed on the skin of their chests bears this out. When a negative stimulus is presented to them, their circulating oxygen levels drop by half. With a positive stimulus the circulating oxygen level goes up significantly. This indicates that even immature cardiovascular systems respond to positive as well as negative stimuli.

Drs. Sprunger and Gorski in my unit at Children's Hospital used this new understanding with dramatic results. They worked with premature babies who had chronic respiratory distress, had not improved for several weeks, and were not gaining weight despite adequate gavage feedings. Their oxygen demands were stationary, and all were on respirators and in incubators. All weighed less than four pounds and were no more than thirty-four weeks of gestational age.

For two of these babies the researchers varied the intensity of the relentless overhead lights that are present in all high-risk nurseries and are said to be necessary for the nurses to monitor each baby's condition. At night they placed gowns over these babies' incubators to darken them. As soon as they did so, the babies' eyes came open, and they began to look around with interest. After a week of this cycling of light and dark, the babies began improving: their weights went up, and their oxygen requirements decreased. So dramatic was this that the nurses began to cover the cribs of all the babies who were not so ill that they needed to be visible. Even an adult would have trouble in an environment with constant light. There is evidence that indicates that proper pituitary function of the brain is dependent on daily cycles of light and darkness.

In another experiment, premature babies had a string tied to one foot and attached to a mobile that hung over them in their incubators. As they moved the foot, the mobile moved. The infants watched it with tremendous interest and quickly seemed to realize that *they* were moving the mobiles. Even such a tiny baby seems to realize when he is having an effect on his environment, and this realization has a positive effect on his growth and development.

I had a similar and heartwarming experience with a less than two-pound premature infant in the high-risk nursery. The baby had severe respiratory distress and had made no progress in opening up his lungs or in gaining weight for the six weeks before I was summoned to test him. His nurses and doctors were discouraged and wondered whether he had suffered severe brain damage. I was asked to test his brain and response. I examined him and began to play little games with him. As I took him out of the incubator to examine him, he was being breathed for by an automatic respirator. It turned out that this was his first experience out of the incubator. As I held this tiny, fragile, wizened thing up to speak softly to him, he stopped his automatic breathing and turned his face toward my voice. He repeated this three times. By then all of the watching nursery personnel were shifting uneasily. I asked his nurse to come to his other side and to compete with me. We both began to talk to him. He stopped the respirator again, wrinkled up his tiny face as if he were thinking, seemed to make the choice, and turned in her direction. By the time he turned to her a second time, she said, "Here, give me that baby!" and looking down into his face, she said softly, "You're gonna be okay, aren't you?" From that time on she began to take him out of his incubator to gavage-feed him, to nestle him, and to talk to him. He soon began to gain weight and had weaned himself from the respirator within ten days. He was out of his incubator within three weeks. He was home within six weeks of that performance, and at fourteen months he came to see me, already walking, smiling, and beginning to talk. He had a minor form of cerebral palsy as demonstrated by a wide-based gait, but he was an intact person otherwise. He had changed the course of his own life by responding so irresistibly to his nurse.

6

Going Home Together

TURMOIL AND ADJUSTMENT

No matter how much parents care about a new baby, no matter how much experience they have had with parenting, no matter how easy the delivery and hospital stay have been, no matter how easy the baby has been to care for in the hospital, going home with that new baby is a major hurdle. The first three weeks at home are likely to be a grueling period under the best of circumstances. Not that there aren't constant rewards in caring for a new baby and watching the many new achievements that he will reach over a short time. But most parents will feel uniquely overwhelmed and out of touch with the rest of the world during much of this time. Learning how to become a new, reorganized family is a major step, and it demands a great deal from everyone. This step comes at a time when the new mother is still depleted and recovering from labor, delivery, and the reorganization of her entire physical system.

The difficulty of adjustment is heightened now that many insurance companies are pressing for twenty-four-hour discharge. A new mother gets no time for recovery and reorganization before she is pushed out. If she wants to stay longer, she is treated like a weakling.

Postpartum blues is the psychological adjustment that accompanies this physical reorganization. The more a mother cares about being a good parent to the baby, the more psychologically demanding this period is likely to be. The new father will have made it through the lying-in period on nerve, alternating between exhilaration and feeling overwhelmed by his new responsibility. Along with the turmoil of these feelings, he is likely to feel shut out by his wife's readjustment and by his still-remote relationship to the new baby. If grandparents come in to help, their vigor and enthusiasm often add too much in the way of stimulation and goodwill—at a time when the parents need a low-keyed environment. The baby is usually just beginning to wake up and gather steam. His sensory world is enlarging rapidly, often overwhelming him. Going home disrupts his rhythms and any balance he may have achieved after delivery. After the initial depression and period of withdrawal that most babies go through on the second and third day, he is likely to come to a wide-awake and highly interactive state. This means there will be a disorganized, somewhat unpredictable baby for the first days at home.

Is there a purpose to all this stress? Why don't more families disintegrate in the face of such crises? I like to believe that such a period of disorganization leads to a new organization at a higher level, developed out of the wide-open systems of the three participants, all in touch with one another, driven by their caring to develop a new set of workable relationships. Fortunately there is a kind of numbness that accompanies this period, largely dominated by physical fatigue. A sort of amnesia makes it all seem worthwhile in retrospect. Meanwhile, parents and baby are learning about one another and learning about coping and working toward the pleasures of making it with one another as a new family. But don't underestimate the turmoil that is liable to occur.

AN IMPORTANT BABY

The Johnsons had waited nearly five years for their baby. Indeed, it seemed longer, for they had known each other for two years before they were married, each hoping for a large family. Cora Johnson had come from a large black family in the South and missed the crazy, shared confusion. In the northern city she missed the massive support system of brothers, sisters, and parents who told their children what to do at every turn, even though they never did it. The shared criticisms, the teasing that met every move amounted to a kind of protective nest within which one could swing wide. Mr. Johnson had grown up in inner-city Detroit and had been an only child. His father had been active in civil rights at a time when this was dangerous for the family as well as for him. As a black child in an activist, thoughtful, striving family he had felt isolated from many of his black peers by his intellectual background and his serious approach to life. He was a quiet, sensitive boy, and he longed for the closeness that came hard to him. When he met his future wife, a good-natured, easygoing, apparently self-assured young woman, he felt she opened up the world for him. He wanted a baby who would be like her and like the companion he'd longed for as an only child.

In their marriage they spent most of their time planning for children. But none came. By the end of the first year they were stunned, silently guilty, and each was beginning to wonder about his or her own adequacy to reproduce. By the end of the second year their relationship was strained by these feelings. They found they were reproaching each other, criticizing each other for absurd minutiae, and hiding the basic question down deep: "Why no baby?" Cora's demanding job as an office manager in a large legal firm helped take up the slack, for she dived into it with extra vigor, but that strained their relationship too.

In the third year their anxiety and their tension with each other drove them to seek medical advice. The horrors of sperm counts, of probing manipulations of sexual organs, of X rays, of keeping temperature charts, and of forced and timed intercourse made each of them feel unnatural. Old feelings of inadequacy were revived and were raw and on the surface all the time.

By the fourth year of their marriage it seemed apparent that they would not have the family they'd dreamed of, and the question was whether they could stay together. Those four trying years had proved that each cared deeply about the other, but every little disagreement loomed as a large one in the face of such raw feelings. They began to try to adopt a baby and had been promised one when they found out that Cora was pregnant. They were so surprised, so overwhelmed with a mixture of joy and disbelief that they could barely take it in. At first they dared not believe in it and wavered between keeping Cora quiet and letting her lead an active, normal life. Each day the miracle seemed more real. They were in real conflict about whether to pursue the adoption anyway. They were afraid to give up the promised baby for fear that they'd lose the pregnancy. Yet deep down they wanted to save all their resources for their own baby. At last, and with the assurance that there was another home for

the adoptive infant, they braved it and took a chance on Cora's
pregnancy.

It is always amazing to me how often this happens. Parents who
have been told they were infertile and for whom efforts at conceiving
have been unsuccessful do conceive when the pressure is off. Either
they give up and relax or the promise of an adoptive baby changes
some internal balance; whatever the reason is, a pregnancy follows.
Too often the pregnancy follows an actual adoption and saddles a previously childless family with two babies. The strain sets up conflicts
so that they cannot quite devote themselves to either baby.

In the Johnsons' case the emotions and the feeling of responsibility that led up to the decision to adopt a baby made it very hard to
give up that baby, even when they were expecting their own. Parents
become committed emotionally to the prospective adoptive baby in
very much the same way that one does to the developing fetus. To
give him or her up is a wrenching decision.

It is hard to raise two babies at once, and the Johnsons did well
to decide to save all their resources for their own baby. A first baby is
an overwhelming experience, and one needs to be as conflict-free as
possible. There are inevitable moments—the parents of twins could
vouch for this—when two babies can press your resources to the
breaking point. With twins the economy of lumping them together
into a single unit makes it just possible to survive. With an adoptive
and a natural baby of slightly different ages, this would be less possible.

*The pregnancy went surprisingly well. Every bit of advice was
followed to the letter. Mrs. Johnson consulted her doctors, her
mother, books on pregnancy. She stopped smoking; she gave up
wine and beer; she refused aspirin for headaches. She was determined to give this baby the best possible chance. Mr. Johnson
participated with her in all this, and they felt cemented as a
family in a way that reminded them of their courting days.*

The stresses of infertility on each partner and on the marriage
and the investigations designed to get at the source of the couple's
inability to reproduce are certainly demoralizing and dehumanizing.
Such an experience can undermine anyone's self-image. Many mar-
riages disintegrate, but the ones that survive such a stressful period
may well be strengthened.

As the end of pregnancy and delivery loomed, the Johnsons became frankly anxious. The anticipation was combined with anxiety, and each withdrew from the other's tension in self-protection. Finally Mrs. Johnson asked her mother to come up—as a strong support for each of them. Mrs. Moore was an experienced grandmother as well as mother by now. She kept her peace, said very little, but offered each of them a kind of silent strength, which they needed.

The delivery progressed well, and Mrs. Johnson delivered a perfect eight-pound baby girl almost on her due date. The ease with which her labor and delivery were carried off did not match the tension in her mind. She and Mr. Johnson worked through labor together, and he was present when she delivered the baby. They were ecstatic, as though they had reached the end of a long nightmare. All of the fears of imperfection, the anxiety about whether the baby would be damaged or not, melted away when they saw and held her and when the obstetrician looked her over to pronounce her perfect. He capped this by pronouncing her Apgar scores as nine, nine, and ten—"about as perfect as they can be."

The Apgar score is a measure of five responses taken in the delivery room at one, five, and fifteen minutes after delivery. It measures heart rate, skin color, adequacy in breathing, motor tone, and responsiveness, and the baby's reaction to a slightly painful stimulus on the sole of the foot or the earlobe. Two points are given for optimal responses in each of these five areas. Since most newborns are slightly blue or cyanotic for a brief period after delivery while the circulation changes over from a parasitic one dependent on the mother and the placenta to an independently functioning one, an initial score of one on skin color is most likely. Hence a nine immediately after birth is about as perfect as it can be.

The Apgar score has been used as a prediction of the baby's future well-being and is too often treated like an IQ score of the future, which it is not. It is simply a test of how he has responded to the immediate stress of delivery and to the initial readjustment to his new world. Its value in the delivery room is that it forces someone to pay close attention to the new baby as these attributes are measured.

Parents are often told the Apgar scores, particularly if they are good, as if they could relate to the baby through them. But they have limited predictive value and are merely an indication to parents that their baby is intact at delivery.

THE FIRST HURDLE

Mr. and Mrs. Johnson learned a great deal about the baby, whom they named Anna, over the next three days in the hospital. She was such an easy baby to adjust to. She seemed to do nothing but eat and sleep. The nurses all said, "She's perfect." And indeed, she seemed to be. Mrs. Johnson's breasts became painfully engorged, and she seemed to have plenty of milk by the third day, when they were discharged. Anna sucked well and seemed wide-awake and eager each time she came in to feed. Everyone was ready for discharge, and the Johnsons could barely wait to get together again. So confident were they that they could handle her by themselves that they sent Mrs. Moore home. She had seen them through the crisis, and now they wanted to do the rest by themselves.

The first afternoon and evening were a breeze. Mrs. Johnson's family doctor had told her that she should warn away well-meaning visitors, and she stuck to this. Several friends and relatives telephoned to congratulate them. Each ring of the telephone made all three of them startle. Anna whimpered a bit after each of these interruptions, but she fell quickly back to sleep.

I cannot stress enough the importance for a family of guarding its privacy through this critical period. Every well-meaning intruder amounts to a disruption, a set of new stimuli to adjust to, and the drain on overtaxed systems is out of proportion to the value of a social visit. As a result, I always urge new parents to restrict their visitors to one or two of the closest family members or friends—and then only ones who will pitch in to help. In this way parents can protect their energies for the big job ahead.

The first several hours were surprisingly easy. Mrs. Johnson felt confident about handling Anna, and she felt well enough to cook dinner for them all. Anna woke for feedings every three hours until about 2:00 A.M. Then she began to be more fretful and woke every two hours. She would nurse on only one breast, gulping down Mrs. Johnson's overloaded milk supply. By the 6:00 A.M. feeding Mrs. Johnson was so engorged with milk that it fairly spurted as Anna began to suck. Anna gulped and choked. Mrs. Johnson panicked and turned her almost upside down as she tried to get the spit-up milk out of her nose and mouth. As she clapped her on the back, Anna disgorged the entire feeding, milk covering her mother's lap and running down her legs. Anna began to gasp, cry, and choke again. Mrs. Johnson nearly dropped her, she was so upset. Mr. Johnson came to their aid, picking Anna up out of her mother's lap to soothe her. Anna lay back exhausted. Mrs. Johnson began to weep. "I thought I'd lost her!" she cried. Mr. Johnson remained calm and helped her pull herself together. He told his wife to go back to bed, promising not to put Anna down for fear of her choking if she spit up again. Mrs. Johnson was sure that her milk had turned "bad" and had caused this upset.

So close to the surface is the natural turmoil around a new baby that any untoward event will set it off. It is amazing that any new family gets through these times.

Anna was restless in her father's arms. As he tried to keep her quiet so that her mother could rest, she began to be more and more fretful. Soon she was screaming with loud, piercing wails, and nothing he could do would calm her. Neither parent had heard her cry like this before, and they wondered frantically what was wrong. She sounded as if she were in acute pain. Mrs. Johnson no longer trusted herself and phoned her doctor for advice. When he heard the story, he tried to be comforting, but he saw the upset as pretty trivial. He told her that she was "too upset" about one vomiting episode and that a baby could not choke very easily, so they should calm down.

It is true that a new baby is set up with marvelous protective systems that will not let him really choke. If he weren't, he wouldn't be able to handle the initial mucus with which a newborn must cope. What the doctor didn't do for them, which might have defused some of their turmoil, was to explain why Anna had spit up. In all likelihood it was mechanical. When a mother's breasts are very engorged, they are likely to let down a lot at once, to overload the baby all of a sudden in the initial rush of stored-up milk. As they do so, they often make the baby choke for a moment, and even if he can gulp his way through the first letdown, a large amount of milk goes down in a hurry. With each gulp the baby swallows a gulp of air. This gulping contributes to a large bubble, which stays under the milk, ready to bring it up. What goes down like an elevator will probably come up like one. There are several things Mrs. Johnson could have done to help. She could have fed the baby more slowly and carefully at the beginning of a feeding. She could also have hand-expressed the initial rush of milk so that her breasts would let down more evenly. After a noisy feeding I always recommend that a baby be propped at a thirty-degree angle for a period before being bubbled. In this situation gravity helps hold down the milk and bring up the gas bubble without all the milk along with it. The baby may still spit up, but it won't be the whole feeding. A large percentage of babies spit up after nearly every feeding, and they can go on gaining weight and progressing well in spite of it. The Johnsons' doctor was right about the fact that babies are not bothered by their spitting up. But parents are.

Mrs. Johnson felt shaken up for the rest of the day. She felt tense in a way that she hadn't in the hospital, and she hated herself for being so upset. She wanted to call her mother to come back. She wanted to go back to the hospital—anything to be able to unload the responsibility for Anna for a while. Yet she couldn't quite trust her husband to take over. She kept feeling that he wouldn't know what to do if something happened. The ominous feeling of something about to happen kept cropping up.

This is a normal part of the postpartum depression and readjustment. The feeling is irrational, yet it cannot just be dismissed. Time and experience will make it pass. Meanwhile, the fact that the new mother doesn't dare trust herself renders her unable to trust her spouse. Her feelings of competition for the baby begin to show in this kind of feeling about him.

In spite of his wife's open mistrust, Mr. Johnson was able to manage with Anna. He changed her diapers, talked to her, and kept her calmly alert for a while after each subsequent feeding. And when she fussed, he put her in her crib. Mrs. Johnson couldn't leave her there. She rushed in to her at each whimper, turning her over to see if she was all right, picking her up to the breast.
After another feeding in which Anna choked at first but managed to keep the milk going down, Mrs. Johnson began to realize that the mechanics of so much milk were what was confusing the baby. But she didn't know what to do about it. She

certainly thought of giving up on her breast feeding, but she'd waited so long to be able to breast-feed this baby, and she still wanted that very much. Mr. Johnson wouldn't hear of her quitting, and he called her mother. Mrs. Moore listened quietly to the description of the two rather frantic feedings, recognized the mechanical problem, and urged her daughter to feed the baby in a lying-down position. This seemed absurd to Mrs. Johnson, who was sure that Anna would choke if she were lying down. But it worked, and the next feeding went much more smoothly.

I have no idea why a reclining mother and baby have an easier time, but they often do. One would anticipate that without gravity helping, it would make it more difficult for the baby to swallow a large amount of milk, but it doesn't seem to do that. Perhaps the mother is more relaxed lying down. Then she won't handle the baby in a tense way, and the baby is freed to concentrate on his job of swallowing.

Mrs. Moore also suggested propping the baby up after feedings and leaving her alone for a bit, but neither parent could do that. They were so eager to hold her, to handle her, and she was wide-awake after feedings, so they continued to play with her. She spit up about half of the feeding after she'd gotten particularly excited by her father's tickling her. He felt so guilty that he swore never again to disturb her.

That would be too bad, for her father seemed easy with her, and that was an asset for all three of them. A certain amount of spitting up is worth the pleasure and warmth of a play period after a feeding. Any father needs encouragement to keep coming back to the baby. His inexperience and his own unresolved anxiety are likely to deter him from getting close to the baby at first.

Nothing in this generation has been as good news as the trend toward fathers' participating more equally in nurturing the family. At a time when there are so few supports for the new mother, a father's role can be absolutely critical. Not only can he back up the mother, but he also adds an often keen set of observations about baby care at such a time. Margaret Mead once told me that the one thing that might save the nuclear family in our society would be more equal participation of fathers in the care of their new infants.

MIXED EMOTIONS

Over the next few days Anna became more and more difficult. Feedings were unpredictable. Mrs. Johnson was afraid that they'd come up and handled her gingerly, but she felt like a failure every time Anna spit any breast milk out. She kept wondering whether her milk was agreeing with the baby. She restricted her diet and continued to worry and fuss over Anna. In the process Anna became more and more restless. She had crying periods now for no discernible reason. She quieted down when she was held, but when she was put down, she started to fuss again. Mr. Johnson handled her more easily and thought of getting her a cradle. Rocking her became the best way of getting her to sleep. There was a sure art in figuring out just the right pace and rhythm, not so slow as to alert her or so fast as to overwhelm her. Mr. Johnson could always figure it out, to Mrs. Johnson's consternation, for her rocking technique was not as effective. She started rocking one way but gave up too quickly when it didn't work. Her indecision came through in her rocking as it did in her behavior the rest of the day. She felt herself going to pieces and began to resent her husband's success with Anna. She even found herself resenting Anna when the baby was particularly unreachable. What made it harder was that Anna was so perfect and adorable when she was at peace. Sometimes Mrs. Johnson even found herself longing to be back in the old childless days. This frightened her.

It needn't have, for all mothers (and fathers) feel this kind of ambivalence when things are not going right. Of course, this mother has mixed feelings about her new baby. Mothers fear that their negative feelings will harm the baby. In other cultures women talk of having the evil eye at such times and of damaging the baby with their evil thoughts. It is a universal fear, and the resentment underlying it springs from the need for self-protection. Mothers find it a great disappointment not to sail right through this initial adjustment. They tend to blame everyone and everything around and inevitably will blame the unreachable baby.

But there are feelings to balance this. If these helplessly angry, negative feelings persisted, there would be extensive child abuse and desertion at such a time. For most mothers, who have been nurtured themselves and have support from those around them, instincts for nurturing the helpless baby take over. And the responses of most babies reinforce these instincts. After a crying period, the gentle relaxation of the baby becomes a great relief and pleasure. After a successful feeding, when the baby is alert, every response becomes a reward for having made it through the fretful, unresponsive times.

MOTHERS AND FATHERS: DIFFERENT RHYTHMS

After feedings, sitting in her reclining chair, waiting for the bubble to come up, Anna began to develop periods when she would be alert and responsive. As her mother leaned over to talk to her, Anna's eyes would widen and her face would soften. As her mother talked quietly to her, her pupils would widen, then contract, alternating in a slow, regular rhythm, taking in and responding to her mother's face, voice, and gentle touch. Her hands and feet would move slowly out toward her mother, then curl up in a slow grasp to return into her body. All of her movements were in rhythm with her mother's soft-spoken voice (see Condon, 1974). If her father came into sight, speaking in more clipped tones and reaching out to poke or jiggle her, she sat more upright. Her shoulders took on a hunched look, her eyes widened in anticipation, and her face became still as she watched him for more. His inclination was to stimulate her to a more excited response, and he seemed always to get it. Her movements were jerkier; she spent more time with him both in a stilled posture and in jerky, excited movements toward him. Even her breathing was quicker and more jagged with him than with her mother.

In our lab at Children's Hospital in Boston, we (Dr. Heidelise Als, Dr. Ed Tronick, Dr. Barry Lester, and I) studied these patterns of interaction between small babies and their parents by means of videotaped play periods using a split screen. Also at Children's Hospital, Drs. Suzanne Dixon and Michael Yogman demonstrated that clear differences show up as early as four to six weeks in the baby's responses to his mother versus those to his father. For instance, with the mother in sight the baby is likely to set the pace of their interaction. His face will brighten; his hands and legs "reach" out toward her gently, curling back in rhythmic, smooth fashion. If we watch his face and eyes, we see that they brighten with an intensely interested look as his mother attempts to engage him, alternating with a dulled look as he withdraws into himself. Often he lowers his lids or averts his gaze in order to recover from the intense looks he gives her. Since these cycles of intense looks alternating with withdrawal are going on at the rate of four per minute, we can really see them only in slow-motion film. What we see by gross observation is a quiet but alert, soft-looking baby relaxedly slumped in a chair.

The mother, too, looks gentle and smooth as she softly plays vocal or facial games with her baby. These are rhythmic, too, and are directly tied to the baby's rhythmic behaviors, following his alertness and withdrawal. As the infant becomes alert, the mother may vocalize softly or give a bright look or even a gentle gesture. As the infant's eyes grow dull or start to close, the mother automatically subsides or slows down. On slowed-down film one sees that she is playing the infant's game, turning in and out, with her advances and withdrawal timed exquisitely to his. She looks at him all the time, offering a kind of containment lest he fly apart, with her hands on his legs or buttocks, or holding him with her gaze or with soft, continuous vocalizations. On top of this background of touch or sight or sound, she adds the play signals: touching/withdrawing; smiling/subsiding; vocalizing/quieting; patting/stopping; head leaning forward/head leaning back. Each of the baby's attentive periods may receive a different signal, which subsides as he does, allowing him to maintain his basic rhythm—of attention and recovery—which dominates his behavior and stems from the need for homeostatic control over his immature physiological systems. As I said earlier, it is costly for a baby to get too involved or excited in response to the world around him. He will shut out quickly if he is overexcited. If he is to pay prolonged attention, as his mother wants him to, she must adapt her responses and her cues to his low-keyed rhythms. Then she can maintain his attention and slowly but surely enlarge upon the wealth of cues she can offer him. My colleagues and I see this as the basis for the baby's earliest ability to communicate socially (Brazelton and Yogman, 1986). As the mother and baby respond to each other's rhythms, they are saying to each other that they are really in touch, locked into each other at several levels. We see this as the beginning of his emotional development and an opportunity to begin to learn about the world around him. And as he learns the inner controls needed to maintain longer and longer periods of attention, he learns about himself. His mother can provide him with the basis for this kind of learning by locking into his rhythms and, via her synchrony, can help him stay in a state of alert interaction.

I once saw an impressive example of this "containment" while following a baby with a cleft palate and harelip. So severe was the defect that it gave him a distorted, frowning facial expression. Whenever he got excited and breathed rapidly, he choked on excessive secretions in his throat, which he could not swallow because of his defective palate. As a result, if he became interested in a stimulus, he began to breathe more rapidly and secrete more saliva, and he ended up choking. Hence any period of attention was inevitably cut short. When his mother brought him in at four weeks of age, we noticed that she was making distorted faces at him. Her grimaces matched his, and we worried that her concerns about him were leading her to such unattractive expressions. Then we noticed that she imitated his jerky, noisy breathing as well, and we felt she was surely in the midst of a grief reaction. But gradually we began to realize what she was doing. By directly imitating his grimaces and his breathing, she could capture his interest, lock into his rhythms, help him control his overreactions as he got excited, and keep him in a state of alertness. By containing him in this way, she could teach him to smile, to vocalize, to become excited, and to subside without "going overboard" in his reactions and choking.

As I mentioned before, a father is likely to set up a different pattern with his baby. In our studies we have seen that fathers are much more likely, as was Mr. Johnson, to excite the baby by heightening the rhythm of their playful interaction. A father is more likely to use rhythmic games of tickling or tapping on parts of the baby's body, often tapping right up the body to the face, in order to produce a heightened response from the baby. Exaggerated gestures or expressions seem to say, "Now let's play." At first the baby will watch

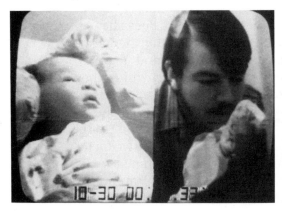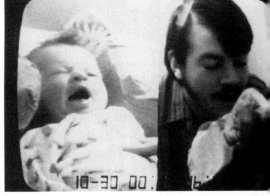

the father's antics as if he were trying to adjust to them and to take them in. His shoulders will hunch, and his eyebrows will become raised in eager anticipation. As he gets older, he will laugh out loud, bouncing up and down in his eagerness to continue this kind of playful interaction with his father.

The baby's awareness of the differences between his parents becomes steadily clearer. By three weeks of age this becomes so pronounced that we can block out the screen to watch only a toe, a finger, a hand, or a foot and predict successfully whether the baby is in an interaction with his mother or his father. The heightened, jerky responsiveness reserved for his father invades his whole body. We have films that show this. At three weeks, if a baby is propped in an infant chair and hears his mother's voice behind him, he will begin to mouth, his face will soften, and his legs and arms will begin to move in a slow, smooth, predictable fashion. If his father's voice is substituted, his shoulders will hunch, his face will elongate, and his eyebrows will shoot up; his movements will first stop in anticipation, and when they do start again, they will be jerky. These patterns are predictable and are repeated for each appearance of the parent. These distinct patterns indicate the importance for each member of the family of having a predictable set of signals that say to each other member, "I know who you are! You are important to me!" The fact that these patterns are set so early is testimony to their adaptative value. They lock each of the parents to the baby in a special way.

Mr. Johnson was already able to elicit a bright-eyed look from Anna, which said to him, "Let's play." Her mother looked on jealously, for the look Anna gave her always seemed to be more se-

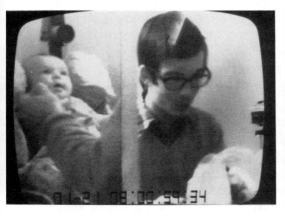 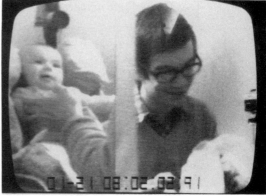

rious and to mean business. She mouthed at her with glazed eyes, rooting toward her breast when she was held. Mrs. Johnson felt a bit like a milk machine at such a time. She could never get a bright look from her until after she'd fed her. This seemed mercenary somehow, and she felt used.

SLEEPING AND WAKING: HELPING THE BABY FIND A PATTERN

After a few turbulent days the feedings began to settle down gradually. Mrs. Johnson found that she was feeding Anna as often as every two or three hours, but at least the feedings were mostly staying down. When she finally followed her mother's advice about propping her after feedings, that did the trick. At one point Mrs. Moore had ventured a bit of wisdom about the turbulence: "You can't always find out what a baby is fussing about. If feeding her, carrying her around, and changing her won't work, maybe she's got to settle it for herself." Mrs. Johnson couldn't take this in at the time and continued to rush to Anna every time she whimpered, every time she moved in bed. She continued to carry her around, to the point of exhaustion for both of them. Then, when she finally dared to put her down, Anna would rouse and start to fuss again. One day, reinforced by her mother's advice, Mrs. Johnson dared let her cry for a few minutes. To her surprise Anna fussed around, squirmed as if to find a comfortable place in her crib, and settled down to sleep. After only a few minutes of fussing, the baby seemed almost relieved to be left to work it out. The Johnsons took this in and began to leave her more often to work out her own means of getting to sleep.

As I discussed in an earlier chapter (Chapter 4), a baby needs to be pushed toward organizing his own cycles of waking and sleeping. He seems to do better if he is gently pushed by his environment. Research on sleep using electroencephalographic techniques (Parmelee, 1967) has shown that the more immature the central nervous system, the less clear the sleep states. More time is spent in indeterminate states—neither deep nor light. The cycling of states—from awake to light to deep sleep—is not well defined either. As the central nervous system matures, the cycling and the definition of these states become clearer—both by behavioral observation and by EEG. In a well-organized, responsive environment the states become defined, and the predictable cycling proceeds more rapidly than it will in a disorganized or insensitive environment. This is a clear indication to me of the role of the environment in pressing a baby to master his own states. Ideally, appropriate reinforcement from the environment to prolong his alert states should be coupled with appropriate reinforcement to prolong his sleep states, to "learn to sleep." In my practice I can see how the constant interference of an anxious parent can add disorganization. The baby will be encouraged to come to an awake state with every REM (rapid eye movement) cycle. REM can be a transitional state and should be interspersed in deep sleep in a regular way. Sleep at night follows a pattern of periods of deep sleep (between thirty and fifty minutes) with periods of light, or REM, sleep around it. These hour-long cycles are then set in a three- to four-hour matrix, at the end of which there is a period of even lighter sleep and alertness. In other words, in order to maintain a long cycle of sleep, the baby must learn to manage the bursts of REM that are interspersed at regular intervals in deeper sleep. He must find techniques to keep himself quiet and to get himself back down into deeper sleep. One of our children would rouse regularly, talk to her beloved doll, relate the day's events, put her fingers in her mouth, and subside into deep sleep again. At such a time she was not really awake. If I went to her, she had to be roused to get any cogent response from her. If a parent inserts himself into each of these REM cycles, he can easily become the mechanism through which the child learns to subside. If he doesn't, the infant or child will find his own ways of settling and quieting.

As long as Mrs. Johnson was rushing to Anna, she was interfering with these cycles. I am convinced that there are many babies who cannot subside easily and quietly from alertness to sleep but must fuss and cry first. Once Mrs. Johnson recognized this, she was able to let Anna establish her own pattern.

Anna began to be clearer about her sleeping and her waking periods. She slept better than she had and soon began to sleep for three- to four-hour periods, especially at night. In the daytime she began to be up for thirty-minute stretches. By the time Anna was three weeks old, they were beginning to feel surer of each other, and the Johnsons could plan a day and night around her. Mr. Johnson felt he could go back to work. Mrs. Johnson felt a sense of relief and of renewed competence.

John Benjamin (1959) first alerted me to the age of three weeks as being a period of renewed organization—or disorganization if things are going badly. It's certainly true in my experience that a family becomes aware of reaching a new plateau of organization in the period between two and four weeks. There are factors at work— the mother's recovery from the physiological changes after delivery, the baby's maturation and recovery from the effects of delivery, the father's and mother's feeling of having learned from their experiences—and all of these things may be helping them reach a period of consolidation. Recent research is beginning to indicate that the baby may have achieved a new stage of central nervous system organization by this time. His more predictable cycle of sleeping and waking and the clearer signals he is able to give his environment would reinforce this. The relief and positive feedback from having been through such a period fuel the family toward the next steps in their development with each other.

NEW WAYS OF COMMUNICATING

New developments in Anna's behavior began to appear rapidly. By four weeks of age she began to have a brief, transient smile in the midst of each play session. Her parents were so overjoyed with it that they responded too eagerly and overwhelmed Anna. The first time she smiled, they laughed out loud. She startled and began to cry. After that they tried to react more gently, and soon they found that they could get her to prolong her smiles. When she began to build up to a vocalization, they worked hard to encourage her, tickling her, talking to her, jazzing her up by every technique they could think of. Finally they found that a low-keyed, rhythmic approach had the best results. If she were in an alert state, they would start to build up in a slow, rhythmic way, talking gently, then quieting down; smiling on and off; cooing, then becoming quiet; touching her gently, then withdrawing. In the quiet, silent intervals Anna would come out with a slow, tentative smile or an attempt to gurgle or coo. She worked so hard to produce these minimal responses that they could tell that she "knew" what she wanted to do. If they responded too enthusiastically, they shut her off. If they kept to her rhythm, adapting the quality of their responses to hers, they gradually began to prolong these "play" periods from a few to fifteen minutes or more.

This is an extension of the patterns of interaction that they began to learn with each other earlier. Now the baby's signals are clearer, and she has begun to master her goals of producing a smile and a vocalization. When the parents draw her into a reciprocal rhythm, this provides her with control over her motor and state systems, so that she can focus on these specific goals. As her parents lock into her rhythms, imitating her behaviors in her way and on her own level, they provide an external source of feedback that leads her on. This subtle rhythm between parent and infant can be manipulated at any moment by either one of them. If the baby changes it by a smile, the chances are that the mother will smile back, and thus she learns about the effect of smiling, on herself as well as on those around her. If the baby vocalizes, the mother is likely to vocalize back, and she will see her own rather fuzzy attempt made into an adult word. Imitation and identification with each other at several levels underlie this interaction. No one leads the other all the time; the controls are switched back and forth imperceptibly. And at any time either one can turn the other off. This ability to turn off is especially critical to the infant, whose immature systems can be overloaded so easily.

This communication between parent and baby makes possible learning about many kinds of behavior at the same time. For instance, in our studies, when we analyzed in detail what was going on when a mother smiled or spoke to her baby, we could see that she led up to it with at least four to six other gestures or actions. She stopped extraneous movements, looked directly at the baby, quieted her expression in anticipation, sat gently forward, reached out to touch the baby's leg, then smiled or spoke. The smile was thus embedded in a cluster of other signals. The baby might respond to one cluster with a sigh, another with a smile, another with a vocalization, but he also embedded his response in a set of other behaviors, such as a squirm or a cycling of arms and legs followed by a withdrawal of his head and arms. He seemed to need to do all this in order to achieve a smile or vocalization. In other words, many kinds of behavior went into each response from each partner. When the parent smiled or spoke to him, the baby had the opportunity to learn about a whole cluster of other behaviors. And since each parent behaves differently with a baby, his chances for learning are multiplied by two.

We have seen that there are at least four kinds of learning the baby and parent must master in order to communicate successfully. The first is learning control over motor discharge, over the imbalance in the autonomic and central nervous systems that attention and involvement in a response are likely to cause. In order to offer control, the parent must learn how this happens in the baby. The second is learning how to set up a rhythm of attention and withdrawal that will fit the needs of the particular infant. Again, parents must sensitively fit their own response rhythms into those of the baby. The third kind of learning involves the ability to embed important signals—words, expressions, gestures—into clusters of other appropriate behavior in order to set up meaningful communication with the partner. A fourth is learning how to imitate and enlarge upon the signals made by the other. Of course, the adult is more adept at this, but very soon the infant strives to match and even enlarge upon the adult's verbal and nonverbal signals.

In the second month Anna began to lead her parents in smiling and vocalizing. They were easily captured, and she began to show that she knew this. As they diapered her, she would begin to smile up at them or to vocalize softly. Diapering was forgotten as they got "caught." Her power over them was already becoming apparent.

We have seen that even diapering styles differ from mother to father. A mother will lay a baby down gently to be diapered, lift the buttocks up slowly, and as slowly lower them onto the clean diaper, gently sponging the area off before closing the diaper. Meanwhile, she will continue to hold on to part of the baby, the legs or buttocks, as she leans over to talk or croon to him. All of this has a gentle, slowed-down air about it. A father, on the other hand, uses a much different, less smooth, and less gentle approach. He will usually lift the baby's buttocks up by his straightened legs, holding him in the air by the feet while he slides the diaper under him. Then, with an almost imperceptible drop, he lets go, and the baby startles slightly as he drops a half inch or so onto the diaper. This wakes the baby even more, so the father leans over him to click and coo in a playful way. Often he will begin to excite him in the typical poking way described before, and they carry out a playful sequence before he finally closes the diaper. Each interaction—whether feeding or diapering—is set in just such a different context by the two parents.

We have observed these behavioral sequences with primary-caretaking fathers. We thought naïvely that maybe primary caretakers all would behave more or less alike, whether they were male or female—and that they would settle on the gentle, rhythmic control systems described for the mother earlier in the chapter. Not at all. If the fathers became more like mothers over time, we never saw it. At four months they are still more like fathers in their rhythms and in their playful approaches to all interactions. Perhaps they might have changed over time if it was up to them alone, but when they approached the baby to diaper him, the baby himself set the tone for their interaction, watching the father with wide eyes, lifted eyebrows, hunched shoulders, his whole body ready to start the expected playful interaction. No father can resist these nonverbal signals. How powerful they are and how early they set the tone of the interaction!

"COLIC"

When she was three weeks old, Anna forced her parents to learn about another aspect of her development. She began to fuss and cry hard every evening at about the same time. Usually this followed the evening feeding. She would stop if they picked her up; she would keep quiet if they carried her around or if they played with her actively. She quieted down if they turned up the television or if they drove her around in the car. But if they stopped any of this activity, she soon began to build up again to crying. As she cried, she looked at them reproachfully as if to say, "Do something!" Their efforts were becoming more and more frantic, and they felt more and more at her mercy. By six weeks she seemed determined to fuss and cry for about two hours every night. Meanwhile, she was gaining weight, feeding more and more effectively, her days were delightful, and after her crying episodes she slept peacefully. They knew she was all right in every other way, but they felt helpless to prevent this period of crying. Their doctor offered them a sedative for the baby, assured them that she was all right, and told them to calm down, assuring them that she'd calm down if they did. Mrs. Johnson was not too pleased with his implication that she was an "anxious mother," so she took his help with a grain of salt. Again she turned to her own mother, who assured her that "all babies cry; it seems to be a necessary part of their day." This reassured Mrs. Johnson, and she found she could live with it if she knew Anna was all right. She had turned to her mother for magic—with the belief that there must be a "solution" to this crying. Hearing her mother's calm response reassured her that there need be no "magic." She was not the inadequate mother she felt in the midst of Anna's fussing. And she began to see Anna's crying with different, calmer eyes.

Early in my practice I realized that fussy crying periods were a real threat to new parents. They felt completely helpless and inadequate with their babies. They were sure that crying in a baby meant that he was in some sort of distress—colicky or in pain—and that if they only knew what to do for him, they could "cure" him. Their anxiety and their desperation to find the magical cure they were sure must exist drove them to call me day after day. Their anxiety was matched by my own as a new, inexperienced physician. I, too, felt that a baby's crying should be alleviated. I, too, felt that there must be a "cure" that I didn't know about. I, too, felt helplessly inadequate with these babies. When I asked my more experienced colleagues what they did, they laughed knowingly and said, "It's colic. Colic is a psychosomatic disease—of anxious parents. Give the parents a sedative, and the baby will quiet down." In other words, other physicians had no answers either. They warned me about not missing physical reasons for the crying such as milk allergy or an allergy to foods the mother might be eating, pain from a hernia or an obstructed bowel, and so forth. I watched for all these, but saw no pattern that helped. Despite all our dietary manipulations, all our attempts at sedation, at reassuring their parents, many babies in my practice cried every evening. I examined them repeatedly to reassure myself that there could be no real physical reason for this crying. The fact that the crying came at the same time each day, that it was self-limited, and that it stopped at the onset of the parents' temporary "solutions" but started again when they ceased whatever they were doing, the fact that these babies all seemed healthy in every other way and stopped crying when they reached the magical age of ten to twelve weeks—all of this began to make me wonder if this was really a "disease," or should it be considered as a part of the baby's developmental process? The evening crying period seemed to be almost predictable for babies under three months and was part of their day.

In a study of evening crying, described in *Doctor and Child,* I showed that normal babies begin to cry for a significant period of time by three weeks of age, building up to two hours by six weeks (several of them cried as much as four hours at this time). As they begin to smile, to vocalize, to watch and play with their hands, as they become more organized in other social responses after four weeks, the crying periods begin to decrease, and they stop by the time they are twelve weeks of age.

For most of these babies there was a regular fussy period at the end of the day, just as Father got home and Mother wanted peace and quiet. (This was thirty years ago.) In an attempt to account for this, I remembered Anna Freud's statement that "children's egos are likely to disintegrate at the end of the day." Indeed, it seemed that mothers' egos might be pretty stressed after a long day and that perhaps this was a period of disintegration for the small baby as well. The mother's and the baby's disintegration could well be evidence of another kind of synchrony.

Anxiety in the household increased the crying, but it didn't account for it in the first place. All of the parents blamed themselves for this crying. All felt it was their fault. Only the experienced mothers knew it would pass and could accept it as part of the day. New, inexperienced parents fussed over the baby, trying desperately to calm him, and seemed to increase the amount of crying by their own fussing. In other words, anxious parents could add to the baby's crying, but they weren't the reason for it.

At the time I realized something else: that my own tension and rather frantic efforts to alleviate the crying, blaming the parents when they couldn't carry out successful programs, just increased their feelings of failure. I was adding stress to an already stressed relationship. This study helped me to feel less concerned about a pattern of cyclical crying at the end of the day. The study helped me to see it as a "part of a baby's day," and as a result, I could be of more help to parents in trouble.

When parents call me about "colic," I now suggest that they go to the baby soon after he starts, trying to find out whether there is anything wrong or they can help him by their maneuvers. When the maneuvers no longer work, I assure them that it may be necessary to leave some of it to him to handle. I recommend a routine, low-keyed approach at such a time. Letting a baby cry for periods of ten to fifteen minutes, followed by picking him up to comfort and soothe him, then putting him down again to let him cry for another period, may be necessary until he can reach the magical age of three months and substitute other, more gregarious activities at the end of the day. Letting him cry isn't easy to do, and no one feels it is a "solution," but it does get one through such a period without intensifying the problem. Even in Mayan households, where babies are breast-fed entirely on demand, often as many as thirty-six times a day and the breast is often left in the baby's mouth as a pacifier at night, the babies of this age are restless and fussy for as much as two hours during the night—always while their mothers sleep and cannot quiet them. The parents say, "When everyone else is quiet, it's the baby's turn to do the talking." This reassures me about the inevitability of such a crying period. At least it doesn't seem unique to our culture.

One must wonder about the adaptive reason for such a crying period. Is there an overall purpose behind it? Whenever there is an almost universal pattern in behavior, we must look to see what goal it serves. This leads me to look at the crying period as an organizer or as a time to discharge tensions that have built up during the day. Since there are so few ways for the baby to discharge his energy, an active, fussy period could serve such a purpose. The crying period may have to be looked at as a time in which input from parents won't help very much. This period may serve to become the first experience for them of the child's autonomy. Parents who can accept this will be better able to let the child develop independence later.

A PERSON OF HER OWN

As the Johnsons learned to accept Anna's crying as a part of her day, they realized they'd come through another milestone. They no longer saw themselves as completely in control of her. They realized that she had an independence from them that was reflected in this fussy period. As long as they "left it up to her" and did what they could to comfort her from time to time, her fussing never got out of control and was over after an hour or so. If they tried to shut it off, they were not only unsuccessful but likely to make it last and last. Postponing it was the best they could do. As they talked about it, they realized that she had needs beyond their control. It made them become more objective about her, and Mr. Johnson first said it: "You know, I think it makes me feel she's a person of her own."

As she began to turn this same fussy period into a communicative period at the end of the day, they felt they'd really attained a new height of elation. Each day Mr. Johnson rushed home to see what new things she'd learned. They put her out on a quilt in the living room to watch her by the hour. She played games with them—gurgling games, cooing games, smiling games, watching games, which started with her watching them carefully as they approached her to tickle or bounce her and ended up with squeals of laughter. Each game was more exciting than the last.

Daniel Stern, in his excellent book on attachment (1977), analyzes these games in detail. He points out their rhythmic quality, the subtle timing and buildup that lead to a crescendo and then to a short period of rest before the next game is instituted. He talks of the difference in "mother" games and "father" games. He speaks of the underlying synchrony between adult and infant and how critical this is to the success of the game. We feel that these games are an extension of the interaction system we described earlier in this chapter. They are built on the same rules and have the same goals—of creating a powerful interlocking system between a mother and father and their baby. Within these games each participant learns about the other. He learns about himself as well. He learns that when he does certain things, he sets the game of communication in motion, and within certain limits he can control the behavior of the other partner. When he does certain things, he will change the rhythm or change the game or even bring it to a halt. So he learns a great deal about communication and about turning it on and off. He learns about "others" and even more about himself. Parents learn as much about themselves as do the babies. And it is in this system, I think, that a baby first learns that he is what we call "loved."

7

Going Home with a
Premature Baby

ANXIETY BEFORE DISCHARGE

The day for Tony's discharge arrived. The Campbells had built themselves up to it in grim silence. For the week prior to this they'd hardly spoken. When they did, they snapped at each other. The air crackled, and an observer would have thought that they were angry. In truth it was all Mrs. Campbell could do to make the necessary preparations. She found herself tired all the time. Her stomach was acting up, churning, and she had frequent diarrhea. Mr. Campbell hardly ate or slept. The prospect of taking Tony home filled them both with more tension and depression than they'd anticipated.

This is an almost universal experience. In nurseries where the parents are encouraged to come in and get to know their babies before discharge, records are kept of the number of phone calls and visits from parents. The nurses in our hospitals now take great pride in how firmly attached the parents seem to be, after all the encouragement to learn about their babies. So when the records begin to show a drop in the number of visits and phone calls just before a baby's discharge, the nurses worry about the depth of the parents' attachment to the baby and often fear that their work has been in vain. Not at all. This is a sign of the inevitable anxiety parents must feel as they try to face up to their approaching responsibility. Of course, they are overwhelmed and frightened. No matter how much they have learned about the baby, such feelings will still be there. This last chance to face their fears openly may also be therapeutic. For I have seen that the approaching responsibility of caring for the baby revives all of the old, unresolved anxiety and grief over having produced a potentially damaged baby in the first place. No matter how much "grief work" (see Chapter 3) they will have done by now, it cannot be completely resolved. The feelings of having been responsible for the baby's condition, the fear of damaging him even further, the wish to leave him in a safe place ("safe" from them), all of the old defenses against their grief and their feelings of inadequacy are bound to come surging back. Klaus and Kennell (1976) say they expect such parents to be unavailable for visiting the baby and for being taught during the last week, so they plan for it by trying to get in the necessary instructions before they announce the time for the baby to go home. Parents may well need to withdraw in order to gather energy for coping when they first take the baby home.

> *When the Campbells came in to get Tony, the nurses were very encouraging. His nurse told Mrs. Campbell how well Tony was doing. She showed her how to administer physiotherapy to his still-weak left leg and arm. She assured them that his left-sided weakness was disappearing. The young doctor in charge confirmed this and attempted to reassure them that this in itself was a good sign about the condition of Tony's brain. "In fact," he said, "we expect Tony to recover completely. But it will be up to you. You must keep up all his exercises." As he spoke, he emphasized this in an almost threatening tone, for he felt as if the Campbells weren't hearing him.*

This kind of "not hearing" is another sign of how anxious and distressed they are. They are hearing, but they need to protect themselves. They certainly do feel the responsibility he is urging on them. In fact, they feel overwhelmed by it. Denial, or acting as if they don't hear, is a defense against these feelings. Denial can certainly be an effective defense mechanism, and it's one we *all* use. But it can also interfere with one's ability to take in necessary information or even to act appropriately. Just getting angry or accusatory, however, with people who need to use denial at such a time does not help them. It would have been more effective had the young physician sat down with them, let them tell him how frightened they were, assured them that all parents feel this way, and then gone on to lay out the minimum necessary instructions. He could have written them down so that they could digest them later. Parents can take in very little at such a time.

ACCENTUATING THE POSITIVE

Tony's special nurse showed them how much better his left leg was, how strong the grasp in his left hand was becoming, and in an effort to show them how little affected his neck and face were, she stroked his left cheek. He rooted quickly toward her finger and almost snapped it into his mouth. At this they all laughed, and the air of tension was reduced. His nurse showed them how to play with Tony—by rocking him up and down until he was wide-eyed and would follow her face. She showed them how alert and quiet he was when she cuddled him close to her. As she showed them all of this good behavior, concentrating on his responsive eyes and his alert head turning to her voice, they began to relax and to talk about him as if he were a real baby.

There is nothing so powerful in reducing parents' natural anxiety and fears about a handicapped or slowly developing infant as showing them the things the baby can do. If they can see some evidence of positive behavior, then they can more easily take in the information they may need to absorb about problems or handicaps. If hope can be centered on the positive, it can help them face the negative. No matter how devastated parents may be by defects in their infant, if they can identify with the baby's positive responses, they can then see their job more clearly as working with these responses to help him. If they are allowed to "wallow" in the deficits, they are more likely to be overwhelmed with the destructive aspects of their grief. Showing a parent the baby's capacity to handle his "states," to wake up and remain alert, to respond to touch, and to become alert in response to a parent's face and voice helps the family get off to a better start.

We saw a dramatic example of this while working with the parents of a blind infant. At birth she had only one sightless globe, and her other eye was missing completely. We never knew what led to this defect, and our concern was that she might also have other associated congenital defects. In order to allay our own fears about whether she had an intact brain, we tested her with the Neonatal

Behavioral Assessment Scale (Brazelton, 1984). This is a twenty-minute exam, designed by me and many helping colleagues, that brings a newborn baby from sleep to awake, on to crying, and back down to quiet alertness. In the process one can test his reflexes for neurological integrity, his alerting responses to all kinds of attractive stimuli (face, voice, rattle, bell, a red ball, rocking, cuddling, singing, and so on). One can also see how he handles his own states, as well as his other attempts to keep himself under control as he reacts to the examiner. In this baby's case we had planned to have the mother present as we examined her baby, for we wanted to demonstrate to her the baby's intact behavioral responses. Although her lack of vision rendered her oversensitive to auditory and tactile cues, if one quieted one's voice and touched and handled her gently, she was extremely responsive. Watching us demonstrate these behaviors, the mother sighed as if tremendously relieved and said, "So she's not completely damaged. I was afraid she'd be a nothing." She had been told by the neurologists that the baby was all right except for her eyes, but she hadn't been able to take it in. After seeing her move from sleeping to an alert, responsive, listening state and seeing her turn to our voices, and after seeing her suck on her own fist, her mother began to see her as a person and to be able to hear what she needed to hear. This one demonstration freed her to be extremely sensitive to the baby. At three weeks, she said to me on a visit, "The difference between Susan and my older child is that when Susan is waking up, if I'm not there to hold her with my voice or my soothing hands, she'll wake up to scream. She could spend all of her day screaming and out of control or sleeping. Looking around helped the older child hold on to things and stay alert so that he could pay attention and learn about life around him. If I'm not there, Susan can't get hold of herself, stay awake, and begin to learn how to handle her world." I found this remarkably perceptive and marveled at her ability to understand Susan so soon and to understand the kind of hypersensitivity that a baby with any sensory deficit will have. She had already figured this out and was at work to help Susan learn about herself. Both she and I felt that the early demonstration of her assets had freed her to be more available to Susan and less overwhelmed by her own inevitable disappointment.

A TENSE DAY

The Campbells had fed Tony on earlier visits, so they felt less uneasy about that, but they asked if he had any "new quirks" about feeding. They would have liked to feed him once more in the nursery—in safety. But the nurses and the doctor seemed in a hurry to get him out, and they dressed him quickly for discharge.

Once a baby is up for discharge, every one of the nursery personnel seems under pressure to get rid of him. They push the parents out, often rushing them through instructions that would be much better learned if they allowed time for the parents to take them in at their own pace. This may reflect the nurses' feeling that now they've done their job and it is time for the parents to get on with theirs. Their attitude can be almost punitive. One also sees the elements of competition in it—competition with the parents for the baby. Nurses will talk a lot about how difficult it is to work hard for and get attached to such a sick baby. When they must discharge him, they feel a real loss, and there's no way to express these feelings. Naturally they feel somewhat angry and competitive with parents who may not understand him and may even harm him. Barbara Korsch, a pediatrician at the Los Angeles Children's Hospital, instituted sessions for nurses in high-risk nurseries in which the nurses are encouraged to ventilate these feelings and to see them as natural ones, necessary to their roles of identifying with and caring for such needy infants. The effect of these sessions has been dramatic. Not only are the nurses freed from the strain of repressing their feelings and more able to act generously toward the stressed parents, but their own lives are easier and richer. The attrition, or turnover, rate in nursing personnel in such nurseries can be as high as 30 to 40 percent a month, for it is very painful to work hard with a baby only to lose it one way or another. With someone to share these feelings of loss, the turnover rate is reduced dramatically.

The Campbells wrapped Tony in four layers of quilted clothing to leave the hospital. So well wrapped was he that his head and face kept disappearing into the wrappings. Mrs. Campbell sat rigidly in the car, watching his every breath, praying that they wouldn't drive off the road or hit another car. Mr. Campbell turned so often to look at Tony in his car seat that such a disaster became a more likely reality. He, too, felt as if he were accident-prone with Tony in the car. When they finally crept up to their apartment house, Mr. Campbell helped his wife bring Tony out of the car as if she were carrying a package of very fragile eggs. The climb up three flights to their apartment seemed interminable—each parent afraid Mrs. Campbell might trip. As she climbed the stairs, she began to realize how unlikely it was that she'd go down again with Tony for a long, long time. She felt a sense of the apartment closing in to trap her with the baby. She was to feel this often in the next few weeks.

Yet she welcomed the safety of having him home and away from dangerous others. They had thought of everything—keeping the heat way up, reducing noises, pulling the shades in his room to keep it dark, a rocking chair for his room. But they hadn't prepared a bottle. As soon as she unwrapped him, Tony woke up, flailing arms and legs, screaming in tiny piercing wails. Each cry sent a shiver through his parents, who were all but immobilized. When they recovered from the sudden shock of this rapid shift—from fragility to demandingness—they began to rush around the apartment, trying to collect the necessary ingredients for a feeding. In their haste they forgot the prepared formula that the hospital had sent home with them. By the time they remembered it and warmed it, Tony had long since stopped crying, exhausted.

Crying in a premature or fragile baby is an excellent sign of strength. Crying demands a lot from a baby. Not only can premature babies not muster the strength to cry until they are fairly well organized, but they cannot maintain the effort for very long.

Tony was so tired that he could hardly be roused to eat. His sucking reflexes were disorganized (see Chapter 5); he couldn't muster the strength to pull on the nipple; the nipple of the bottle was so soft that it let milk out too quickly for him, and he choked a bit, the milk coming out of his nose. His breathing became labored and noisy, to the horror of his "new" parents.

The Campbells would have done well to let Tony have a rest and recovery period before they fed him. Feeding, like everything else, is demanding for such a baby. Even pushing to have a bowel movement is a major effort. When such a baby is overtaxed, even his reflexive behaviors fall apart. More organized behaviors—even such a primitive one as sucking—can disintegrate with fatigue or stress. One sees this in all sorts of ways: If one tries to set off a startle, it may not be forthcoming. And at a more critical level, his breathing apparatus and the controls over it at a central nervous system level can show the strain. A baby like this may breathe shallowly and irregularly. He may even demonstrate apneic spells, when his breathing will cease for periods at a time. His color may change to mottled or slightly cyanotic (bluish) at the tips of his fingers, toes, and around his mouth. All of these are signs of his being stressed, and parents of such a baby should pay careful attention to them. If they have been asking too much of the baby, by bathing him, playing with him, feeding him, or leaving him undressed for too long, they would do well to wrap the baby securely and to leave him to rest for a period. After an amazingly short time, in which he can recover his autonomic balance, the baby can go on with a necessary procedure or activity. Since these necessary activities, such as eating, cost him so much, it is no wonder that he has little energy left over for learning or for paying prolonged attention to his new world. *Of course,* a premature will be slow in catching up. *Of course,* he will be more difficult for his parents to get used to. Parents should be prepared for this beforehand so that their natural anxiety won't be increased by it—and so that they won't press such a baby too hard and too fast. All parents of premature babies will be dominated by their wish to see the baby grow up fast. In their minds, it is easy to equate the baby's growing up or maturing with survival and with proving himself intact.

> *After his choking episode they put Tony down in his crib. They propped his bed up a bit so that his head was higher in case he choked again. They'd seen and remembered that his nurses always did this in the hospital after such an episode.*

I always marvel at how much parents can learn at such a time. Unconsciously as well as consciously they model their behavior on the nursing techniques they see in the premature nursery. When Sylvia Brody (1956) published her ideas about assessing maternal feeding behaviors, demonstrating that mothers who were at risk for failure with their babies did not cuddle their babies or nestle them in their arms at feeding time, she and others ignored the source of this behavior in certain mothers. The mothers of premature or sick babies have seen their infants fed on the laps of nurses, propped in front of them in a sitting position, head and shoulders supported by one hand. In the nurse's case this is a way to watch the baby eat and to watch for difficulty in feeding. Mothers will, of course, model their own feeding techniques on this observation and may be labeled "cool" or "nonnurturing" as a result.

THE FIRST SMILE

The Campbells watched Tony anxiously for the next weeks. Each feeding was an ordeal. Each night one of them slept next to him, with one eye open—waiting for something to happen. They fed him on the minute of an every-three-hour schedule. If he wasn't awake, they woke him. If he woke early and got restless, they walked him or rocked him until the three hours were up. Each episode of spitting up, each bowel movement, every upset were examined carefully. Mr. Campbell's work suffered again. Mrs. Campbell never left the house or Tony's bedside. When anyone called to ask them out or to inquire about Tony, they felt it was an intrusion. Every ounce of energy was directed to him. They had none left over for lives of their own.

Four weeks later, Tony by now forty-two weeks old, they were still in the same, dogged routine. They changed his diapers and exercised his legs and arms to try to strengthen them. Time seemed to have come to a standstill. Anyone who might have observed them in the midst of this would have felt it was pretty joyless. It might almost have seemed as if they were working out a penance, with no prospect of a reward. Meanwhile, Tony was gaining weight and beginning to look a little sturdier.

At forty-two weeks they took him to the clinic for his checkup. It was an important event for them. They were both eager to see whether Tony was making headway and afraid of what might turn up if he wasn't. Their relief at having him examined was enormous. The doctor who saw him had never seen him before, but he congratulated them on the progress of his left side and encouraged them to keep at his therapy. He also gave them a real present by saying he'd gained two and a half pounds and was in excellent shape.

Premature infants start gaining rapidly after they have recovered. In fact, they can get encased in fat to such an extent that they are somewhat immobilized by it. I always warn parents of prematures that at about the time the baby may be ready to start moving, he may be too lumpy and heavy to crawl or walk on time. Since parents of premies are worried about their being "slow," the difficulty an overweight baby faces may compound and confirm their worries.

The Campbells had hoped to see one of his old nurses so that they could show him off. But the visit came and went without their seeing anyone they knew. Mrs. Campbell realized how much she'd looked forward to this excursion and how tied up she'd been with Tony. The doctor gave her permission to take him out on walks, but she hardly listened to him. She couldn't yet conceive of exposing him to the outside world.

After another monotonous month of routines, Mrs. Campbell realized that Tony was getting easier. He now slept soundly at night; he cried in a more vigorous way; he even stayed awake for thirty minutes at a time during the day. She realized he was a "different baby." With this realization she and her husband began to feel easier about playing with him and jostling him.

As the baby settles into a more predictable pattern, the parents unconsciously assume he is becoming sturdier. Their responses are guided by changes in him.

Mrs. Campbell began to allow her husband to play with Tony in a more vigorous way. It was in one of these playful episodes that they first saw him really smile. They had been aware of fleeting smiles before and had even dared try to produce them, but now he smiled at them and with them. They smiled back, and he seemed to know it. Although this big event was marked in his baby book, it took him another five days before he smiled again.

As we've said before, reflex smiles are present at birth, and fleeting smiles are seen in prematures before their due date. So smiles start out as reflexes. If they are responded to and encouraged, they begin to be "responsive smiles" by the age of four to six weeks. Parents see these as "real smiles" because they can be reproduced at will, under appropriate circumstances. Freedman (1964) studied them in blind infants, saw them appear as "voluntary" at six to eight weeks, but then they began to disappear, *unless* parents found ways of reinforcing them that didn't depend on vision. If they cooed or touched or responded with each smile, the blind baby continued to smile both responsively and in an eliciting way. In other words, smiling is an expectable developmental milestone, but it needs appropriate fueling. A premature infant may be slower in producing this kind of social behavior. As in Tony's case, some of the reasons for delay may be: (a) the rather monotonous, task-oriented climate that anxious parents provide and (b) the need for physiological systems to stabilize before a social behavior can emerge.

FEARS AND OVERPROTECTION

By now the Campbells were ecstatic about each smile. They called up their friends; they called up their parents. Mrs. Campbell wanted to show him off. For the first time she felt the urge to take him out. She spent nearly an hour getting him dressed—in layer upon layer of clothing. Taking him down the three flights of stairs and out in the carriage was such an ordeal that she ended up by walking down an empty street with him and then going straight home. She saw no one to show him to. Tony seemed shaken by this "trip" and fussed for thirty minutes afterward. This upset his mother so much that she resolved to stay at home with him. However, she noticed that after his fussing, he ate well and went into a sound sleep, so her fears of having disrupted him were not well founded. As Tony began to get more sociable— cooing and smiling for ten minutes at a time—the Campbells felt more and more that he would "make it." They hadn't dared voice the depth of their fears to each other, but as he proved himself, they became braver. It turned out that each of them had had the same ominous dream each night, had waked with a start, and then could hardly wait to check on him each day. Tony himself was proving these fears groundless—but it had taken him ten weeks to do it.

There is no real way of overcoming these hovering fears of losing the baby. The stress of seeing him through all he's suffered is so great and so telling that it's bound to leave its mark. Tony is proving to them by his increasing social behavior that he will survive.

In this country infant mortality has become low enough that most parents never have to go through what the Campbells have experienced. In third world countries a mother must guard herself so that she doesn't get too attached before it is safe for her to expect her baby to live. In cultures where one-third of infants will die in the first few months, the culture sets up taboos to guard against overattachment on the part of the mother. In the Greek islands midwives warn a mother not to name her baby until he's three months old, for he's not a person until then but rather a phoenix who can fly away all too easily and unexpectedly. There are other adaptive superstitions: "You should never take a new baby out under the stars, for his soul will fly away to one of the stars. Never show him to others, for they may have the evil eye and damage him." These taboos protect a baby from exposure and infection. Another one is: "If you let the gods see that you care too much about him, they'll be jealous and take him away." This one, to protect a mother from letting herself get attached, is reproduced in many mythological tales in which heroes were snatched away in infancy and raised by the gods. The parents of a premature infant must not dare to care too much. Hence each milestone in his progress allows them to open up a bit more.

The other result of overconcern is that parents don't "dare" push such babies to learn for themselves. A mother of a full-term baby will try out new toys and new tasks and will even tease a baby to learn new things. She and his father will, by these actions, stir him on to practice a new acquisition and to become frustrated enough to want to do it by himself. And when he tries to do it by himself, they can allow him "space"—the space to try and fail, the space to keep trying it without their interference. In other words, they reinforce his autonomy.

This is difficult for the parents of a premie. They continue to wrap him in their overpowering attention. If he tries something, it is hard for them to see him fail. They cannot tolerate his frustration. So they continue to do everything for him, to rush to him before he's had a chance to try anything out for himself. They encase him in cotton wool—the cotton wool of anxiously caring parents. As a result, they create a kind of monotonous environment for the baby, and they interfere with his development of a "sense of competence," which would fuel further learning.

Dr. Kate Kogan did an experiment on four-year-olds who had experienced early difficulties such as prematurity, matching them with normal four-year-olds. She filmed them while their mothers presented a learning task and taught them how to do it. The mothers of normal children showed them what they were to do, then sat back and waited for them to learn each step by themselves and to put it together at the end. The mothers of prematures hovered over the four-year-olds (who had now long outgrown any residual effects of their immaturity), showing them the task repeatedly, never allowing them the time or the independence to try a step, fail, but try again and succeed. Not only did it take the second group twice as long to learn a task, but there seemed to be no pleasure in it for them when they did finally succeed—just a sense of relief.

The Campbells found themselves hovering over Tony, trying to get a smile or a coo out of him whenever he was awake. They

overloaded him with solicitation, and he spent a lot of time turn-
ing away from them. If they came into sight, he first monitored
them warily with his eyes to see whether they were uptight or
low-keyed. If they were the latter, he seemed more responsive
and would look them in the eye to smile or vocalize. When they
were too eager or too anxious to get a response, they found that
he averted his gaze, turned his head away, and nothing they did
would get him back.

This is a combination of his high degree of sensitivity, now de-
creasing (see Chapter 3), and their tendency to overload him with
attention. Finding the "appropriate" level of stimulation and remain-
ing sensitive to the cues that would let them know when he is overloaded make for a hard job in getting such a baby started.

SLOW PROGRESS

On his four-month birthday (thirty weeks plus four months) he
really fell apart. The Campbells couldn't resist having two other
couples and their babies over for the birthday party. The noise
and confusion and the excitement of having other people around
were too much for all of them. Mrs. Campbell found herself
watching the other babies with longing. A three-month-old was
already "talking," kicking her arms and legs in glee as an adult
talked back to her. She even attempted to reach toward an object
if it was held out for her. She was miles ahead of Tony, and Mrs.
Campbell felt depressed after they'd left. Would he ever really be
all right? Was it brain damage that held him back, or was the
progress of a premature infant always slow? These questions
racked her after she'd seen the other babies. She could see how
much slower, how much more limited Tony's progress was.

The grief reaction is close to the surface, ready to be mobilized
by any setback. Even a chance to observe the smoother, more easily
integrated behavior of a normal baby will show a mother what hard
work she must do to be able to help her baby get going. We found
that mothers of prematures spend a lot of time comparing their baby's slower, sparser progress with that of normal babies. And the
comparison takes a lot out of them. If they can focus on the individualized progress of their own baby, they will be spared some of this

anxiety. But a mother who is as isolated as Mrs. Campbell also needs input from other mothers; she needs it for Tony's sake as well as her own. By watching other babies and talking to other mothers, she will get ideas for keeping Tony's progress going as well as the kind of support and companionship she needs for her own peace of mind. Self-doubts are bound to plague her. A group of mothers with premature babies of the same age, who have been through the same experiences, would be ideal. But unless premature nurseries set them up, it would be difficult for someone as retiring as Mrs. Campbell to find others in her same boat. "Therapeutic" day-care centers, where parents could participate along with their infants, would also serve this kind of purpose.

After the party Tony was still disorganized. He fell apart at the end of the day, fussing and crying for several hours. He ate poorly, waking off and on each hour through the night. When his parents tried to comfort him, he quieted down briefly but then continued in this disorganized pattern. Mrs. Campbell reproached herself. It had all seemed like a disaster. Mr. Campbell pointed out that it was a good thing for both of them to see friends, and he tried to convince her that of course, she and Tony would be raw the first time but that they'd learn how to cope. He felt it would be good for Tony, but this just made her angry at him, so he shut up.

Tony continued to be upset for several more days afterward. He slept poorly, ate less, and seemed frustrated, as if he were looking around for something whenever she picked him up. After this rather brief period of disorganization, however, he began to settle down again to more easily observable progress. By now he could stay awake for long periods. He gurgled, he cooed more regularly; he smiled over and over again as he communicated with his parents. Although he was more tenuous about it and more easily overloaded, he began to set up short periods of communication with them, similar to those described in the last chapter with the Johnsons and Anna. Tony's ability to maintain these periods for more than a little while was not yet developed. Mr. and Mrs. Campbell were so overjoyed when he responded that they often overwhelmed him and broke the rhythm.

In a longitudinal study of premature infants and their parents we have had a chance to study this. At four months of age (thirty weeks plus four months), the ratio of baby behavior to mother behavior and the degree to which mothers dominate the interaction is comparable with that of a two-month-old normal infant and his mother. So habitual has it become for the mother of a premie to do everything for him that she continues to do so long after the need for it has gone. This leads to a kind of unconscious insensitivity on her part that would surprise her were she aware of it. In fact, when we ask her to remain still and inactive in front of the baby, she sees the baby come alive. He begins to elicit her to be responsive in all sorts of ingenious ways. He demonstrates reaching behavior that she's never seen before, and each mother realizes that she's been doing too much in the interaction and overpowering his spontaneity. This lag in a mother's realization of her baby's developing skills is not a matter of not caring but of caring too much. It is a natural, expectable reaction to the baby's initial long period of helplessness.

Tony's regressed behavior just before he made new strides demonstrates that there is a more obvious period of falling apart in premature babies that precedes each new developmental step. All infants go through a kind of jagged progress of development, but for premature babies the periods of reorganization are interspersed with more horrendous periods of disorganization. The parents' tendency to overreact plays into this. For example, just before he sits up or crawls or stands or walks, a premature infant can be expected to fall apart. He will cry more unpredictably and will be harder to comfort; he will start waking up at night all over again; he will cry whenever one turns one's back; he will act as if nothing can really satisfy him. Unless his parents can learn that this precedes another spurt in development and thereby gain courage, they, too, will fall apart. And each will drag down the other. Learning about each other, about how to help the baby learn controls, how much it is good to do for him and how much he has to learn to do for himself—all of these are lessons learned the hard way in such a period. So it's hardly wasted. But it can be a painful period.

OUTSIDE HELP

By the time Tony had been at home for six months, it seemed like a year. His mother was depressed a great deal of the time, angry with her husband when he came home, longing for relief from her isolated life with Tony, longing to be out in the world work-

*ing yet trapped by her fears about leaving Tony with anyone
else. She saw very few people. Most of her friends had babies, and
she spent her time comparing Tony with their "normal" babies—
always unfavorably. She hardly saw any of the good things Tony
was learning anymore. She felt she'd "had it." She'd worked so
hard, hovered over the baby for so long, yet when she compared
him with other babies eight months of age, he seemed to be behind them in his development. At his checkup the doctor said
that his left hand and leg were strong and returned to normal.
He felt that Tony was making good progress, gaining weight that
made him equivalent in size to other eight-month-old babies. He
felt that physically Tony couldn't be doing better, and he congratulated Mrs. Campbell on his progress. This relieved some of
her worries, but after a day or so she felt exhausted and discouraged again. She barely played with Tony these days, leaving him
in his chair to watch his mobile or propped in front of the blaring
television.*

This was the end of a long siege of worry and hard work, without
the usual rewards that an eight-month-old baby would be giving
back. Tony was slower, duller, and more monotonous in his responses. But his mother's depression and her hidden anger were undoubtedly affecting him too.

What could be done? I can think of several options for them.
Mrs. Campbell could use help in some form—a substitute caregiver
or a day-care setting where she could be freed up part of the time—
either to go to work or to do something on her own for at least a few
times each week. The relief to her and the added source of stimulation for Tony would pay off for them both. Another possibility is that
she could sign up for one of the so-called "early intervention" programs. These are outgrowths of an increasing awareness of the fact
that vulnerable babies like Tony do not do well in environments
where the caregiver is overloaded—with too many other responsibilities or with poverty or undernutrition—or in households like the
Campbells' where the mother is isolated and doesn't know where to
go for help. When the mother participates in a program to set up
developmental goals for her interaction with the child, not only does
she get a chance to see where she as a person is going, but she can
focus her interests and attention on the baby in a more productive
way. Maybe most important of all, the mother feels as if she is being
cared about in her role. The isolation, the depression, the hopeless

feeling of not getting anywhere with the baby, which are added to her grief at his premature birth and her leftover fears about his normality, are met head-on in such programs. In addition, the other mothers in the programs offer tremendous support, the programs focus the mother again on what the baby can do and set up stimulating sequences for her to follow with her baby. All this provides a most important source of fuel for the child's recovery. Unfortunately these programs do not exist everywhere.*

A third source of help might come from an increase in father support. But this can be difficult. The role of the father in such a situation becomes even more critical. Realizing this, he may feel overwhelmed too. For he has been through a long crisis with his wife and baby. He may well have become "burnt out." His wife's resentment of his job, of his relative freedom, her anger at the situation, which she will tend to project onto him, can push him away rather than toward the family. Fathers should be urged to participate for everyone's sake.

> *One of Mrs. Campbell's old friends came to see Tony and was struck by how lifeless and withdrawn he was. When she went over to talk to him, he put his outstretched hand in front of his face, as if to hide behind his fingers. Instead of responding to her overtures, he watched his fingers moving slowly in front of his eyes. She couldn't get him to smile, and he averted his face if she tried to remove his hand. When she picked him up to hold him, he arched back as if to get away from her, and when that was unsuccessful, he clung to her in a way that let him face away from her. She was very upset with this withdrawal, which seemed to dominate his behavior. She found Mrs. Campbell almost as hard to reach. And she sensed her depression. After this visit she called Mr. Campbell in real distress. She urged him to get them into some sort of program and even found him one that was set up to follow babies like Tony.*
>
> *Mr. Campbell approached his wife with this suggestion. He didn't expect the blast he received. She was furious. "You think*

---

*The United Cerebral Palsy Foundation, 330 West Thirty-fourth Street, New York, New York 10001, would be an excellent source for finding out about such programs. As far as I know, the baby does not have to be a CP patient to join many of the outreach programs. Other stimulation programs are connected with day-care centers. Another source of information is the National Center for Clinical Infant Programs, 2000 14th Street N., Suite 380, Arlington, VA 22201.

I'm a failure too. You won't help me, so you want to send me off to a psychiatrist. You don't care a thing about Tony. You just want to get at me!" At first she refused to go, and Mr. Campbell was stymied. He called the center for advice, and it offered to send a trained worker to see Mrs. Campbell and Tony.

Anyone who is depressed and senses the need for help must defend himself or herself against these thoughts. For the longing for such help is coupled with the fear of failure and the deeper realization of how desperate one can be at such times. Anyone who wishes to offer help must risk braving the storm with a depressed person. Mr. Campbell is wise to follow through, for his wife and Tony are both at risk of developmental failure. He needs to be playing more of a role.

The worker convinced Mrs. Campbell that Tony's reactions were expectable and would improve if she could get some relief for herself as well as some ideas about how to bring him along. She convinced Mrs. Campbell that Tony was a depressed little boy but not a damaged one.

In the center both Tony and Mrs. Campbell met an extremely sensitive, caring environment. The caregivers didn't push Tony too fast. They let him begin to relate to them at his own speed before they introduced any of their program. They let Mrs. Campbell talk and helped her feel less overwhelmed and isolated. They kept her near Tony, for they knew she'd feel torn away from him if they didn't. And they taught her what to do to help him, so that she could be the one who brought him along.

This is critical. A program that concentrates on just the infant and excludes the mother could do more harm than good. Mrs. Campbell has invested too much and needs to see that her own efforts will help Tony. Any success on the part of an outsider would either make her feel devalued, diluting their relationship in a serious way and forcing her away from Tony for good, or cause her to fight back and pull him out of treatment. Her natural feelings of competition for her baby would not allow him to be "taken from her."

We have seen confirmation of this in many national programs, all designed to help. In their zeal to be of benefit to the infant or child directly, they ignore the needs of the family. The inevitable competition more than negates any gains the child may have made. In assessments of the effects of the Head Start programs around the country, designed to improve preschool children's readiness for school, one thing became very clear. The programs that included families and enriched the families' lives as well as those of the children were successful in raising IQs and in instituting permanent gains in the child's outlook toward life and his success in school performance. The ones that ignored families or had no effect on them established only minimal and transient successes in the children they tried to help.

So protecting and encouraging Mrs. Campbell's feelings about herself by helping her participate actively were absolutely critical parts of any program for Tony.

As the caregivers worked with these two, they asked Mr. Campbell to join a fathers' group at night. Here fathers aired their concerns, clarified their roles in supporting their wives, and faced some of their own ambivalent feelings about parental responsibility. Mr. Campbell was an eager and active participant.

Mrs. Campbell found her own sessions rewarding and exciting. The rewards came in two ways. Not only did she feel encouraged by the group for what she'd already done for Tony—because everyone kept saying, "Think how far you have brought him," as

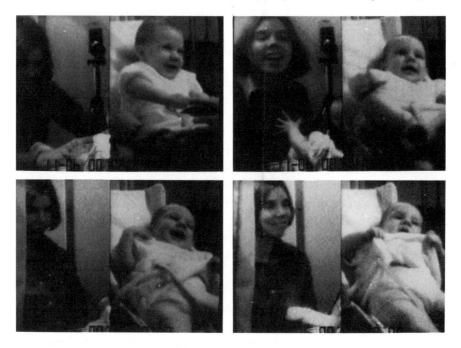

if it were a miracle—but she found Tony a new person because of all the exciting activity around him. It made her realize that she'd been depressed for quite a while. Now Tony's eyes blazed with excitement as they played exercise games with a song attached. She would present him with a toy to reach, and as he'd reach for it, she would make a game out of it by pulling the toy a bit out of his reach. He seemed to love to be teased. When he would finally capture the toy, he'd pull it away from her, then attempt to tease her by offering it and pulling it away again. He was a new Tony!

Had the Campbells lost time in not getting help earlier? Probably not. For they were not yet locked into irreversible patterns of depression or failure. But it was close. The value of letting a family realize they need help is that when help actually comes, everyone is ready for it. There is always a timing for intervention that is critical. If an outsider forces help on a family before they are aware of the need for it, it may not stick. Their resistance may even keep them from accepting it. In this case all three Campbells were relieved and revived by this outside support. However, the danger in postponing it too long can be even greater than the danger of suggesting it too soon. I know that in my practice I keep postponing the suggestion of outside help even after I suspect that a family is experiencing trouble. My denial reinforces the natural denial of the parents, who are trying hard to make it on their own. As soon as I am aware of this, I can help them recognize the situation with me, and they are more likely to accept a referral to outside help.

THE EXPECTATION OF FAILURE

The danger of postponement lies in the possibility that patterns of failure will become firmly established. Not only are they likely to be fixed and hard to eradicate, but there are critical periods that can be missed, critical in that an opportunity for learning about a developmental milestone may be lost. And when the baby and his parents begin to sense failure, the child quickly builds up an expectation within himself for failure. He will learn to perform as if he expected to fail, and at some point he will see himself as a failure. We see this in learning-disabled children. By the time their disability is identified, at three or four years of age, they often demonstrate an expectation of failure. They see themselves as always failing, and they devalue what they can do. This danger makes the actual processing disorder the least of the child's problems. Treating the child for his poor self-image becomes the most critical aspect of any rehabilitation program.

I have been struck with how early this pattern of expecting to fail gets going in a small child's mind. In our unit at Children's Hospital we have seen it in an eight-month-old. This baby, who was later identified as having an information-processing disorder (or learning disability), would set herself up to fail on every test in the Bayley exam. Similar to Gesell tests of infant competence, the Bayley can be administered and scored at each month of infancy. For example, at eight months a baby is supposed to be able to put two cubes together and to show thereby that he has a concept of spatial relationships and of the equivalence of the two cubes. This infant would get them almost up to each other (showing us clearly that she had the concept), and then she'd actively make them miss each other. She made them pass each other so adeptly and so consistently that we knew she could have done the task easily. She would then look at us to be sure we'd noticed her failure. We felt, as did her mother, that she already *expected* to fail and would henceforth set it up for herself.

For a child with a motor disability or any kind of handicap, it may be even more critical to make sure that patterns of failure and the expectation for failure do not get incorporated into the baby's performance or the mother's mind. A mother may give up and stop doing the very things her baby needs most from her in order to overcome his handicap. She may unconsciously cease to expect him to succeed and may transmit this to him. If his own performance becomes derailed, he may learn patterns that will actively interfere with more successful ones. Hence, in the case of minor or major brain damage, early intervention becomes even more critical. The Bobaths' work in rechanneling disordered motor pathways is a real example of how much we now know about how to help a child detour around his deficits. The success of these programs depends largely upon capturing the motivation in the child *before* it is derailed by failure and capturing the parents' energy for carrying out the program—with an *expectation* from them that the child will succeed. This latter is critical and may be hardest to revive if it has faded.

NEW STRIDES

Tony began to play at home. He lay in his crib in the morning, before they got up, talking to himself. He tried all sorts of cooing, vowels, trilling, coughing, and gagging sounds. He seemed to go over all the possibilities for using his vocal apparatus. When he first learned to gag and cough, Mrs. Campbell jumped out of bed in alarm. As she approached his room, she heard him repeat the sounds on purpose, and she realized that it was all part of his new repertoire. His trills could be seen as almost mimicking some of her inflections. She heard him try out a two-part sound that seemed to mimic the way she said "To-ny" to him. He tried it over and over again without the consonants. With all of this practice his vocal abilities increased rapidly, and he said "da da" to his father on one red-letter day. A week later, after much repeated encouragement from her, he whimpered "mum-mum" to Mrs. Campbell.

At the same time he began to watch his hands. He practiced rotating them in front of his face, playing with the fingers of each hand with the other. The stereotyped pattern of covering his face with his hands dropped out as he began to find more exciting uses for them. He began to reach for toys in his crib, and within a week he had mastered two-hand reaching, one-hand reaching, and transferring of objects from one hand to the other (see Infants and Mothers*). In a short time he had covered the achievements of two months of practice and learning. His new drive to learn kept him going, and he began to catch up with others his age.*

The most obvious aspect of all of this new learning was that the capacity had been there but had not been utilized. He had fallen into monotonous, stereotyped patterns of behavior, which covered over these more complex capacities. The excitement of learning new, richer ways of doing things had been repressed by the rather dull, unrewarding, and unrewarded atmosphere between him and his mother. As Mrs. Campbell became motivated and excited again, Tony did too. Their communications were now on an entirely different level. Very quickly they began to enjoy each other, to fire each other up. Mr. Campbell looked on at all of this with awe. He was also a bit jealous. But the relief of coming home to a cheerful, lively atmosphere was a new experience, something he had not felt since Tony's birth.

The effect of such programs is not always so dramatic, of course. But they certainly can offer support and a new outlook for the whole family. When they do, they enhance the attachments within the family in a very significant way. *Now* if Mrs. Campbell wanted or needed to go to work, she could do so with a very different feeling—about herself and about Tony. If she'd left him in failure, if she'd "deserted" him to a day-care center or a special program for Tony alone, as she might well have wanted to at the time, she would have seen his recovery and achievements as theirs, not hers and his. This latter difference is crucial—not only to her future feelings about Tony but to her own self-image as a competent mother and person. With this renewal of her firm feelings of attachment to Tony, separation from him was no longer a threat. It could become another stage of development in their attachment. For successful detachment is the ultimate goal of attachment after all.

8

Adoption and Attachment

Attachment to an adopted child can be surprisingly complex. In many ways parents who have waited and searched for an appropriate baby bring more passionate feelings to the process. They feel that they are ready to give their all to this baby. Because of the intensity of these feelings, it can come as a surprise if they and the longed-for baby can't make it with each other right away.

For parents who adopt, the longing for a child has been tested by a devastating fertility work-up. The experience of being examined repeatedly, searched for defects, is bound to undermine any adult's self-concept. The intimate nature of the tests, and the psychological questions which imply that there is a psychosomatic problem, cannot help making a couple doubt that they can be adequate as parents. All parents but especially adopting parents worry about this. When one takes on the responsibility for another person's child, the question of one's competence is likely to be heightened. The zeal to provide an abandoned or unwanted child with a safe haven covers up these insecure feelings for a while. But the underlying questions about one's adequacy as a parent will surface as the work of attachment proceeds.

Today a prospective parent usually must search at home and abroad for a baby. Only certain agencies can be trusted. For the majority of parents who want a healthy newborn baby, there are limited choices available. Alternatives such as surrogacy raise highly complex psychological issues that are well beyond the scope of this book.

Parents whom I have interviewed tell me of the long, complicated searches they go through to find an agency they can trust. Waiting lists can be eight to ten years long. The great longings of infertile couples have been exploited. Some agencies can be paid large sums for an immediate baby. This corruption faces many families in the same situation. Often when they give up the idea of adopting a child of their own race or turn to foreign adoptions, they find the same corrupt process. Babies are treated as marketable. Parents willing to accept an impaired infant can get a bargain. An intact child is expensive. Such a situation is naturally horrifying and demoralizing to would-be parents.

In working with an agency, including the reliable ones, the most caring parents-to-be must face questions about their life-style. Are they really able to live up to this precious responsibility? Why have they turned to adoption? Were their own chances at natural parenting completely explored? Many parents adopt and then find they get pregnant. Even after a diagnosis of hopeless infertility, something about making the decision to adopt appears to free up both physical and psychological potential, which may not be identifiable in an infertility work-up. As the agency does its job and delves for reasons not to give a couple a baby, a parent will also question his or her own motives. "Am I really adequate?"

For most would-be adoptive parents, as the self-questioning proceeds, their resolve is strengthened. Their motives become more fervent. In such a situation one does not dare question oneself too deeply. Any chink in one's armor would be found by the agency, and the chance of an adoption curtailed. A waiting parent builds up a passionate hunger. By the time a baby is found, parents-to-be are aware of the hunger and of the long wait. They are ready for any baby. The usual work of readying oneself in pregnancy finds a parallel in these anxieties and the waiting process. For most parents this leaves an intense readiness to fall in love with the baby.

The younger the baby, the easier the adoption. Not only does a newborn's appearance summon up an adult's nurturing response, but the vulnerability of the newborn is bound to appeal to hungry parents. They can easily fall into passionate bonding to a newborn. Every movement, every response is greeted as miraculous. Parents who are lucky enough to make a newborn adoption know that they are in better position to shape this baby's future and to help the baby fit into their own family. It is easier to develop as a parent when one starts with the newborn.

An older infant will have been in a placement before the adoption. When moved into the waiting family, the child must make a new adjustment. A baby of any age must withdraw in order to make this adjustment. Even a four-month-old has adapted to the environment he or she is in. Expectancies have been developed. When the environment changes, the baby must readapt to new expectancies. New noises, new faces, new rhythms must replace the ones to which the baby has become accustomed. It is well known that a baby will have to "grieve" over the lost environment in order to adapt to the new. Part of grieving is a kind of withdrawal. The baby will become unavailable to stimuli for a period. The more attractive the stimulus, such as a tender voice, a loving face, a nurturing cuddle, the more it will remind the baby of the previous nurturing. Even when the previous placement was relatively empty and depriving, the baby will have made an adaptation. New nurturing cues will cause the baby to pull away. Babies undergoing this withdrawal will look away, arch their bodies, cry in protest, or sleep a great deal.

Adoptive parents who are prepared for this period of withdrawal and adaptation will understand the reason for this disappointing behavior. Without preparation, they are likely to take this behavior personally. The initial period of meeting a new adoptive baby can be painful unless the baby's need for time to adjust is considered. When the baby arrives, parents are full of enthusiasm and excitement. Their need for the baby is at its peak, and they are bound to overwhelm the baby with well-intentioned stimuli. "We are so glad you are here!" "Look us in the face." Parents will find it hard to put the baby down, to give the baby time to adjust. The very intensity of their caring makes the necessary restraint difficult.

When met with hypersensitivity and averting responses, any parent will feel rejected. The vulnerable parent who has been through fertility tests before he or she has decided to adopt is likely to feel this rejection even more strongly. Pediatricians and professionals involved in an adoption can prepare parents for this period of reorganization and urge them to wait until the baby is ready to meet their hungry enthusiasm. The baby's own hunger for attachment will then make the transition smoother.

Today parents-to-be know a great deal about intrauterine conditions and their effect on the developing fetus. Intrauterine malnutrition, for instance, can interfere with as much as 40 percent of the number of cells in the fetal brain, the thyroid and adrenals (organs important to activation and paying attention). Drugs, alcohol, and smoking by the pregnant mother have powerful effects on the behavior of the newborn. In earlier days a parent might assign difficult behavior in an adopted baby to "genes." Now, when things go wrong, a new parent is likely to wonder if the baby hasn't had a depriving pregnancy.

When parents wonder about the mother who would give up her baby and the likelihood of unhealthy behavior while she was carrying this rejected fetus, they can see the baby as vulnerable and potentially damaged. As long as things go well with the baby, such worries may not surface. But any behavior on the baby's part that causes turmoil in the parent-infant relationship can too easily lead to labeling the baby as less than perfect. For example, the intractable, fussy period that occurs in most infants in the first twelve colicky weeks can lead to an unconscious reaction in new, eager, adoptive parents. They think, "Oh-oh. She's not an intact baby. Was she already damaged?" Instead of looking to the reasons for such normal patterns as fussiness each day, an adoptive parent may all too easily attribute the troubles to the baby's past history. Understanding this tendency in themselves can help prevent such inappropriate anxiety. Adoptive parents need extra support and an understanding person who can evaluate conflicts at each stress period. The initial period of adjustment is bound to be stressful for parents who really care.

All through childhood in an adoptive family's experience, questions about the heredity and the prior experience of the baby will keep surfacing in a parent's mind. His or her own questions of adequacy to meet the parenting needs of this child will also arise at each stress. Natural competitive feelings arise at each period of readjustment: "Would he have been better off in his natural environment? Have we failed?" A parent of natural children will recognize that these questions arise in every parent's mind as he or she questions problems with a child's adjustment. In an adoption, the tendency present in all parents toward vulnerability and toward a sense of personal failure is liable to be enhanced.

When does an adoptive parent begin to feel like the infant's "real" parent? When does a parent become less vulnerable to questions like "Will she want to look up her natural parents someday— and desert me?" "Will her birth mother come and take her away from me?" "When should I tell her she's adopted—and not really mine?" "How do I tell her? Will she then reject me?" "How do I protect her from the feeling of rejection she will get when she knows her natural mother gave her up for adoption?" "How could she do it?"

When adoptive parents realize how universal these questions are to anyone in their situation, their feelings of insecurity will gradually be balanced by feelings of solid attachment. Competitive feelings with the birth parents are bound to be there. The more an adoptive parent learns to care, the stronger these feelings can become. Understanding that these feelings arise from the depth of their caring frees parents to enjoy the process of attachment. As with the natural families described earlier, the responses of adopted babies will provide clues to their adjustment and reassurance to the parents.

When the adoptive parents get beyond the magic of falling in love and enter the working phase of staying in love, then they will feel like that baby's "real" parent. Adoptive parents tell me that when they've handled a few crises and have survived them, they are no longer vulnerable to a child's question: "Are you my *real* mother?" They *know* they are the parents that child needs.

Detachment:
The Goal of Attachment

FOSTERING INDEPENDENCE

In the work we are doing at Children's Hospital with parents and infants, we are attempting to understand the stages, as well as the behavioral markers, of the attachment process. We have come to realize that the purest sign of attachment is the ability to detach at appropriate stages in the infant's development. This is critical to his ability to act for himself and to learn about the excitement of autonomy. Autonomous achievements are the foundation for the baby's own belief in himself—and form the ingredients of his ego. If he is overwhelmed even by the most caring parents or acted for over too long a period, the opportunities for testing out these capacities in himself may be missed. Hence there seem to be critical stages for fostering independence.

If autonomy is not developing properly, it is likely to be demonstrated in a baby's behavior. For example, he may fall back on a kind of monotony or repetition, which indirectly shows that he doesn't dare add on new facets to what he can already achieve. He may subtly wait for his parents to perform the task for him. Or he may retire behind a pattern of failure, in which each task ends up with an incomplete or missed goal (see Chapter 7). These patterns are hard to interpret in early infancy, yet the foundations for autonomy or the lack of it may well be laid in infancy. For the parents, unconscious forces are at work: fears of failure and preference for the baby as he is—safe and immature. These feelings make it hard for them to allow frustration in him, to see the value of small failures and their attendant frustrations, which motivate the baby to practice toward success in a goal. The same feelings perpetuate a parent's need to contain the baby long beyond the stage when simple containment is appropriate. A truly reciprocal attachment will allow periods of disruption and detachment. In these periods, when the old patterns no longer work, when the baby shows that he is no longer satisfied with the old, monotonous interactions, when he is no longer satisfied with himself, the parents realize that they have moved into a period of disorganization. Their own reactions are likely to be surprise, disappointment, and a feeling of desertion, followed by a feeling of being at a loss to know where to go next. All of these mark a stage, and a reorganization of parenting skills is called for at these times. One must follow the baby. By observing the baby's new attempts, by looking at him for cues to what he is trying to do, where he is going, parents can begin to see their new role. At the same time this very process of sitting back, of watching and waiting frees the baby toward autonomy and allows him to learn more about himself. When the new stage of development is reached, the parents' joy in the baby's achievements and in their own new role will reinforce the baby. He will feel a double reward—one of having explored and learned a new step and one of feeling the response from those around him.

This is a complex way of saying that anything a baby learns for himself is likely to be more rewarding for him than if it is entirely taught to him. As we have tried to demonstrate in the previous chapters, this kind of detachment on the part of a caring parent isn't always easy, but it certainly is necessary. By four to five months, in the play session we videotape between mothers and infants, we expect to see the baby leading the mother just as often as she leads him. She may institute a sequence, but she rapidly turns it over to him. She may model a new task for him, but then she ducks out and leaves it to him to practice, fail, and try again, until he has mastered it. Her pleasure matches his when he can do it for himself.

We saw an eye-opening example of this in our research with mothers and babies in western Kenya. We were trying to gain some understanding of the kind of motor precocity seen there in older infants. They walked well by nine months, they sat alone at four months, and their reaching behavior was often advanced by a month or so. The excitement that these babies demonstrated as they achieved a milestone was remarkable. In our research over a two-year period we learned a great deal about how this motor excitement was generated, both from within the baby and from those around him (Super, 1980). One of the most striking ways was demonstrated in a teaching task. We set up a situation in which the mother would "teach" her baby to perform a task from the Bayley exam, which was designated as being one month ahead of his present development. We filmed this and planned to score the mother for her capacity to model it for him in intelligible stages, to wait for the baby to try each step of the task, and also to score her behavior as either "shaping, showing, or shoving" (K. Kaye, 1979, has demonstrated that these are the three patterns used by U.S. mothers to teach a task to a one-year-old). However, when a black mother in Kisii sat a baby on her lap, it turned out that she would model the entire task for him. Then she'd sit back to wait for him to do it after her. She'd keep his interest on track by saying repeatedly and monotonously, "You do it, you do it, you can do it." At the point at which the baby performed the first stage of the task, she became completely silent. When he had time to digest this step, she started in again, urging him on, until, at the next stage of success, she got silent again. We had been so thoroughly indoctrinated by our culture to think of positive reinforcement as critical to a baby's becoming aware of what he has just done that we thought she wasn't helping the baby at all. We had to watch the tapes repeatedly really to absorb what had happened when she became silent. Not only was her silence the reinforcer for his achievement, but in the silence his face brightened, and he returned to the task with renewed vigor. What her silence provided for him was the opportunity and time to realize that *he* had done it himself. His excitement and vigor drove him on to more achievement, and these babies showed motor skills advanced for their age. This experiment seemed to show us at least one of the forces for motor precocity in these babies.

When we tried a similar experiment in our own culture, we found a different picture. Mothers in the United States would routinely demonstrate the task one step at a time, talking about each step in an instructive manner as they went along. (The talking could also be seen as distracting and intrusive.) After a baby performed each step of the task, his mother would crow, "That's it! That's wonderful!" Then she'd say, "Now go on. Do this or this or this." She gave him several choices, but not necessarily his own, and certainly she left little of it up to him. We began to view positive reinforcement very differently after this. Depending on *how* it's used, it can be very manipulative, and it can become a way of stripping an infant of his own choices and sense of achievement. At least in this comparison, it was obvious that U.S. mothers were more controlling with their reinforcement, and the opportunity for the baby to realize his own autonomous achievement was diluted.

By the time a mother has taught her baby how to control inner states and how to direct and prolong his attention (see Chapter 5), it is time to turn the control back to him, both subtly and overtly. This is what I mean by detachment—the process in parenting that allows a baby to begin to take over and to realize that he can become independent. Margaret Mahler (1963) calls this new awareness "hatching." She describes the new expressions it brings to a baby's eyes and face. When his mother or another adult interacts with him, he has the capacity to sit at a distance, taking in her approaches and giving off signals of his own that are rich and variable. There is a gradual change not only in his awareness but in his ability to communicate that he is more independent. Mahler describes this as "a new look of alertness, mixed with persistence and goal-directedness." The baby can maintain a more permanent alert state on his own, and within that he demonstrates an increasing capacity to check on people and things, mixed with an intention to act upon these observations. He can now reach and point, as well as inhibit these actions. This gives him a range of foci for his attention and relationships, over which he now has control—and he *knows* it.

THE SINGLE PARENT

These first steps toward "separation" and detachment were vividly demonstrated to me by a single mother and her baby. In my experience, raising a child alone makes this process harder.

Ms. Hardy came to me when her baby was three months old. She had heard that I respected single parents and was willing to help them raise their children alone. She was indeed alone, for even her own parents lived far away. The baby's father was a professor in England, whom she had never intended to marry. She'd always wanted a baby and was delighted when she found herself pregnant. She never looked back with regret, and told me that her pregnancy was a period of "blissful fulfillment." She said that she'd never felt so complete and that she had treasured every minute of it. Her high-powered job brought her to Boston when

she was four months pregnant, so she'd not seen her baby's father again, nor had she been to visit her own parents. She was an insurance executive, a vice-president, and doing extremely well professionally. In addition, she loved her work. She had asked for and received "as much leave as I need for the new baby." She was convinced that everyone at her work respected her decision. In no way did anyone seem to resent her being a single parent or taking time out. "However," she said, "it's been lonely. No one has asked me out, and I haven't wanted to go, of course. But there are no social events that are even appropriate for single women who are already committed. There's no real way for me to meet anyone else like me. I'm so happy and proud to be a single parent that I'd like to share it with others. But how does one meet other single parents?"

I suggested some single-parent support groups as a source of companions.* She told me that she'd been to some meetings to try to ally herself with other single women. But she hadn't met anyone in her situation, and although she met a few single mothers who were raising children, their children were older and these mothers seemed "so angry." She didn't feel comfortable around all that anger. I asked her about the anger, and she re-

---

*The Family Resource Coalition, 230 North Michigan Avenue, Suite 1625, Chicago, Illinois 60601, can be a source of help in locating such groups.

plied, "Angry that they are alone, that they aren't being backed up by anyone—husband, mate, or society. And the women's movement doesn't really back them up for their mothering role either, so they feel isolated. I don't want to get angry. I'm not; I expected this to be hard, but it's so rewarding!"

Ms. Hardy is right. Many women's groups have been slow in backing their members for roles as nurturers—an important part of every woman's (and man's) makeup. The woman's collective in Cambridge that wrote a book entitled *Ourselves and Our Children* (1978) made an effort to correct this. Some feminists, such as Adrienne Rich and Phyllis Chesler, have written of the importance of supporting this side of a woman's life. Such recognition would add powerful steam to the women's movement, which has already done so much to back up women's self-fulfillment in other areas. This role needs it too. Ms. Hardy needs the support of her peers. All of this effort going in the direction of clarification of two important roles for women makes the current so-called men's movement of considerable interest. Men need as desperately as women to reevaluate themselves and their goals—both their professional roles and their roles as part of a family and larger community. Few men ever see themselves as successful in achieving success in both potential roles.

Ms. Hardy was laying out her needs for me in a very open, challenging way. I had had a number of single parents in my practice— mostly females but a few males too—and found the opportunity of backing them up very rewarding. Their loneliness and inability to meet people in their situation were certainly a disturbing aspect of most of their personal lives. My job was to make the parent-child interaction as rewarding as possible for both members. In past cases I could see that there were problems that would arise at times within the relationship between a single parent and his or her child that could be predicted and with which I could be of help. Over time I've come to the realization that it is more effective to prevent problems than to deal with them *after* they've arisen and are defined as problems. But there is also danger in anticipating problems that may not develop as such. This recognition does slow down one's zeal in identifying all the vicissitudes that might plague a developing family. So I've begun to set up a kind of "contract" with single parents when they first come to me. If they see my approach as that of a "borrower of trouble," they can leave to find a more useful doctor for them and their children. If they see my efforts to prevent problems as useful, they can take or leave what I suggest. "There are certain times in a baby's development," I tell them, "when he will be ahead of you and your expectations. Your tendency will be to maintain the status quo. My part in the contract will be to show you his need to be let go of, to be encouraged to try a new step *on his own,* for allowing a baby to step out and become independent is one of the most difficult jobs a single parent may have to deal with."

GOING BACK TO WORK

This contract really surprised Ms. Hardy, for she said she'd not expected me to be in favor of a baby's being pushed to be independent. "Does that mean that you think it's time for me to go back to work?"

I hadn't implied anything of the sort; she'd overinterpreted my remarks. Part of being tied, of caring a great deal is that one feels the effects of deep ambivalence. One side wants to stay close, but the other side pulls back, saying, "You should get away. It's not healthy to care this much." One of the real problems with a relationship in which there's no margin to test it with a third person in a family is that the relationship can become an either/or kind of thing. "Either I'm all yours or I'm not yours at all." The other side of caring is separating. Ms. Hardy had this ambivalence close to the surface. Her past success in her job and the pull on her to return to it did not make a measured decision easy.

I encouraged Ms. Hardy to give that question more time and to give us a chance to work it out together. I reminded her that I hardly knew her and that although I had seen a number of single parents and had helped them with this decision, I thought it was critical to individualize it each time. She looked very relieved and subsided back into her chair.

She discussed with me her labor and delivery and the first three months. She was breast feeding the baby, whom she called Lee. The breast feeding had been difficult at first, but she'd very determinedly worked through her problems, and she was quite proud to have been able to keep it up. She planned to continue when she started back to work. I reminded her that this was the

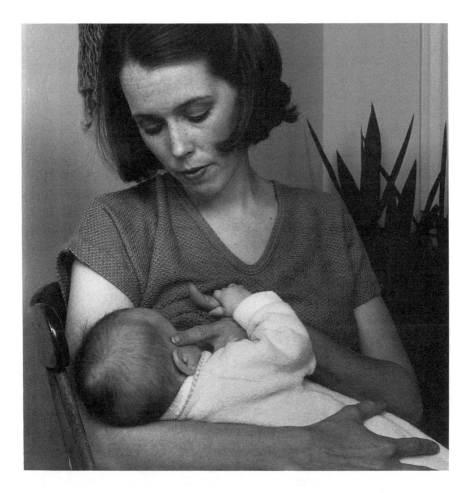

second time she'd brought it up and that maybe she did need help in deciding about her job.

She rushed to assure me that she had it on her mind but that she certainly couldn't give Lee up yet. As she said it, she made it sound as if the act of sharing him with a secondary caregiver would be a kind of finality.

I have seen and heard this before. I feel that this kind of honest, selfish reason should be accounted for in any decision to place a baby in a situation such as day care. So little research has been done to help us know where we stand about this kind of early separation that so far we are on pretty shaky ground. The people in favor of day care feel that it doesn't hurt a baby to be in such a setup *if* the ratio of caregivers to babies is at least one to four—that is, if there are enough adults to ensure individualized care and plenty of it. They also push for competence and training of this personnel. I fully agree with these requirements and would go even further: that the caregivers be chosen for their capacity to nurture under stress as well as in ideal conditions. However, there are also many thoughtful child advocates who feel that infants should not be in day care at all. Those who advocate day care for infants counter that over half of infants (children under three) are already in day care because their mothers must work. Our decision about whether or not there should be day care, they say, is spurious; what we need to be sure of is that there is quality day care available.

I would press for one more set of stipulations on day care for infants: that the care include nurturing of mothers. Unless a mother is included in the planning for her baby, she will feel shoved out and useless at a time when it is critical that she continue to feel important to him. If she is left out, she is likely to grieve about losing him and may begin to detach at an unconscious level in order to defend herself from her feelings about having to share him. This will make her raw and competitive with his caregivers. Since she is likely to blame herself for all of her baby's faults and credit his other caregivers for all of his development, she will be particularly vulnerable to self-criticism and criticism from them. If a caregiver makes a remark such as "He never does that to me!" when she complains about his immediate fussing when she picks up her baby at night, she will be devastated. Since babies not only disintegrate at the end of a long day but are likely to save up the important messages (such as fussing and disintegration) for their mothers, this very likely event should be explained to her as evidence of the fact that he's been waiting all day for her. If she can be nurtured as well and her role as his mother stressed as a crucial part of his care, we can probably mitigate many of the untoward effects of early separation. But we still need research to prove this.

It may also be that there are a critical number of months that a baby and mother must go through together before they can be separated without irreparable losses to both of them. Selma Fraiberg (1959) felt that there is at least a two- or three-year period in which a baby needs to be at home with his mother. My own feeling is that that might be a long, lonely time for them both under the circumstances in which many nuclear families are living. If we do expect from women that long a period at home, we'd better make it rewarding for them in individualized ways, or they'll end up by taking out their negative feelings on their babies without intending to. I feel that while further research is pending, we all should fight for laws to institutionalize a four-month leave from work for mothers and at least a month's leave for fathers. In this way we'd free parents to make their own choices and would, at a national level, place emphasis on the importance of cementing the parent-infant relationship. In order to do this, we'd have to be certain that businesses and professions wouldn't penalize parents for such leaves and that there would be ways for them to keep up in the competitive world of jobs. At present there are no such sanctions. A female pediatrician and chief resident at our hospital snatched only one month to be with her new baby. An obstetrical resident had two weeks at home but is still successfully nursing her baby, against all odds, at six months. It can be done by determined people, but couldn't it be made easier?

I feel that a mother (or father) should be at home and in charge of her or his baby for at least the first four months, as an absolute minimum. There are plenty of times in those first months when any parent would be relieved and happy to walk away from the responsibility. Every crying period raises this likelihood. But if a parent doesn't work through these first turbulent months to reach the tranquil period that follows, the period when the baby is predictable and organized, when he smiles, gurgles, and coos *at* the parent, he or she may never feel the sense of self-esteem that comes from having made it through this early disorganized period. The rewards of the baby's social behavior will never feel as if they were deserved by, and hence belong to, the parent. The relationship may not actually be endangered, but it may never be as rich as it might have been. The early struggles and the effort to find one's way through them may be critical to the feeling of accomplishment that comes for parents when their baby is about four months old.

SHARING DECISIONS

Ms. Hardy asked me more about the "contract," and we talked about her feelings about sharing the baby at all. She said that she felt so much a part of him and that he was so much a part of her that she couldn't even sleep away from him. She hadn't wanted to use a bottle or solids to feed him because she wanted to be solely responsible for his well-being. So far that had worked out well for them both, she felt, but she felt guilty about how close they were. She felt herself overreacting when anyone intruded on this closeness. And she was afraid that this was what I was threatening to do.

The fact that she could speak so openly about it showed how intelligent and flexible she is, but it also came across as something of a challenge. For she was coming to the realization that separation and an end to this lovely period of symbiosis were ahead. I didn't need to push it at this stage; she would come to it on her own.

> *I assured her that I saw my job as one of cementing their relationship and keeping it productive for them both. The times that I might need to help would be those when turbulence was beginning to surface and when they might need outside help in understanding what the turbulence was all about and where it was heading.*
>
> *She said, "I do feel the desperate need for someone who cares about us to help me figure things out at times. It feels awfully one-sided with only me to decide which way to go."*
>
> *At this point she looked down at Lee, who'd gotten tired of my absorbing talk with his mother and had begun to vocalize in loud crescendos. As she looked in his face, he stopped to smile broadly at her. They both began to smile and vocalize to each other in a rhythmic back and forth (described in Chapter 6). The alternating verbal signals, embedded in the lovely softening and brightening of their nonverbal communication, was beautiful to watch.*
>
> *As she looked up from this, I remarked on how warming it was to watch them and reminded her of her last statement: that she alone was making the decisions. I described the two-way sequence I'd just seen. "I think he's helping you make these decisions." She laughed and said, "I think you do appreciate us and will be on our wavelength. Lee and I can trust you."*

Not only is a single parent plagued with loneliness, but he or she must also wonder how much to trust all those outsiders to understand the depth of caring and turmoil that go on in a healthy relationship. It's parallel to being in love and to feeling that no one else has ever been in love like this and that therefore, no one else can understand the joys and the pain. For an unwed mother, society has set up so many disapproving roadblocks that these feelings are bound to be intensified.

The next few weeks went well. I heard from Ms. Hardy at call hour a few times, always with interesting questions, for which she used me as a kind of mirror for her own reactions or as a third ear to which she voiced her pros and cons in order to sort out her own decisions.

In a two-parent family this happens all the time and unconsciously. At mealtime, at bedtime, at all times of the day, one parent will try out his or her ideas on the other. And because they know each other's likely reactions, most such questions are really looking not for answers but for the opportunity for this kind of sorting out, for decisions that are already made but that just need backup.

I didn't need to play anything but a supportive role until a real crisis came. One night Lee ran a temperature. Ms. Hardy called me in a panic. After she'd recited all of his symptoms, his temperature of 101.5, his rapid breathing, and so on, I asked her whether he was in pain or distress. She answered no. I asked her whether he "looked sick." "What a silly question," she said. "Of course he looks sick." I asked her to describe what he was doing, whether he was playing or not, and if he was alert and responsive. "He is, but I can't see what that has to do with it." I assured her that if he were really ill, he'd show it in his behavior as well. Whatever his other symptoms, if he were really "flaked out," acting limp and unresponsive, even with a normal temperature, I'd be more worried. With an alert, actively responsive baby, we could afford to see him in the morning. When I saw him in the morning, he was already on the mend, and I found very little to account for his night temperature, which never returned. Ms. Hardy began to see that she could trust his behavior to tell her when he was in trouble, and she thanked me for teaching her about him.

EXPLORING—FROM A SAFE BASE

Our next crisis came when Lee was four and a half months old. Ms. Hardy came in for his routine visit and inoculation with a long, grim face. "Should I wean him?" was her first question. "Why do you ask right now? I thought you said that you planned to nurse him even after you went back to work." Her eyes dropped to him, and she said, sadly, "He wants me to. He won't nurse any longer. Every time I put him to my breast, he turns away. He actively rejects me."

I have heard this repeatedly at about this age. Mothers who are set on nursing call up with the same question and the same reason. He's turning away. When I analyze the reason for his behavior, I hear the same thing: His interest in the world around him is so great that he can't stay at the breast. If there's the slightest sound or noise or if anyone moves in the distance, he is off the breast and looking around. This sudden burst of intense interest in his environment comes with the baby's burgeoning capacity to act upon it. His new one-handed reach is providing him with much more skill to reach for toys in his environment. Jean Piaget (1969) has alerted us all to "circular processes," or the feedback systems in which a baby knows when he has acted upon an object and his actions have brought about an expected reaction from it. With this comes an increasing interest in performing a task with an object. Hence his ability to reach for and locate an object is linked to this awareness of his influence on his environment.

At this time there is also evidence of increasing awareness of important people, and strangers, around him. I notice this in my office when I lean over to examine a baby of this age. He will watch me come closer with widening eyes, an increasing look of horror on his face, his body perfectly still as I lean over him. As I begin to examine him or come close to him, his horror will break into screaming as if to hold me off or shut me out. If I am clever enough to put his mother's face in front of me and to work around it, he'll let me do anything at all without protest.

A third new development that fuels his increasing awareness and interest in his environment comes out in the cognitive area. He begins to show signs of awareness of spatial relationships, an early form of what Piaget calls object constancy. For example, if a baby this age who has been taught to hold his own bottle is handed it by the wrong end, with the nipple turned away, he will clumsily but surely turn it around to insert the nipple into his mouth. Any other important object would be treated in the same way, with an awareness of what is appropriate and what is not—and of what he can now do to right it. *Of course,* he would be so fueled by these new skills and the excitement of acting on them that he will turn away from his "sure thing"—his mother.

We see this reliance on the mother's presence regularly in our experimental face-to-face situation. Whereas at three months, in the play situation described in Chapter 6, all babies will be engaged by the mother's and father's playful advances, by four months in some very secure babies, and predictably by five months in all babies, the mother can hardly keep the baby looking at her. He first sizes her up, smiles at her politely a few times, vocalizes once, then turns away from her persistent efforts to engage him, to look off into the distance. He will look around our carefully cleaned-up, uninteresting lab as if it were full of fascinating things to look at. If she reaches out to tickle him or turn his face to her, he will look right past her, arching away from her hand and even pushing it away with one of his. With the father he is not quite so nonchalant (or negative) at first and for about one minute enters into the playful interaction his father sets up, but then he will turn the father off in very much the same way as he does the mother.

As one watches this sequence, there is a dawning awareness that this is a new stage and that there must be a very important reason behind such predictable and regular age-linked behavior. Mothers (and fathers) take it personally, as rejection, and are very embarrassed and even put off by it. Another sequence that we have tried in the lab disproves the worry that this is rejection. For we ask the parent to go into the lab and sit in front of the baby with an unresponsive, still face for three minutes. At first the baby cannot believe it, so he starts out with his usual perfunctory greeting, then begins to turn away. Then (and it takes only twenty seconds) he realizes that she is not performing in the usual way, has "violated his expectancy." His eyes widen, his face sets, and he begins very purposefully to try to elicit the expected responses from her. He brightens up, he smiles, he vocalizes with a coo, then a whimper. He fakes a broad smile, a loud protesting whimper. He may cough or sneeze, and we have even had babies who made themselves gag. He cannot believe she won't respond, so he runs through his repertoire a second and a third time trying to get her involved with him. If this still-faced, unresponsive mother persists, he may give up and turn actively away, curling up into a protective ball or arching away and closing his eyes as if to try to shut her out in sleep—all of this brought on by only three minutes of changed behavior from her. When she finally does begin to respond and to play with him in the usual manner, he redoubles his responses with obvious joy.

This kind of concern when the mother is not available as expected leads us to see this new stage as one of using her as a foundation, *as long as she behaves in her usual, expectable way,* on which to build new, burgeoning interests. Bowlby (1969) calls this the "use of mother as a base from which to explore." The universality of such behavior at this age makes me feel that this may not be an optimal time for the mother to wean the baby or to change anything in his environment if she can help it.

> *When I tried to convey some of this to Ms. Hardy, she seemed to understand me, then followed with: "I thought that he was telling me it was time for me to go back to work. I'm relieved to hear that it isn't, for I'm not quite ready myself."*

I agree with her. This may not be the optimal time for a separation—for either of them. All mothers who are contemplating going back to work and are looking for a signal from the baby use this time and this behavior to help them make their decision. I feel that this is a time of rapid acquisition of new skills, a time when the stable base might best be left alone. After it is over and the baby returns to more flexible use of his "base," having assimilated the newly learned skills, there will be another plateau—and a set of optimal times when each new step can be taken. At these times the mother may be ready, and so may the baby.

TRYING HIS WINGS

> *Ms. Hardy had heard my reasoning and saw the value in looking behind Lee's cues to try to understand what they meant. By now she had learned to trust me and to trust herself to interpret some of them. She reminded me of our original contract: that I would prepare her for the times when it would be hardest for her yet most important for him that she encourage him to become independent.*

This mother was remarkable in her ability to learn from the stresses in their relationship. In these two crises she had begun to see Lee as a viable and independent little person—no longer as an extension of herself. She could stand off and evaluate him at a distance now. She could allow me to participate in their relationship. They were both "hatching," in Mahler's sense. Ms. Hardy was learning about the value of distance in an intense relationship, and they both were entering into a new phase of development—a freer and richer stage.

There will be more times in the future when the baby's independence will take a spurt, upsetting the previous comfortable balance. All mothers sense these periods and initially react against them, but in time they are able to rationalize them and see their importance. Eventually they actively foster these spurts of independence that accompany periods of development in the child. A single parent may find it more difficult. His or her needs may be greater—for companionship, for closeness, and for not making the mistake of letting go too quickly. So he or she may automatically and more forcefully resist change. If there were a second caregiver, such as a father, he would be likely to press her to give in or would take up the slack in some way that would make it easier for the mother to let go. The periods of stress that I can predict for single mothers center on new learning tasks. For example, the spurt and the increasing demands just before a baby sits up (around seven months), crawls (around nine months), stands (around eleven to twelve months), or walks (around twelve to fourteen months) are usually accompanied by night waking, demanding behavior during the day, and pushing a parent to set limits. Single parents will inevitably find it difficult to set limits at night or to limit the demands during the day. If they can understand the reason for the demands and can see that limits help a baby channel his

On Becoming a Family

efforts more effectively, they can stand firm. The increasingly delicate pincer grasp of the baby's fingers that comes to the surface at eight months is another exciting development that a mother had better play along with. She must sense the drive toward independence, especially in an area where she and the baby are locked together, such as feeding. She can allow him to finger-feed small bits to himself. If she doesn't, he will become so negative that she won't be able to feed him at all. Many single parents get caught in feeding problems because they don't see the burgeoning independence in this behavioral step. Another important time of separation will come in the second twelve months. The negative second year can be predicted to be stormy, but the separation and independence that take place during it are critical to the baby's development.

Learning anew about the baby at each stage, how to let him go and how to allow him the necessary autonomy to foster his new independence, is critical toward building a relationship for the future. Within the limits of a firm but flexible attachment, an infant can afford to try himself out, to learn about his own potential and about his limits. He can bounce out to try new things and to test his parents with his negativism. He can afford to turn away because he *knows* they will be there when he turns back. By five months both parents and child are getting their first test—a test of the strength of their attachment. If parents can allow a baby to turn away, to try his wings in small ways, to detach himself in such a safe testing ground, they will prove the strength of their attachment to him, and he will build on it to become his own person.

Bibliography

Adamson, L., and E. Tronick. *Brand New Baby*. New York: Macmillan, 1981.

Ainsworth, M. D. S. "Object Relations, Dependency and Attachment: A Theoretical Review of the Infant-Mother Relationship." *Child Development*, 40 (1969) 1–25.

Als, H.; E. Tronick; and T. B. Brazelton. "Analysis of Face to Face Interaction in Infant Adult Dyads." *The Study of Social Interaction*, ed. Lamb, Suomi, and Stephenson. Madison: University of Wisconsin Press, 1979.

Anders, T., and E. Hoffman. "The Sleep Polygram." *American Journal of Mental Deficiency*, 77 (1973) 506–14.

Ball, W., and E. Tronick. "Infant Responses to Impending Collision, Optical and Real." *Science*, 171 (1971) 818–20.

Barnard, K. *A Program of Stimulation for Infants Born Prematurely, Seattle School of Nursing*. Seattle: University of Washington Press, 1975.

Barnett, C. R., et al. "Neonatal Separation: The Maternal Side of Interactional Deprivation." *Pediatrics*, 45 (1970) 197–205.

Bateson, G., and M. Mead. *First Days in the Life of a New Guinea Baby*, New York Film Library.

Bell, S. M., and M. D. S. Ainsworth. "Infant's Crying and Maternal Responsiveness." *Child Development*, 43 (1972) 1171–92.

Benjamin, J. D. "Prediction and Psychopathologic Theory." *Dynamic Psychopathology in Childhood*, ed. L. Jessner and E. Pavenstedt. New York: Grune and Stratton, 1959.

Bergman, P., and S. K. Escalona. "Unusual Sensitivities in Very Young Children." *The Psychoanalytic Study of the Child*, 3 (1949) 333–52.

Bibring, G. L., et al. "A Study of the Psychological Processes in Pregnancy; the Earliest Mother-Child Relationship." *The Psychoanalytic Study of the Child,* XVI (1961) 169–72.

Boston Women's Health Collective. *Our Bodies, Our Selves.* New York: Simon & Schuster, 1972.

———. *Ourselves, Our Children.* New York: Random House, 1976.

Bower, T. G. R. "The Object in the World of the Infant." *Scientific American,* 225 (1971) 30–38.

Bowlby, J. *Attachment,* Attachment and Loss Series, Vol. I. New York: Basic Books, 1969.

———. *Loss: Sadness and Depression,* Attachment and Loss Series, Vol. III. New York: Basic Books, 1980.

———. *Separation: Anxiety and Anger,* Attachment and Loss Series, Vol. II. New York: Basic Books, 1973.

Brackbill, Y. "Obstetric Medication Usage and Assessment of Neonatal Behavior." *Anesthesiology,* 40 (1974) 116–20.

Brazelton, T. B. "The Early Mother-Infant Adjustment." *Pediatrics,* 32 (1963) 931–38.

———. *Infants and Mothers.* New York: Delacorte Press/Lawrence, 1969; rev. ed.; Delta/Lawrence, 1981.

———. "Precursors for the Development of Emotion in Early Infancy." *Emotion, Theory, Research and Experience,* ed. R. Plutcik and H. Kellerman, Vol. II. New York: Academic Press, 1981.

———. *Neonatal Behavioral Assessment Scale,* 2d ed., Clinics in Developmental Medicine, No. 88. Philadelphia: Spastics International Medical Publications, Lippincott, 1984.

———, and B. G. Cramer. *The Earliest Relationship: Parents, Infants, and the Drama of Early Attachment.* Reading, Mass.: Addison Wesley/Merloyd Lawrence, 1990.

———, B. Koslowski, and M. Main. "The Origins of Reciprocity: The Early Mother-Infant Interaction." *The Effect of the Infant on His Caregiver,* ed. M. Lewis and L. Rosenblum. New York: John Wiley & Sons, 1974.

———, and M. W. Yogman, eds. *Affective Development in Infancy.* Norwood, N.J.: Ablex Publishing Corporation, 1986.

Brody, S. *Patterns of Mothering.* New York: International Universities Press, 1956.

Brooks-Gunn, J., and W. S. Matthews. *He and She: How Children Develop Their Sex Role Identity.* Englewood Cliffs: Prentice-Hall, 1979.

Bruner, J. S. "The Course of Cognitive Growth." *American Psychologist,* 19 (1964) 1–15.

Carpenter, G. C., et al. "Differential Visual Behavior to Human and Humanoid Faces in Early Infancy." *Merrill-Palmer Quarterly,* 16 (1970) 91–107.

Chess, S., and A. Thomas. *Temperament in Clinical Practice*. New York: Guilford Press, 1986.

Condon, W. S., and L. W. Sander. "Neonate Movement Is Synchronized with Adult Speech: International Participation and Language Acquisition." *Science,* 183 (1974) 99–101.

Crowe, K., and C. von Baeyer. "Predictors of a Positive Childbirth Experience." *Birth,* 16:2 (1989) 59–63.

Dawes, G. S. *Foetal and Neonatal Physiology*. Chicago: Year Book Medical Publishers, Inc., 1968.

Desmond, M. M., et al. "The Clinical Behavior of the Newly Born." *Journal of Pediatrics,* 62 (1963) 307–25.

Dick-Read, Grantly. *Childbirth Without Fear*. New York: Harper and Row, 1944.

Dixon, S., et al. "Early Infant Social Interaction with Parents and Strangers." *Journal of the American Academy of Child Psychiatry,* 1980.

Donovan, B. *The Caesarean Birth Experience*. Boston: Beacon Press, 1977.

Earls, F., and M. W. Yogman. "The Father-Infant Relationship," *Modern Perspectives in the Psychiatry of Infancy,* ed. J. G. Howells. New York: Bruner/Mazel, 1979.

Eimas, P. D., et al. "Speech Perception in Infants." *Science,* 171 (1971) 303–306.

Eisenberg, R. B., et al. "Auditory Behavior in the Human Neonate: A Preliminary Report." *Journal of Speech and Hearing Research,* 7 (1964) 245–69.

Emde, R. N.; T. J. Gaensbauer; and R. N. Harmon. *Emotional Expression in Infancy: A Biobehavioral Study*. New York: International Universities Press, 1976.

Erikson, E. H. *Childhood and Society*. New York: Norton, 1963.

Fantz, R. L. "Pattern Vision in Newborn Infants." *Science,* 140 (1963) 296–97.

Field, T. M. *Infants Born at Risk*. Jamaica, N.Y.: Spectrum, 1979.

Flanagan, G. *The First Nine Months of Life*. New York: Simon & Schuster, 1962.

Fraiberg, S. *The Magic Years*. New York: Scribners, 1959.

Freedman, D. G. "Smiling in Blind Infants and the Issue of the Innate vs. Acquired." *Journal of Child Psychology and Psychiatry,* 5 (1964) 171–84.

Fries, M. E., and P. J. Woolf. "Some Hypotheses on the Role of the Congenital Activity Type in Personality Development." *The Psychoanalytic Study of the Child,* VIII (1953) 8.

Gewirtz, J. L. "On Designing the Functional Environment of the Child to Facilitate Behavioral Development." *Early Child Care,* ed. L. L. Ditman. New York: Atherton, 1968.

————, and E. Boyd. "Does Maternal Responding Imply Reduced Infant Crying?" *Child Development*, 48 (1977) 1200–07.

Goren, C.; M. Jarty; and P. Wu. "Visual Following and Pattern Discrimination of Facelike Stimuli by Newborn Infants." *Pediatrics*, 56 (1975) 544–49.

Gorman, J. J.; D. G. Cogan; and S. Gellis. "An Apparatus for Grading Visual Acuity in Infants." *Pediatrics*, 19 (1957) 1088–92.

Greenberg, M., and N. Morris. "Engrossment: The Newborn's Impact upon the Father." *American Journal of Orthopsychiatry*, 44 (1974) 520–31.

Gunther, M. *Infant Feeding*. London: Methuen, 1970.

Haith, M. M.; T. Bergman; and M. J. Moore. "Eye Contact and Face Scanning in Early Infancy." *Science*, 198 (1977) 853–55.

Harlow, H. F.; M. K. Harlow; and S. J. Suomi. "From Thought to Therapy—Lessons from a Primate Laboratory." *American Scientist*, 59 (1971) 538–49.

Haviland, J. "Looking Smart, the Relationship Between Affect and Intelligence in Infancy." *Origins of Intelligence, Infancy and Early Childhood*, ed. M. Lewis. New York: Plenum, 1976.

Hooker, D. *The Prenatal Origin of Behavior*. Lawrence: University of Kansas Press, 1952.

Hovey, W. R., and C. C. Wilson. *Caesarean Childbirth: A Handbook for Parents*. 3184 Sing Sing Rd., Horseheads, N.Y. 14845.

Humphrey, T. "Postnatal Repetition of Human Prenatal Activity Sequences." *Brain and Early Behavior: Development in the Fetus and Infant*, ed. R. J. Robinson. New York: Academic, 1969.

Jackson, E., et al. "A Hospital Rooming in Unit for Four Newborn Infants and Their Mothers." *Pediatrics*, 1 (1948) 28–43.

Kagen, J. "The Determinates of Attention in the Infant." *American Scientist*, 58 (1970) 298–306.

————. "Do Infants Think?" *Scientific American*, 226 (1972) 74–82.

Kaplan, L. J. *Oneness and Separateness*. New York: Simon & Schuster, 1978.

Kaye, K. "The Maternal Role in Developing Communication and Language." *Before Speech*, ed. M. Bullowa. Cambridge, Mass.: Cambridge University Press, 1979.

Kennell, T.; M. H. Klaus; et al. "Continuous Emotional Support During Labor in a U.S. Hospital." *Journal of the American Medical Association*, 265 (1991) 2197–2201.

Kitzinger, S. *The Experience of Childbirth*. New York: Penguin, 1978.

Klaus, M. H., and J. H. Kennell. "Human Maternal Behavior at First Contact with Her Young." *Pediatrics*, 46 (1970) 187–92.

————. *Maternal-Infant Bonding*. St. Louis: Mosby, 1976.

————. *Parent-Infant Bonding*. St. Louis: Mosby, 1982.

Korner, A. F., and E. B. Thoman. "Visual Alertness in Neonates as

Evoked by Maternal Care." *Journal of Experimental Child Psychology,* 10 (1970) 67–78.

La Leche League. *The Womanly Art of Breastfeeding.* Franklin Park, Ill.: La Leche International, 1963.

Lamb, M. E. "Father-Infant and Mother-Infant Interaction in the First Year of Life." *Child Development,* 48 (1977) 167–81.

Leach, P. *Your Baby and Child.* New York: Alfred Knopf, 1989.

Leboyer, F. *Birth Without Violence.* New York: Alfred Knopf, 1975.

Leiderman, P. H., et al. "Mother-Infant Interaction." *Early Development,* 51 (1973) 154–75.

Lindeman, E. "Symptomatology and the Management of Acute Grief." *American Journal of Psychiatry,* 101 (1944) 141–48.

Lipsitt, L. P. "Learning in the First Year of Life." *Advances in Child Development and Behavior,* ed. L. P. Lipsitt. New York: Academy, 1963.

———, T. Engen, and H. Kaye. "Developmental Changes in the Olfactory Threshold of the Neonate." *Child Development,* 34 (1963) 371–76.

MacFarlane, A. *The Psychology of Childbirth,* The Developing Child Series. Cambridge, Mass.: Harvard University Press, 1977.

———. "Olfaction in the Development of Social Preferences in the Human Neonate," CIBA Foundation Symposium, No. 33: Parent-Infant Interaction, 1975.

Mahler, M. S. "Certain Aspects of the Separation-Individuation Phase." *Psychoanalytic Quarterly,* 32 (1963) 1–14.

McCall, R. B. *Infants.* Cambridge, Mass.: Harvard University Press, 1979.

McGraw, M. *The Neuromuscular Maturation of the Human Infant.* New York: Columbia University Press, 1943.

Meltzoff, A. N., and M. K. Moore. "Imitation of Facial and Manual Gestures by the Human Neonate." *Science,* 198 (1977) 75–78.

Middlemore, M. P. *The Nursing Couple.* London: Hamish Hamilton, 1956.

Miranda, S. B. "Visual Abilities and Pattern Preferences of Premature and Full-Term Infants." *Journal of Experimental Child Psychology,* 10 (1970) 139–205.

Newman, B. M., and P. R. Newman. *Infancy and Childhood.* New York: John Wiley & Sons, 1978.

Newton, N. *Maternal Emotions.* New York: Paul B. Hocker, 1955.

Osofsky, J. "Neonatal Characteristics and Mother-Infant Interaction in Two Observational Situations." *Child Development,* 47 (1976) 1138–47.

Parke, R. "Father-Infant Interaction." *Maternal Attachment and Mothering Disorders,* ed. M. H. Klaus et al. Sausalito, Calif.: John and Johnson Roundtable, 1974.

Parmelee, A. H., Jr., et al. "Sleep States in Premature Infants." *Developmental Medicine & Child Neurology,* 9 (1967) 70.

———. "The Concept of a Cumulative Risk Score for Infants." *Aberrant Development in Infancy,* ed. N. R. Ellis. New York: John Wiley & Sons, 1975.

Peiper, A. *Cerebral Function in Infancy and Childhood,* trans. B. Negler and H. Negler. New York: Consultants Bureau, 1963.

Piaget, J. "Piaget's Theory." *Carmichael's Manual of Child Psychology,* ed. P. H. Mussen. New York: John Wiley & Sons, 1970.

———, and B. Inhelder. *The Psychology of the Child.* New York: Basic Books, 1969.

Prechtl, H. F. R., and D. Beintema. "Neurological Examination of the Full-Term Newborn Infant." *Clinics in Developmental Medicine #12.* London: William Heineman, 1964.

Provence, S., and R. C. Lipton. *Infants in Institutions.* New York: International Universities Press, 1962.

Raphael, D. *The Tender Gift: Breast Feeding.* Englewood Cliffs: Prentice-Hall, 1973.

Rheingold, H. L. "The Effect of Environmental Stimulation upon Social and Exploratory Behavior in the Human Infant." *Determinants of Infant Behavior 1,* ed. B. M. Foss. London: Methuen, 1966.

Ribble, M. *The Rights of Infants.* New York: Columbia University Press, 1943.

Robson, K. S. "The Role of Eye-to-Eye Contact in Maternal-Infant Attachment." *Journal of Child Psychology and Psychiatry,* 8 (1967) 13–25.

Roffwarg, H. P.; J. N. Muzio; and W. C. Dement. "Ontogenetic Development of the Human Sleep-Dream Cycle." *Science,* 152 (1966) 604–19.

Rosen, M. G., and L. Rosen. *In the Beginning: Your Brain Before Birth.* New York: New American Library, Signet Books, 1975.

Rosenthal, R. "Interpersonal Expectations: Effects of the Experimenter's Hypothesis." *Artifact in Behavioral Research,* ed. R. Rosenthal and R. Roshow. New York: Academic, 1969.

Salapatek, P., and W. Kessen. "Prolonged Investigation of a Plane Geometric Triangle by the Human Newborn." *Journal of Experimental Child Psychology,* 15 (1973) 22–29.

Sander, L. W., et al. "Early Mother-Infant Interaction and Twenty-four-Hour Patterns of Activity and Sleep." *Journal of the American Academy of Child Psychiatry,* 9 (1970) 103.

Schaffer, R. *Mothering,* Developing Child Series. Cambridge, Mass.: Harvard University Press, 1977.

Sell, E. *Following of the Highrisk Newborn—A Practical Approach.* Springfield, Ill.: C. C. Thomas, 1980.

Sontag, L. W. "Implications of Fetal Behavior and Environment for Adult

Personalities." *Annals of the New York Academy of Science,* 134 (1966) 782.

Spitz, R. A. *The First Year of Life: Psychoanalytic Study of Normal and Deviant Development of Object Relations.* New York: International Universities Press, 1965.

Spock, B. *The Common Sense Book of Baby and Child Care.* New York: Duell, Sloan & Pearce, 1946.

Stechler, G. S., and E. Latz. "Some Observations on Attention and Arousal in the Human Infant." *Journal of the American Academy of Child Psychiatry,* 5 (1966) 517–25.

Stern, D., et al. "The Infants' Stimulus World During Social Interaction." *Studies in Mother-Infant Interaction,* ed. H. R. Schaffer. New York: Academic, 1977.

Stern, D. *The First Relationship: Infant and Mother,* Developing Child Series. Cambridge, Mass.: Harvard University Press, 1977.

Super, C. M. *Cross Cultural Psychology,* Vol. IV, ed. Triandis et al. Boston: Allyn & Bacon, Inc., 1980.

Thoman, E. B. "Sleep and Wake Behaviors in Neonates: Consistencies and Consequences." *Merrill Palmer Quarterly,* 21 (1975) 295–314.

Thomas, A., et al. *Behavioral Individuality in Early Childhood.* New York: New York University Press, 1963.

Tjossem, T. J., ed. *Intervention Strategies for High Risk Infants and Young Children.* Baltimore: University Park Press, 1976.

Trevarthen, C. "Conversations with a Two-Month-Old." *New Scientist,* 62 (1974) 230–35.

Tronick, E.; H. Als; and L. Adamson. "Structure of Early Face to Face Communicative Interactions." *Before Speech: The Beginning of Human Communication,* ed. M. Bullowa, Cambridge, Eng.: Cambridge University Press, 1978.

———, et al. "The Infant's Response to Entrapment Between Contradictory Messages in Face to Face Interaction." *Journal of the Academy of Child Psychiatry,* 17 (1978) 1.

Watzlawick, P.; J. H. Beavin; and D. Jackson. *Pragmatics of Human Communication.* New York: W. W. Norton, 1967.

White, R. W. "Competence and the Psychosexual Stages of Development." *Nebraska Symposium on Motivation,* ed. M. R. Jones. Lincoln: University of Nebraska Press, 1960.

Whiting, B. B., ed. *Six Cultures: Studies in Child Rearing.* New York: John Wiley & Sons, 1963.

Winick, M. *Malnutrition and Brain Development.* New York: Oxford University Press, 1976.

Winnicott, D. W. *Babies and Their Mothers.* Reading, Mass.: Addison-Wesley/Merloyd Lawrence, 1987.

————. *The Child, the Family and the Outside World.* Reading, Mass.: Addison-Wesley/Merloyd Lawrence, 1987.

Yarrow, L. J. "Maternal Deprivation: Toward an Empirical and Conceptual Evaluation." *Psychology Bulletin,* 58 (1961), 459–90.

Index

The Author

T. Berry Brazelton, M.D., founder of the Child Development Unit at Boston Children's Hospital, is clinical professor emeritus of pediatrics at Harvard Medical School. Currently professor of pediatrics and human development at Brown University, he is also past president of both the Society for Research in Child Development and the National Center for Clinical Infant Programs. Dr. Brazelton is the recipient of the C. Anderson Aldrich Award for Distinguished Contributions to the Field of Child Development given by the American Academy of Pediatrics. The author of over 180 scholarly papers, Dr. Brazelton has written 23 books, for both professional and lay audiences, including the now-classic trilogy *Infants and Mothers, Toddlers and Parents,* and *On Becoming a Family.* Most recently, together with the Swiss psychoanalyst Bertrand G. Cramer, he has written a book for professionals and parents on early parent-child interaction entitled *The Earliest Relationship.*